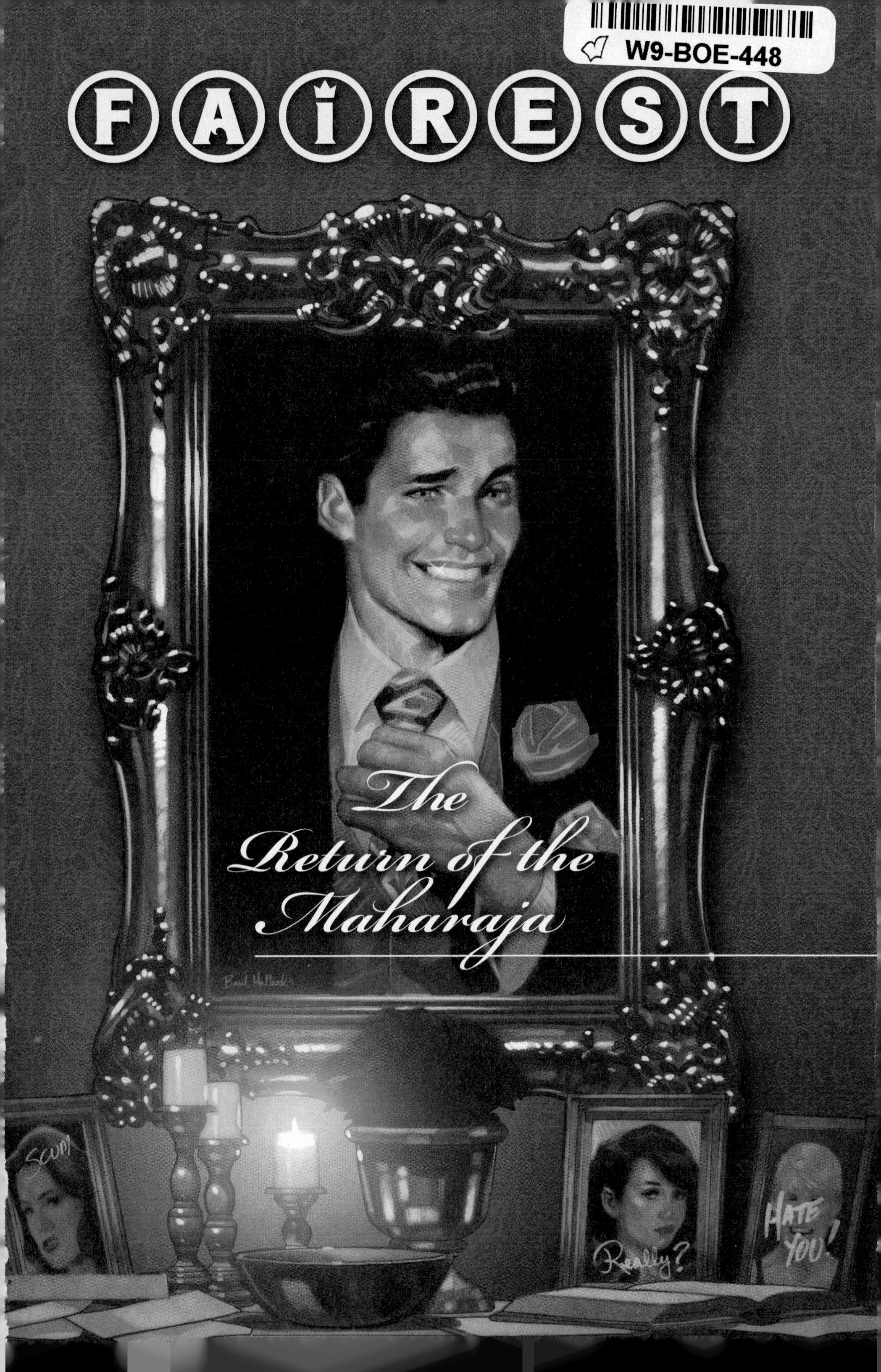
FAIREST
The Return of the Maharaja
Scum
Really?
HATE YOU!

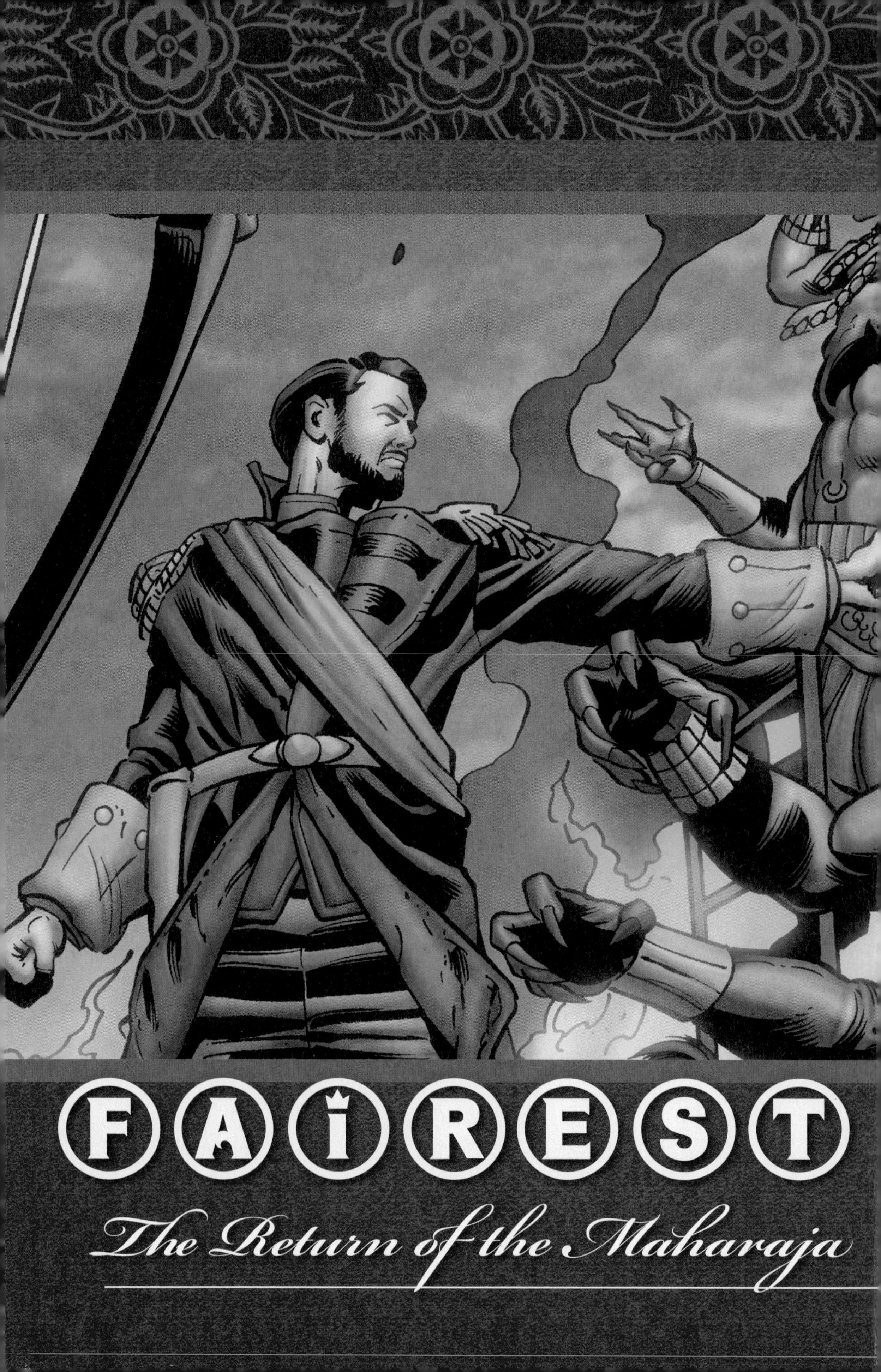

FAIREST

The Return of the Maharaja

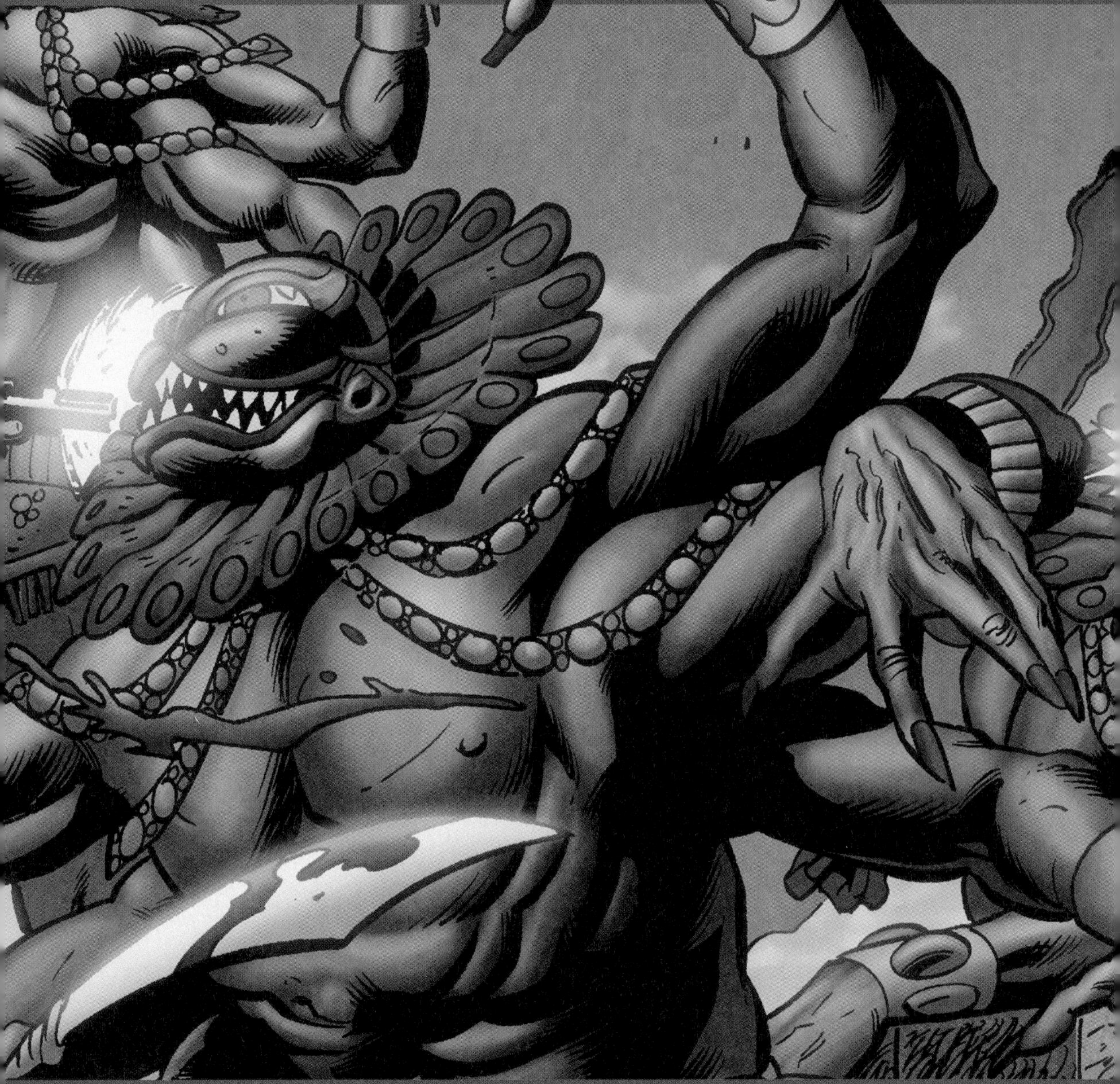

Sean E. Williams
WRITER

Stephen Sadowski
Phil Jimenez
Andrew Pepoy
Dan Green
Russ Braun
Meghan Hetrick
Christian Alamy
José Marzán
ARTISTS

Andrew Dalhouse
COLORIST

Todd Klein
LETTERER

Adam Hughes
COVER ART AND ORIGINAL SERIES COVERS

FAIREST CREATED BY **Bill Willingham**

Shelly Bond
EXECUTIVE EDITOR — VERTIGO AND EDITOR — ORIGINAL SERIES

Gregory Lockard
ASSOCIATE EDITOR — ORIGINAL SERIES

Scott Nybakken
EDITOR

Robbin Brosterman
DESIGN DIRECTOR — BOOKS

Curtis King Jr.
PUBLICATION DESIGN

Hank Kanalz
SENIOR VP — VERTIGO AND INTEGRATED PUBLISHING

Diane Nelson
PRESIDENT

Dan DiDio and **Jim Lee**
CO-PUBLISHERS

Geoff Johns
CHIEF CREATIVE OFFICER

John Rood
EXECUTIVE VP — SALES, MARKETING AND BUSINESS DEVELOPMENT

Amy Genkins
SENIOR VP — BUSINESS AND LEGAL AFFAIRS

Nairi Gardiner
SENIOR VP — FINANCE

Jeff Boison
VP — PUBLISHING PLANNING

Mark Chiarello
VP — ART DIRECTION AND DESIGN

John Cunningham
VP — MARKETING

Terri Cunningham
VP — EDITORIAL ADMINISTRATION

Alison Gill
SENIOR VP — MANUFACTURING AND OPERATIONS

Jay Kogan
VP — BUSINESS AND LEGAL AFFAIRS, PUBLISHING

Jack Mahan
VP — BUSINESS AFFAIRS, TALENT

Nick Napolitano
VP — MANUFACTURING ADMINISTRATION

Sue Pohja
VP — BOOK SALES

Courtney Simmons
SENIOR VP — PUBLICITY

Bob Wayne
SENIOR VP — SALES

FAIREST: THE RETURN OF THE MAHARAJA
Published by DC Comics. Copyright © 2014 Bill Willingham and
DC Comics. All Rights Reserved. Originally published in single magazine
form in FAIREST 15-20. Copyright © 2013 Bill Willingham and DC
Comics. All Rights Reserved. All characters, their distinctive likenesses
and related elements featured in this publication are trademarks of Bill
Willingham. VERTIGO is a trademark of DC Comics. The stories,
characters and incidents featured in this publication are entirely fictional.
DC Comics does not read or accept unsolicited submissions of ideas,
stories or artwork.

DC Comics, 1700 Broadway, New York, NY 10019
A Warner Bros. Entertainment Company
Printed in the U.S.A. First Printing. ISBN: 978-1-4012-4593-1

Library of Congress Cataloging-in-Publication Data

Williams, Sean E., author.
 Fairest. Vol. 3, The Return of the Maharaja / Sean E. Williams ; illustrated
by Stephen Sadowski ; illustrated by Phil Jimenez.
   pages cm
 ISBN 978-1-4012-4593-1 (paperback)
 1. Fairy tales—Comic books, strips, etc. 2. Graphic novels. I. Sadowski,
Stephen, illustrator. II. Jimenez, Phil, illustrator. III. Title. IV. Title: Return
of the Maharaja.
 PN6728.F255W48 2014
 741.5'973—dc23
                                        2014008597

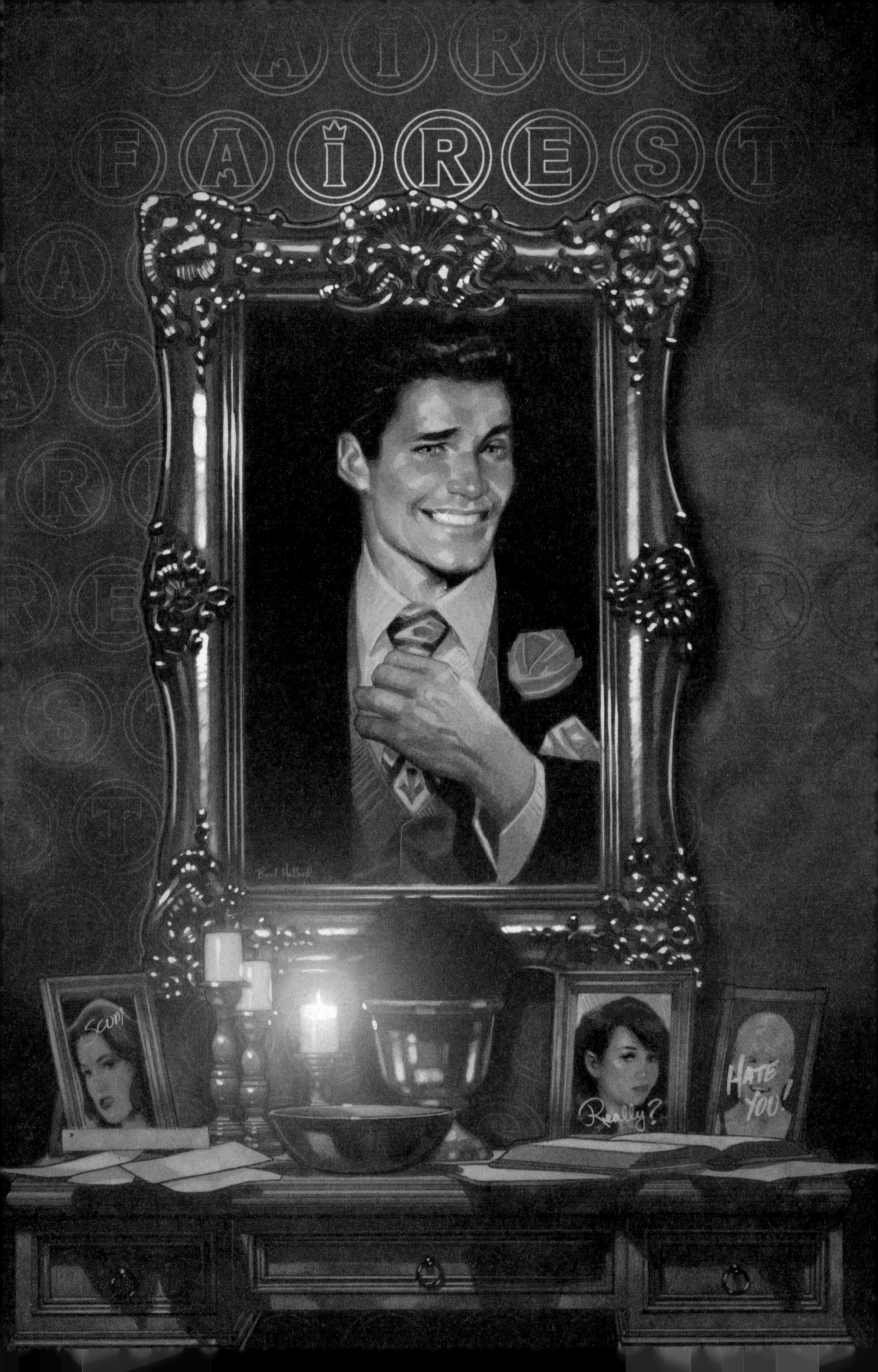
FAIREST
Scum
Really?
HATE YOU

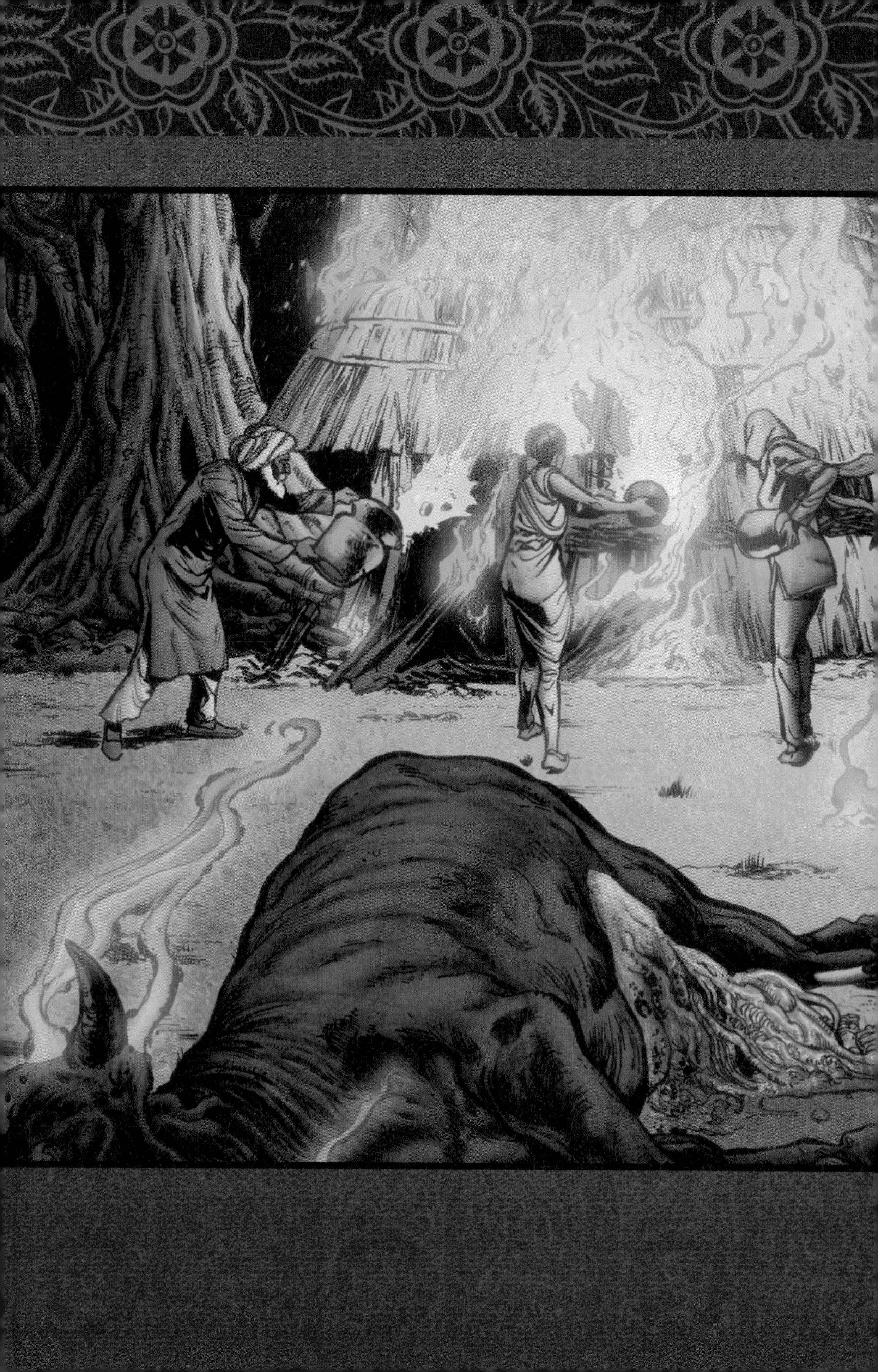

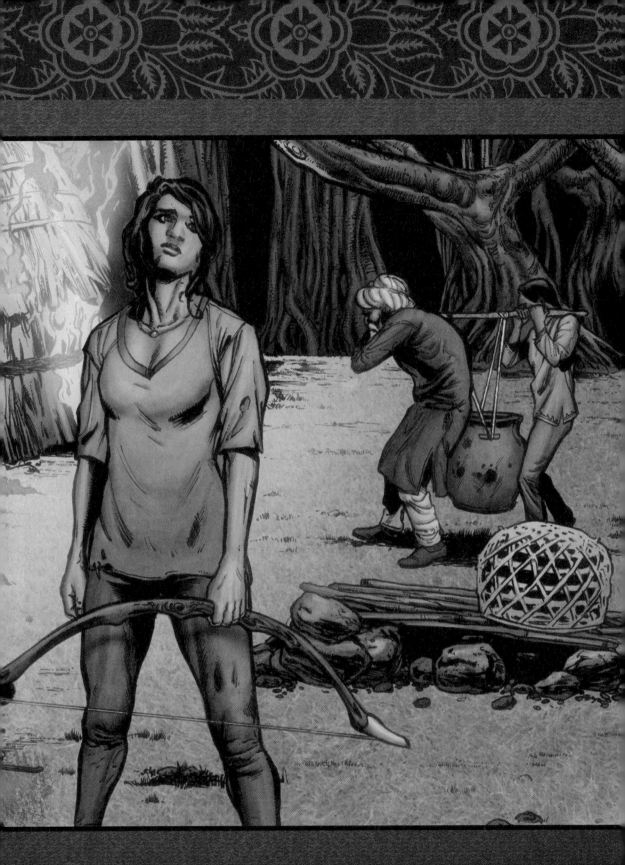

"The gods left this world a long time ago."

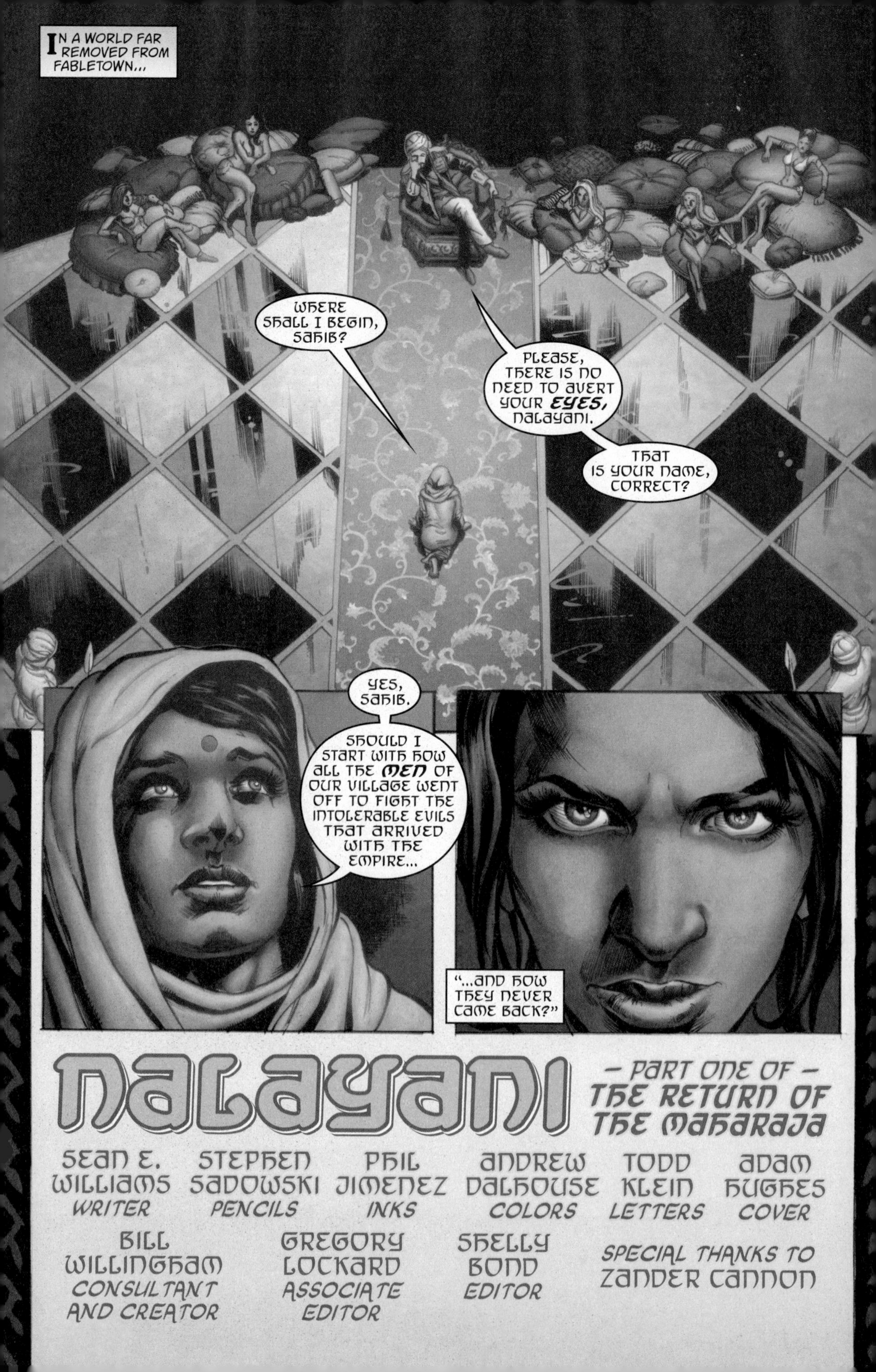
IN A WORLD FAR REMOVED FROM FABLETOWN...
WHERE SHALL I BEGIN, SAHIB?
PLEASE, THERE IS NO NEED TO AVERT YOUR EYES, NALAYANI.
THAT IS YOUR NAME, CORRECT?
YES, SAHIB.
SHOULD I START WITH HOW ALL THE MEN OF OUR VILLAGE WENT OFF TO FIGHT THE INTOLERABLE EVILS THAT ARRIVED WITH THE EMPIRE...
"...AND HOW THEY NEVER CAME BACK?"
NALAYANI
– PART ONE OF – THE RETURN OF THE MAHARAJA
SEAN E. WILLIAMS WRITER
STEPHEN SADOWSKI PENCILS
PHIL JIMENEZ INKS
ANDREW DALHOUSE COLORS
TODD KLEIN LETTERS
ADAM HUGHES COVER
BILL WILLINGHAM CONSULTANT AND CREATOR
GREGORY LOCKARD ASSOCIATE EDITOR
SHELLY BOND EDITOR
SPECIAL THANKS TO ZANDER CANNON

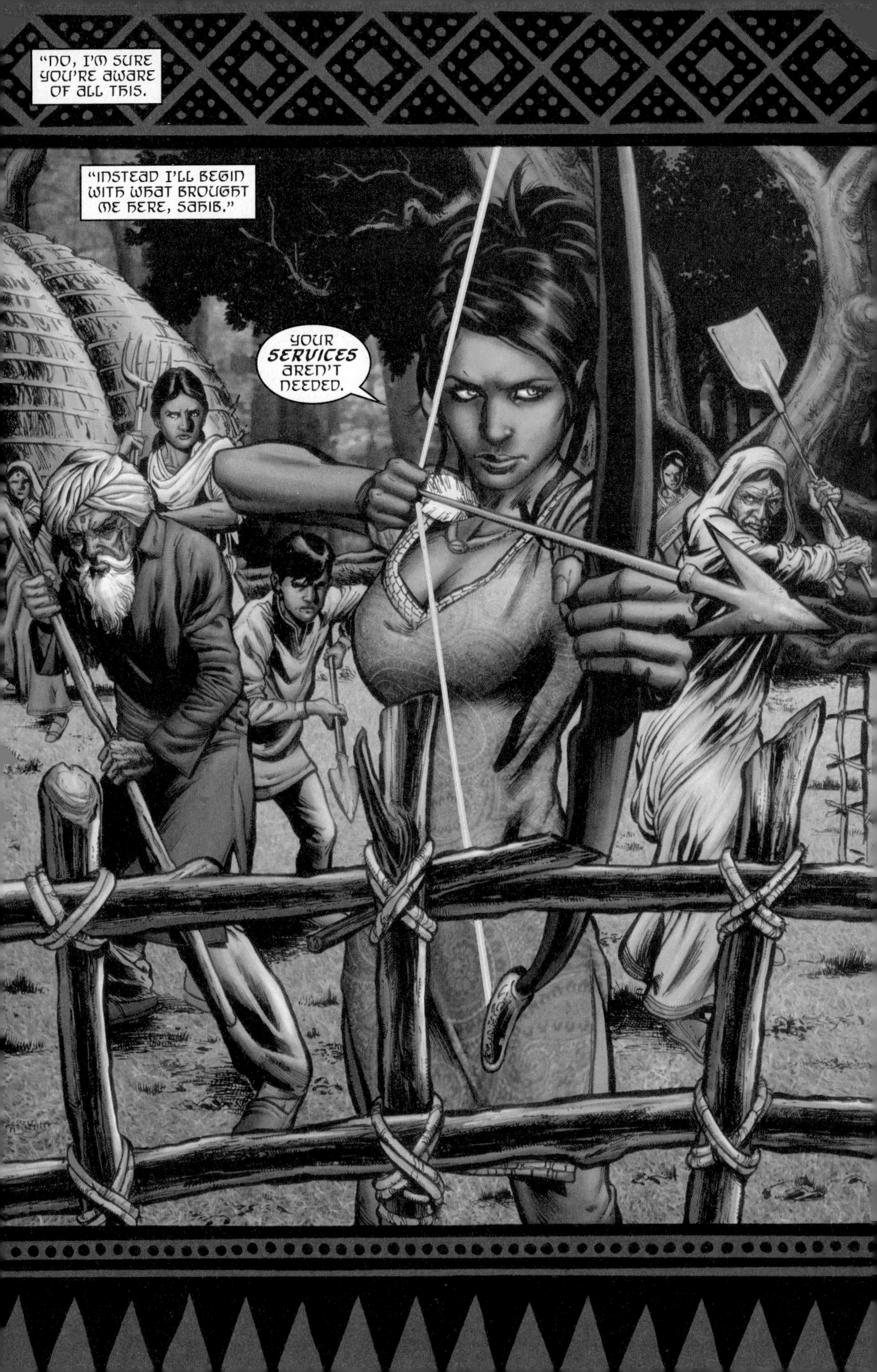
"NO, I'M SURE YOU'RE AWARE OF ALL THIS.
"INSTEAD I'LL BEGIN WITH WHAT BROUGHT ME HERE, SAHIB."
YOUR SERVICES AREN'T NEEDED.

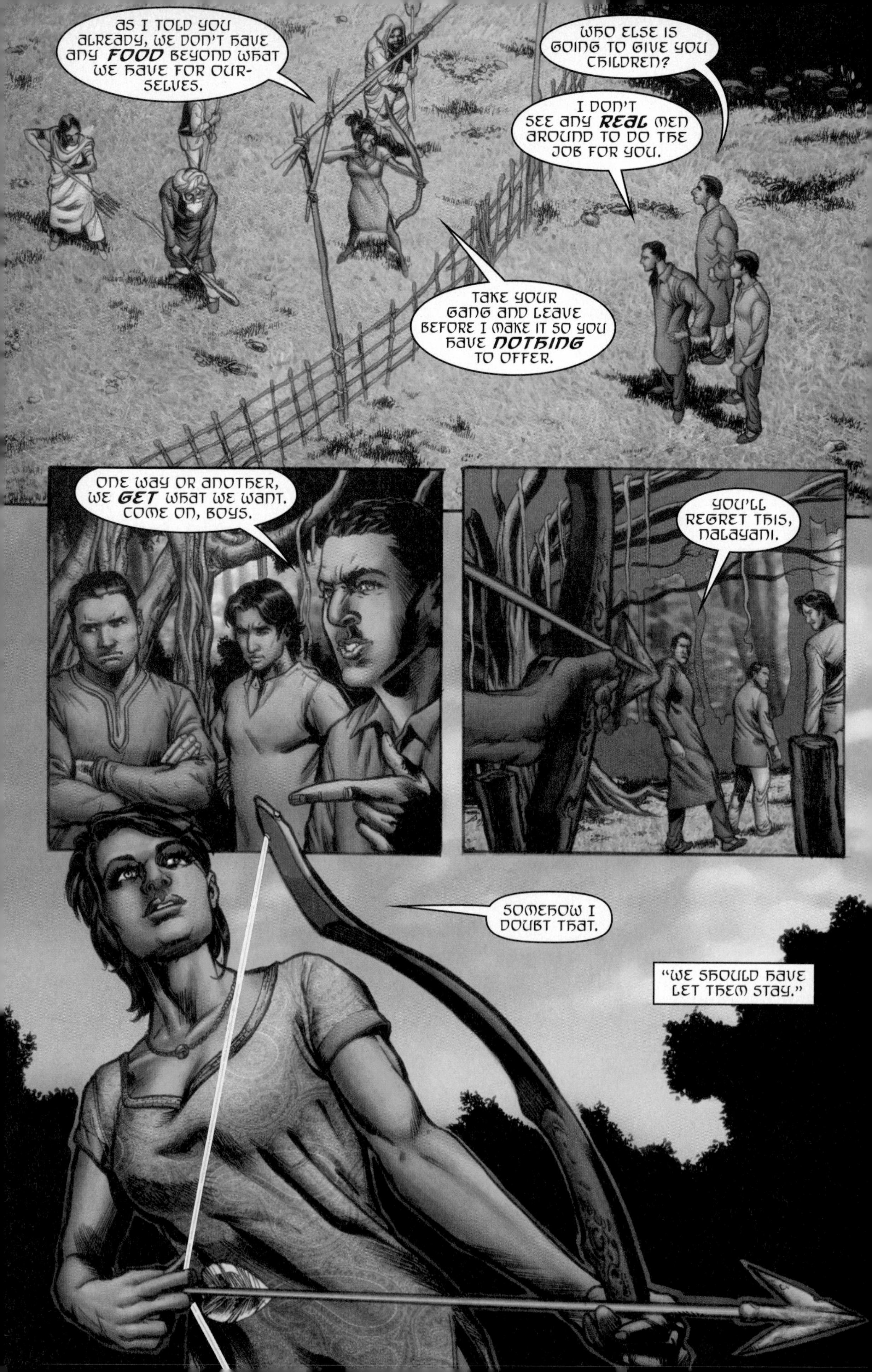
AS I TOLD YOU ALREADY, WE DON'T HAVE ANY FOOD BEYOND WHAT WE HAVE FOR OURSELVES.
WHO ELSE IS GOING TO GIVE YOU CHILDREN?
I DON'T SEE ANY REAL MEN AROUND TO DO THE JOB FOR YOU.
TAKE YOUR GANG AND LEAVE BEFORE I MAKE IT SO YOU HAVE NOTHING TO OFFER.
ONE WAY OR ANOTHER, WE GET WHAT WE WANT. COME ON, BOYS.
YOU'LL REGRET THIS, NALAYANI.
SOMEHOW I DOUBT THAT.
"WE SHOULD HAVE LET THEM STAY."

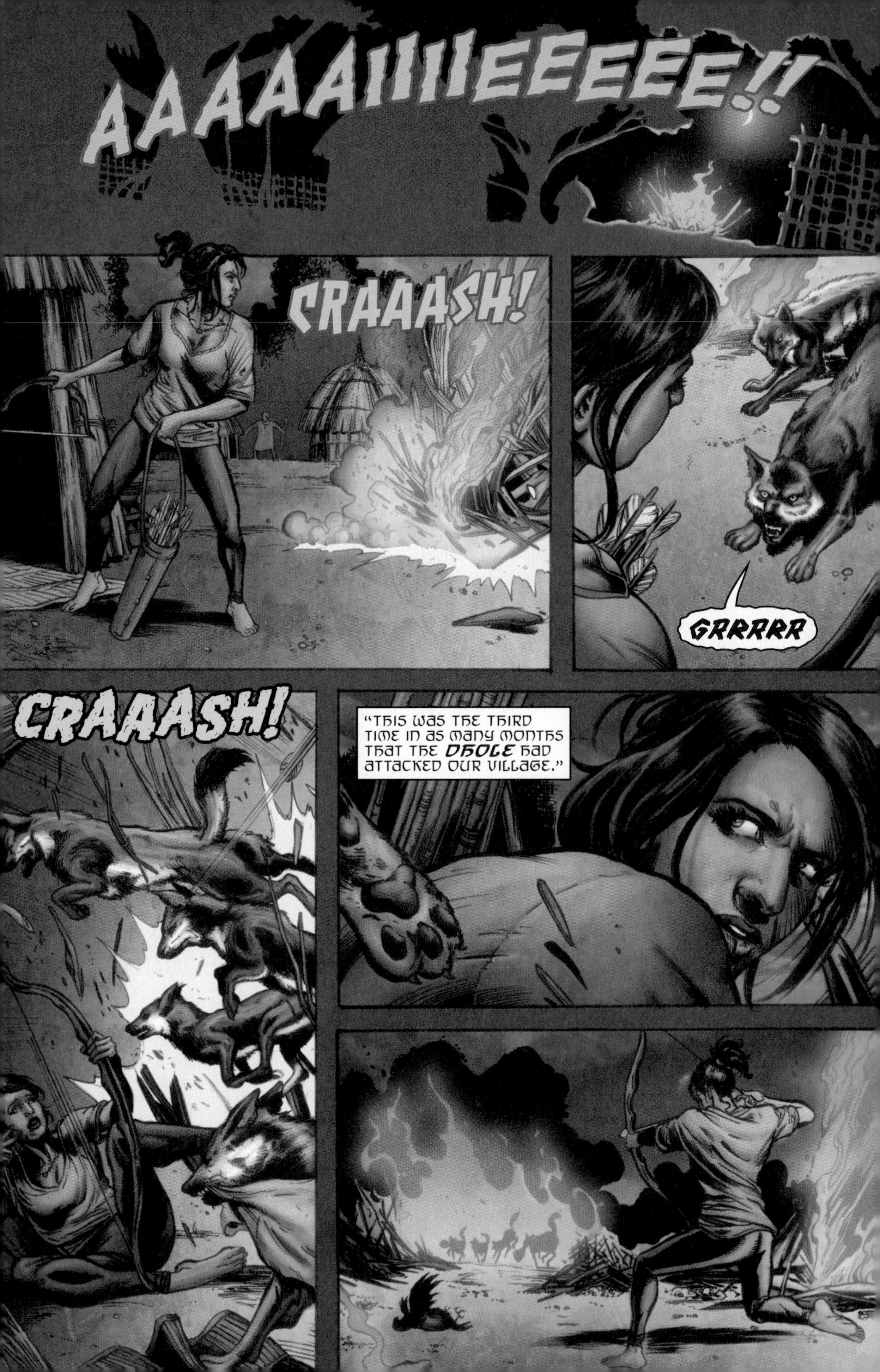
AAAAAIIIIEEEEEE!!
CRAAASH!
GRRRRR
CRAAASH!
"THIS WAS THE THIRD TIME IN AS MANY MONTHS THAT THE DHOLE HAD ATTACKED OUR VILLAGE."

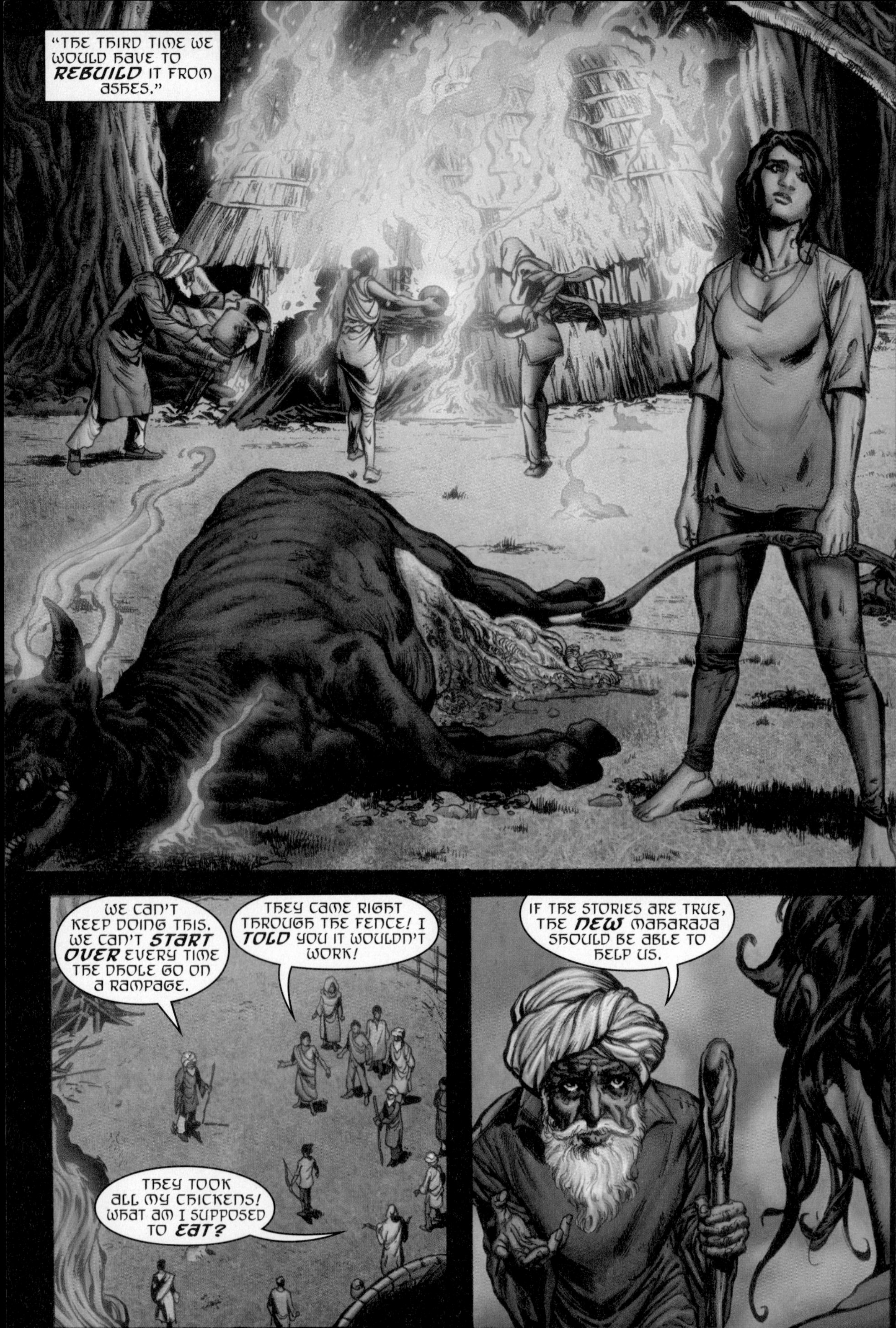

"THE THIRD TIME WE WOULD HAVE TO REBUILD IT FROM ASHES."
WE CAN'T KEEP DOING THIS. WE CAN'T START OVER EVERY TIME THE DHOLE GO ON A RAMPAGE.
THEY CAME RIGHT THROUGH THE FENCE! I TOLD YOU IT WOULDN'T WORK!
THEY TOOK ALL MY CHICKENS! WHAT AM I SUPPOSED TO EAT?
IF THE STORIES ARE TRUE, THE NEW MAHARAJA SHOULD BE ABLE TO HELP US.

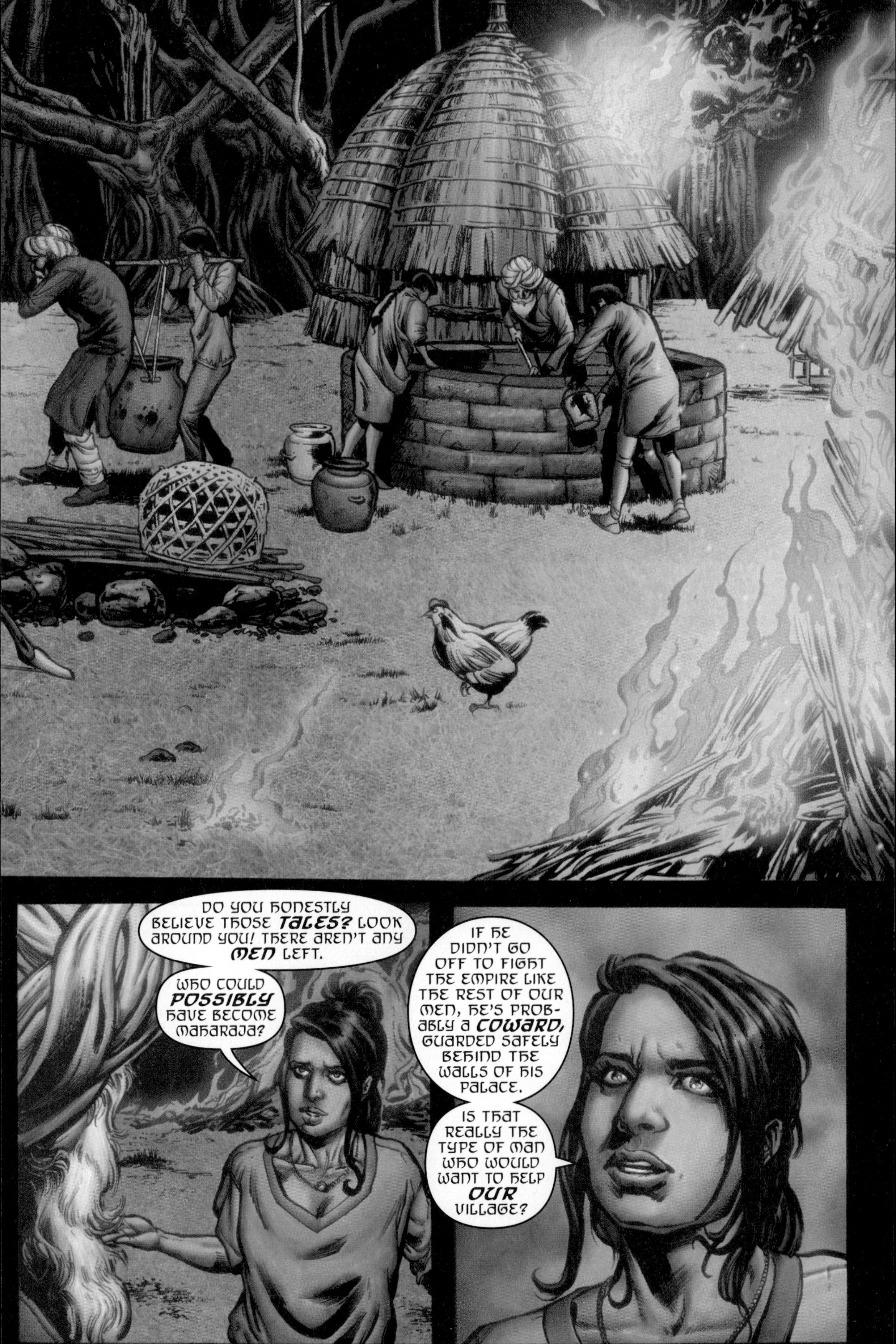
DO YOU HONESTLY BELIEVE THOSE TALES? LOOK AROUND YOU! THERE AREN'T ANY MEN LEFT.
WHO COULD POSSIBLY HAVE BECOME MAHARAJA?
IF HE DIDN'T GO OFF TO FIGHT THE EMPIRE LIKE THE REST OF OUR MEN, HE'S PROBABLY A COWARD, GUARDED SAFELY BEHIND THE WALLS OF HIS PALACE.
IS THAT REALLY THE TYPE OF MAN WHO WOULD WANT TO HELP OUR VILLAGE?

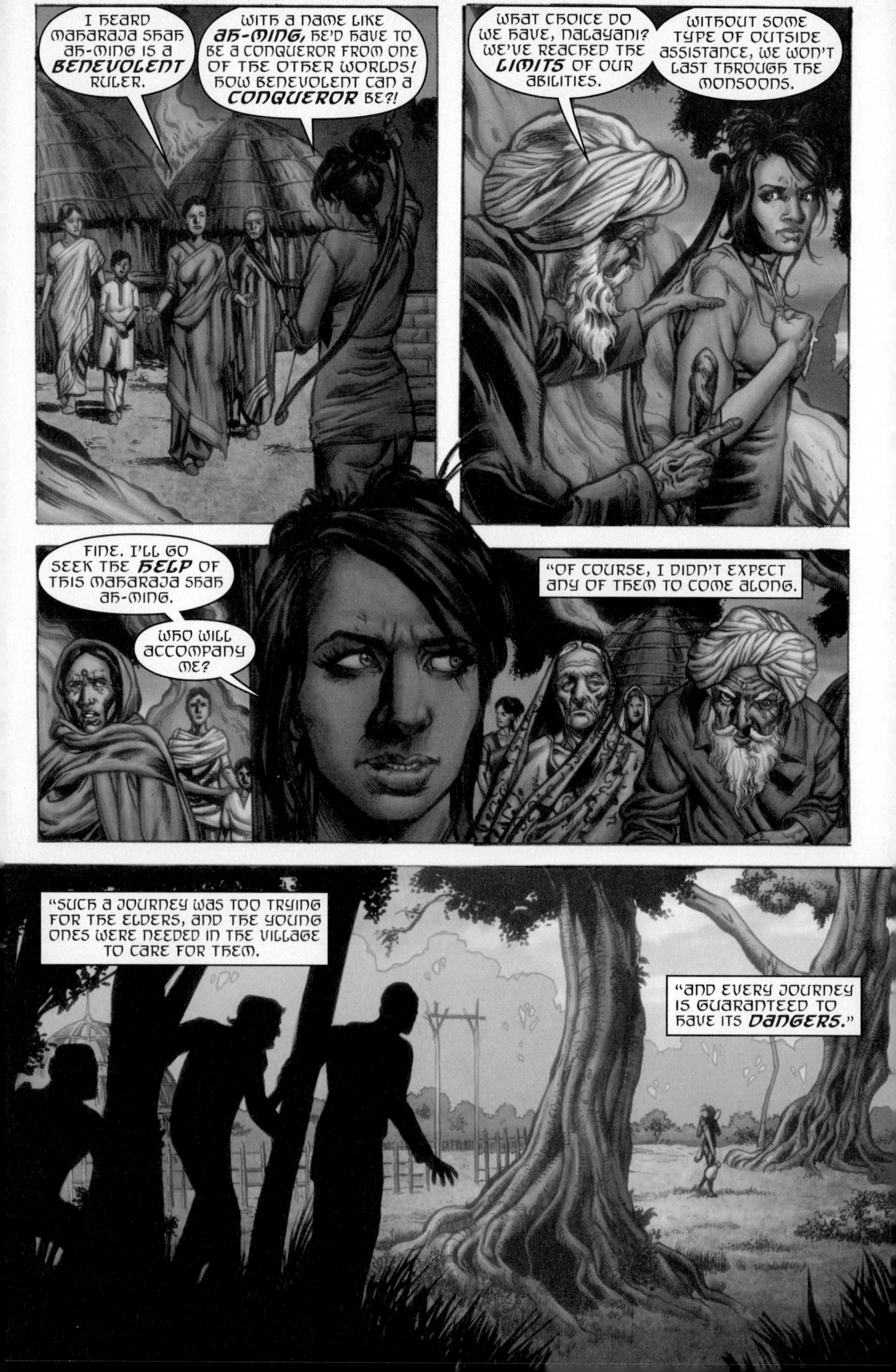
I HEARD MAHARAJA SHAH AH-MING IS A BENEVOLENT RULER.
WITH A NAME LIKE AH-MING, HE'D HAVE TO BE A CONQUEROR FROM ONE OF THE OTHER WORLDS! HOW BENEVOLENT CAN A CONQUEROR BE?!
WHAT CHOICE DO WE HAVE, NALAYANI? WE'VE REACHED THE LIMITS OF OUR ABILITIES.
WITHOUT SOME TYPE OF OUTSIDE ASSISTANCE, WE WON'T LAST THROUGH THE MONSOONS.
FINE. I'LL GO SEEK THE HELP OF THIS MAHARAJA SHAH AH-MING.
WHO WILL ACCOMPANY ME?
"OF COURSE, I DIDN'T EXPECT ANY OF THEM TO COME ALONG.
"SUCH A JOURNEY WAS TOO TRYING FOR THE ELDERS, AND THE YOUNG ONES WERE NEEDED IN THE VILLAGE TO CARE FOR THEM.
"AND EVERY JOURNEY IS GUARANTEED TO HAVE ITS DANGERS."

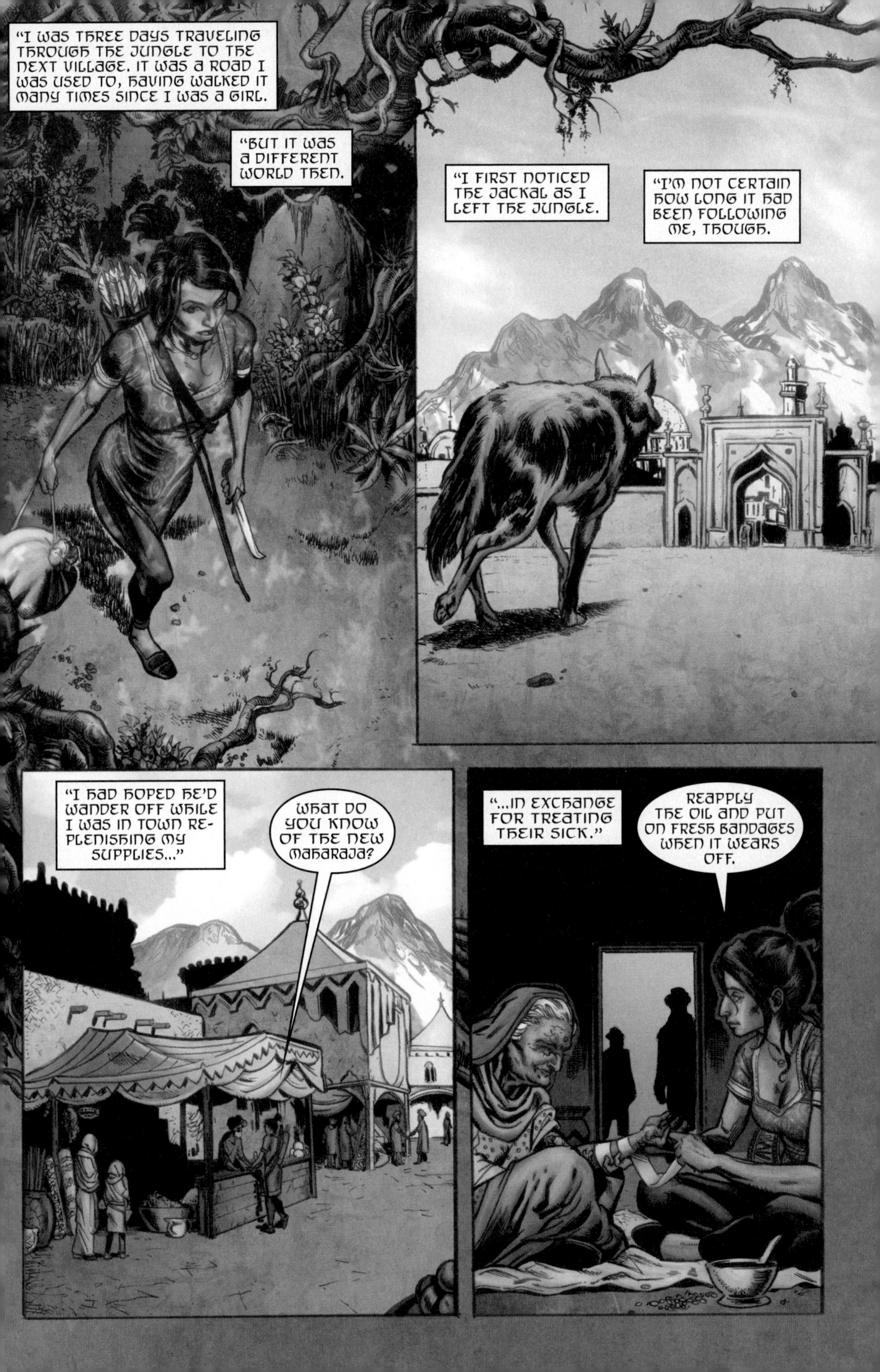
"I WAS THREE DAYS TRAVELING THROUGH THE JUNGLE TO THE NEXT VILLAGE. IT WAS A ROAD I WAS USED TO, HAVING WALKED IT MANY TIMES SINCE I WAS A GIRL.
"BUT IT WAS A DIFFERENT WORLD THEN.
"I FIRST NOTICED THE JACKAL AS I LEFT THE JUNGLE.
"I'M NOT CERTAIN HOW LONG IT HAD BEEN FOLLOWING ME, THOUGH.
"I HAD HOPED HE'D WANDER OFF WHILE I WAS IN TOWN REPLENISHING MY SUPPLIES..."
WHAT DO YOU KNOW OF THE NEW MAHARAJA?
"...IN EXCHANGE FOR TREATING THEIR SICK."
REAPPLY THE OIL AND PUT ON FRESH BANDAGES WHEN IT WEARS OFF.

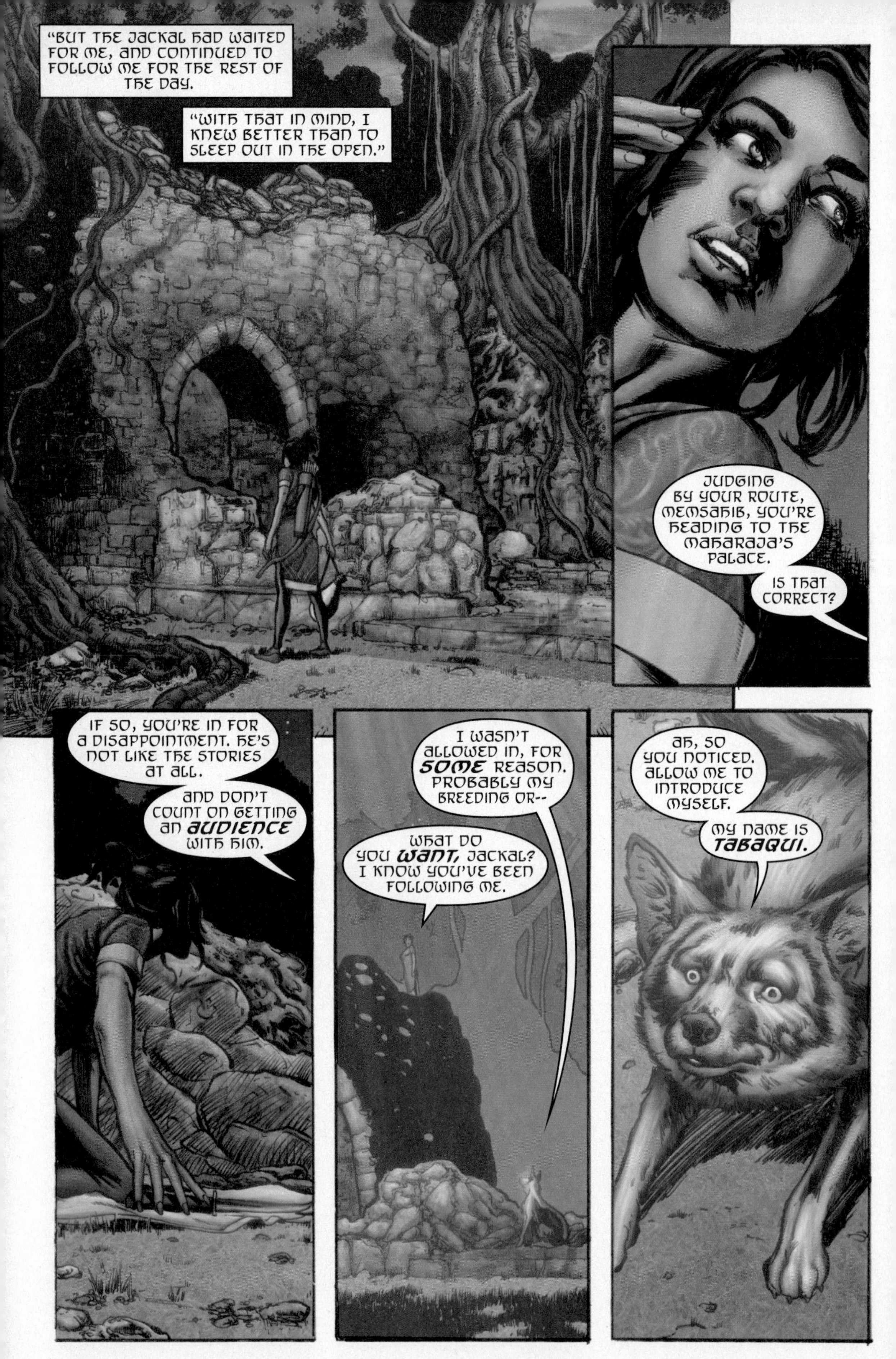
"BUT THE JACKAL HAD WAITED FOR ME, AND CONTINUED TO FOLLOW ME FOR THE REST OF THE DAY.
"WITH THAT IN MIND, I KNEW BETTER THAN TO SLEEP OUT IN THE OPEN."
JUDGING BY YOUR ROUTE, MEMSAHIB, YOU'RE HEADING TO THE MAHARAJA'S PALACE.
IS THAT CORRECT?
IF SO, YOU'RE IN FOR A DISAPPOINTMENT. HE'S NOT LIKE THE STORIES AT ALL.
AND DON'T COUNT ON GETTING AN *AUDIENCE* WITH HIM.
I WASN'T ALLOWED IN, FOR *SOME* REASON. PROBABLY MY BREEDING OR--
WHAT DO YOU *WANT,* JACKAL? I KNOW YOU'VE BEEN FOLLOWING ME.
AH, SO YOU NOTICED. ALLOW ME TO INTRODUCE MYSELF.
MY NAME IS *TABAQUI.*

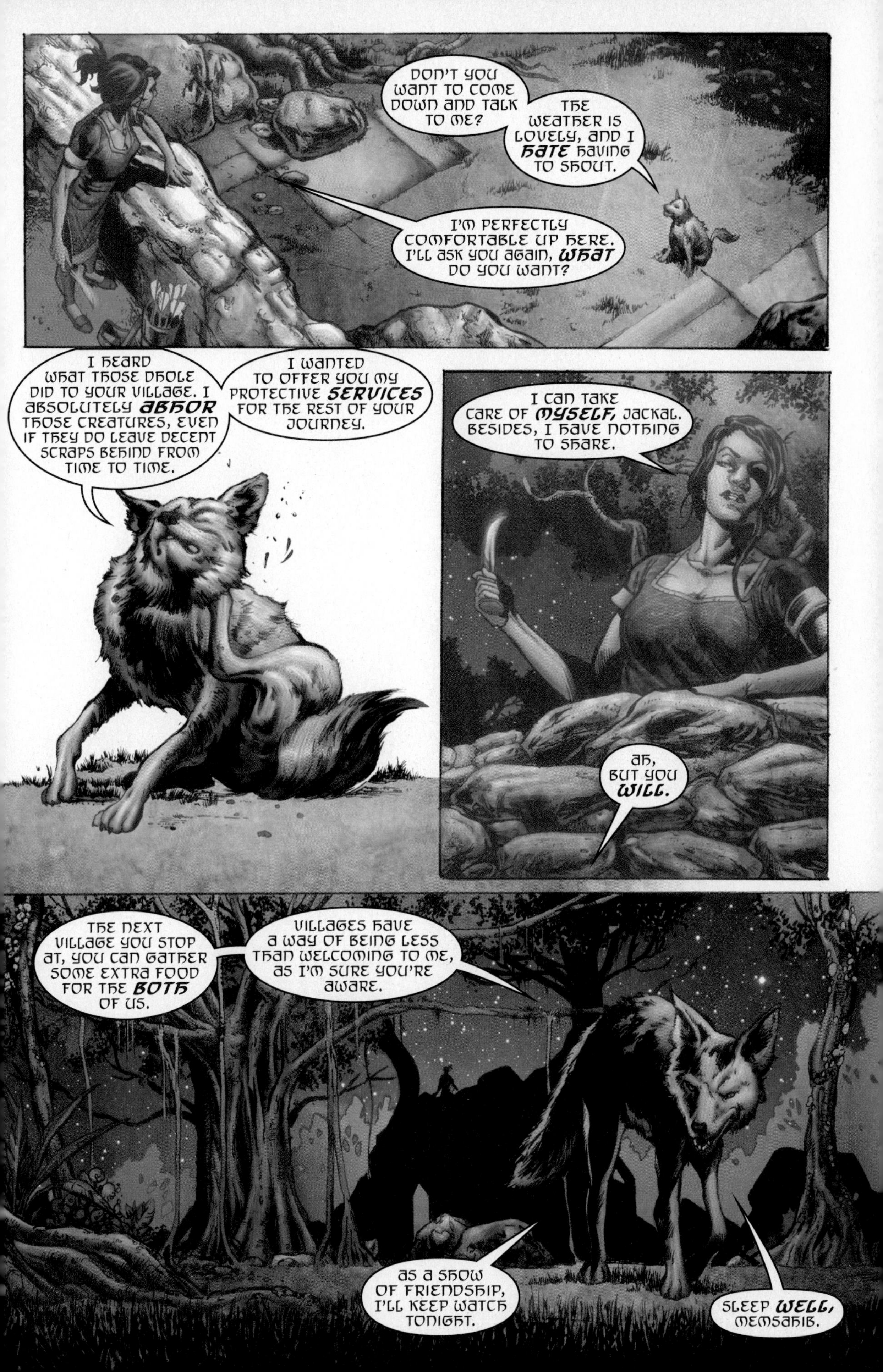
DON'T YOU WANT TO COME DOWN AND TALK TO ME?
THE WEATHER IS LOVELY, AND I HATE HAVING TO SHOUT.
I'M PERFECTLY COMFORTABLE UP HERE. I'LL ASK YOU AGAIN, WHAT DO YOU WANT?
I HEARD WHAT THOSE DHOLE DID TO YOUR VILLAGE. I ABSOLUTELY ABHOR THOSE CREATURES, EVEN IF THEY DO LEAVE DECENT SCRAPS BEHIND FROM TIME TO TIME.
I WANTED TO OFFER YOU MY PROTECTIVE SERVICES FOR THE REST OF YOUR JOURNEY.
I CAN TAKE CARE OF MYSELF, JACKAL. BESIDES, I HAVE NOTHING TO SHARE.
AH, BUT YOU WILL.
THE NEXT VILLAGE YOU STOP AT, YOU CAN GATHER SOME EXTRA FOOD FOR THE BOTH OF US.
VILLAGES HAVE A WAY OF BEING LESS THAN WELCOMING TO ME, AS I'M SURE YOU'RE AWARE.
AS A SHOW OF FRIENDSHIP, I'LL KEEP WATCH TONIGHT.
SLEEP WELL, MEMSAHIB.

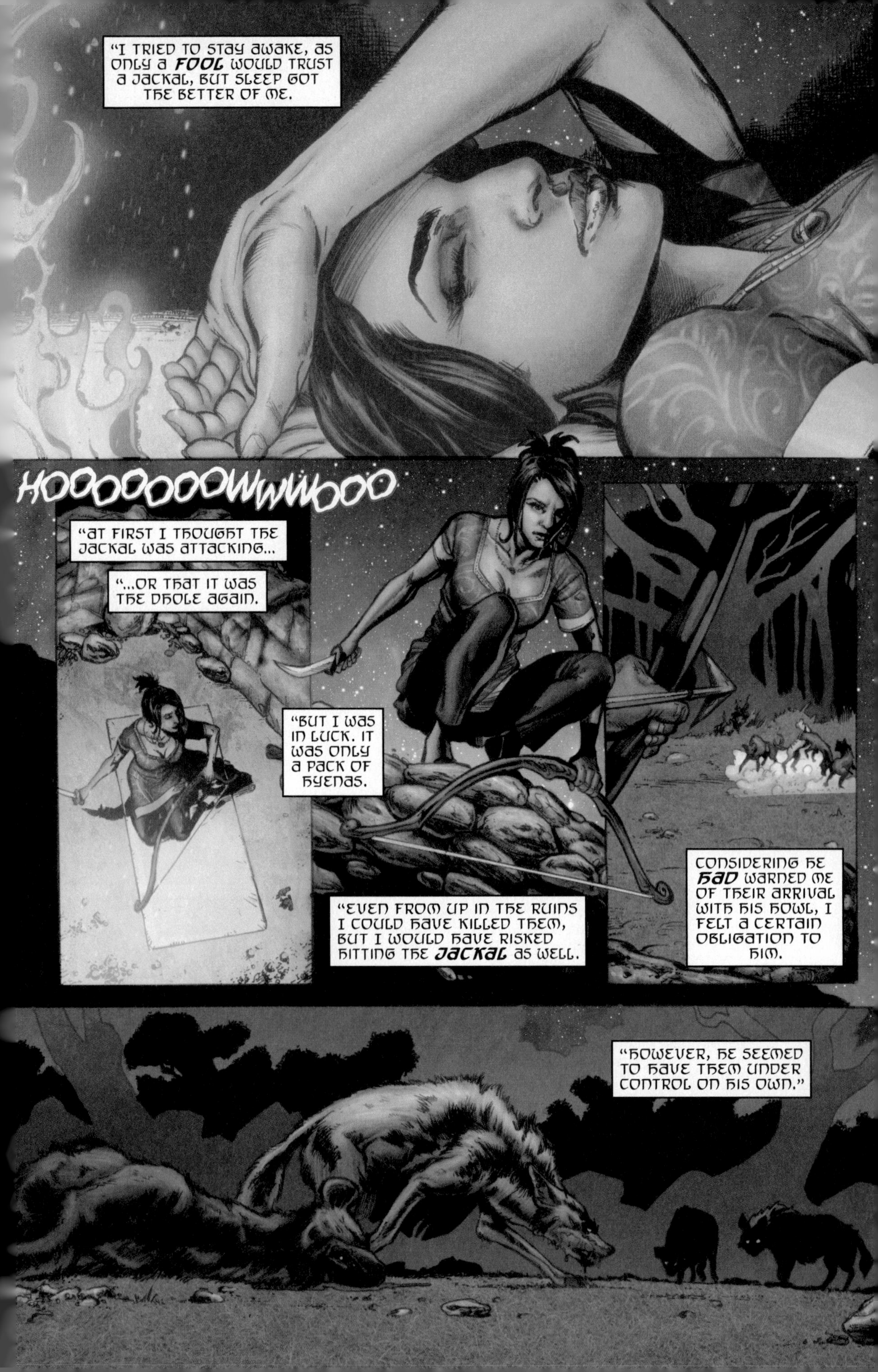
"I TRIED TO STAY AWAKE, AS ONLY A FOOL WOULD TRUST A JACKAL, BUT SLEEP GOT THE BETTER OF ME.
HOOOOOOOOWWWOOO
"AT FIRST I THOUGHT THE JACKAL WAS ATTACKING...
"...OR THAT IT WAS THE DHOLE AGAIN.
"BUT I WAS IN LUCK. IT WAS ONLY A PACK OF HYENAS.
"EVEN FROM UP IN THE RUINS I COULD HAVE KILLED THEM, BUT I WOULD HAVE RISKED HITTING THE JACKAL AS WELL.
CONSIDERING HE HAD WARNED ME OF THEIR ARRIVAL WITH HIS HOWL, I FELT A CERTAIN OBLIGATION TO HIM.
"HOWEVER, HE SEEMED TO HAVE THEM UNDER CONTROL ON HIS OWN."

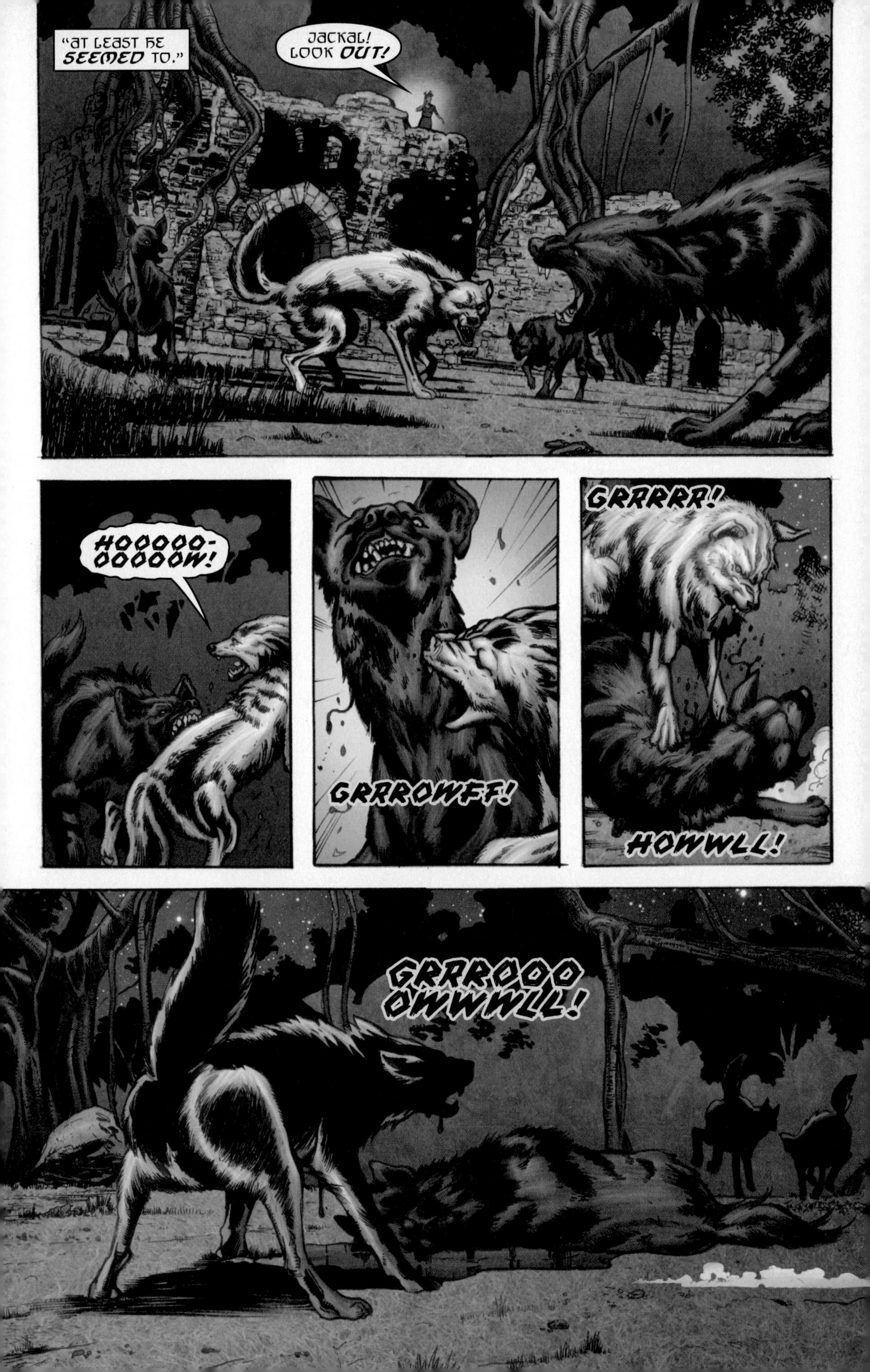
"AT LEAST HE SEEMED TO."
JACKAL! LOOK OUT!
HOOOOO-OOOOOW!
GRRROWFF!
GRRRRR!
HOWWLL!
GRRROOO OWWWLL!

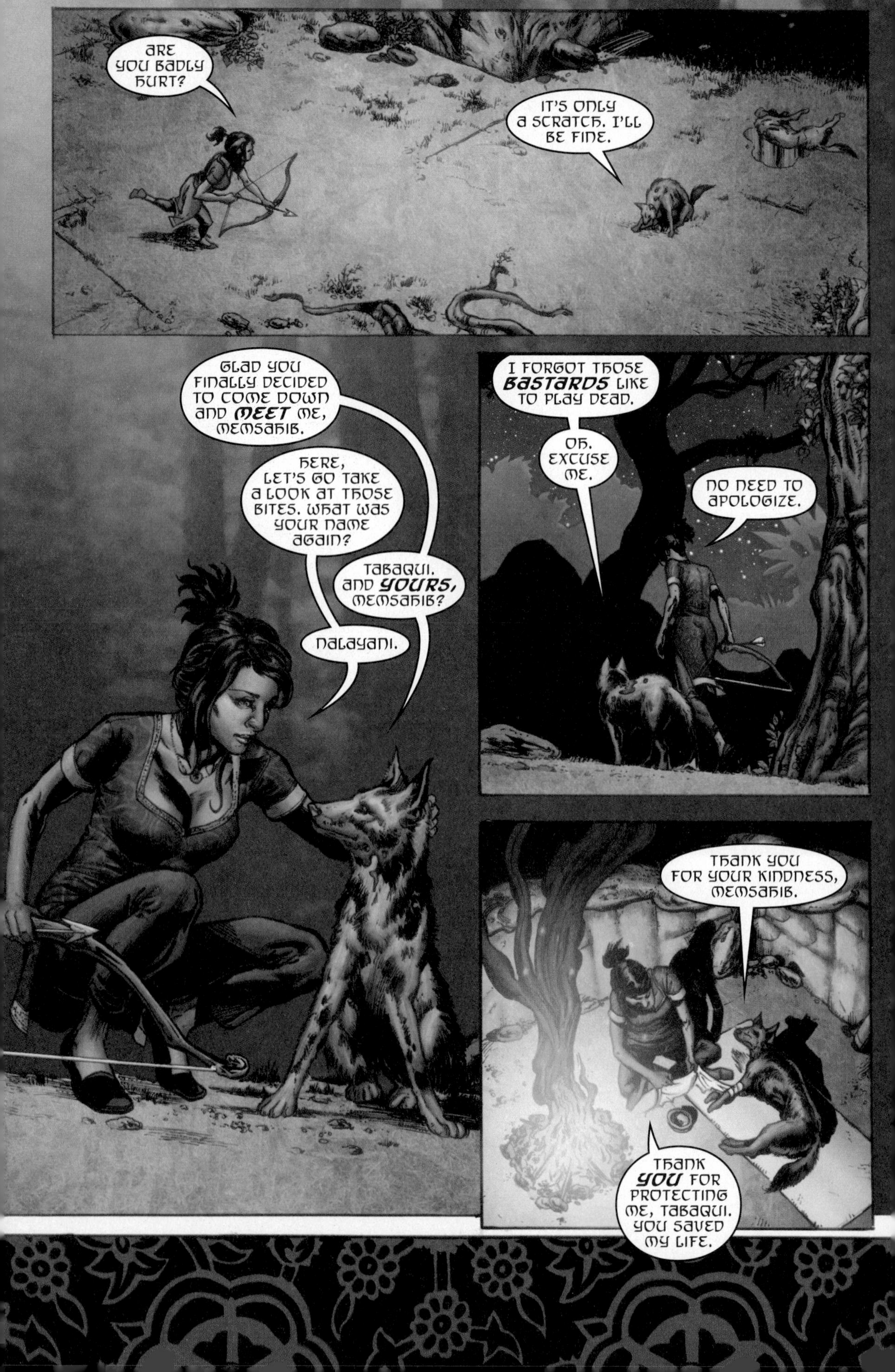

ARE YOU BADLY HURT?
IT'S ONLY A SCRATCH. I'LL BE FINE.
GLAD YOU FINALLY DECIDED TO COME DOWN AND MEET ME, MEMSAHIB.
HERE, LET'S GO TAKE A LOOK AT THOSE BITES. WHAT WAS YOUR NAME AGAIN?
TABAQUI. AND YOURS, MEMSAHIB?
NALAYANI.
I FORGOT THOSE BASTARDS LIKE TO PLAY DEAD.
OH. EXCUSE ME.
NO NEED TO APOLOGIZE.
THANK YOU FOR YOUR KINDNESS, MEMSAHIB.
THANK YOU FOR PROTECTING ME, TABAQUI. YOU SAVED MY LIFE.

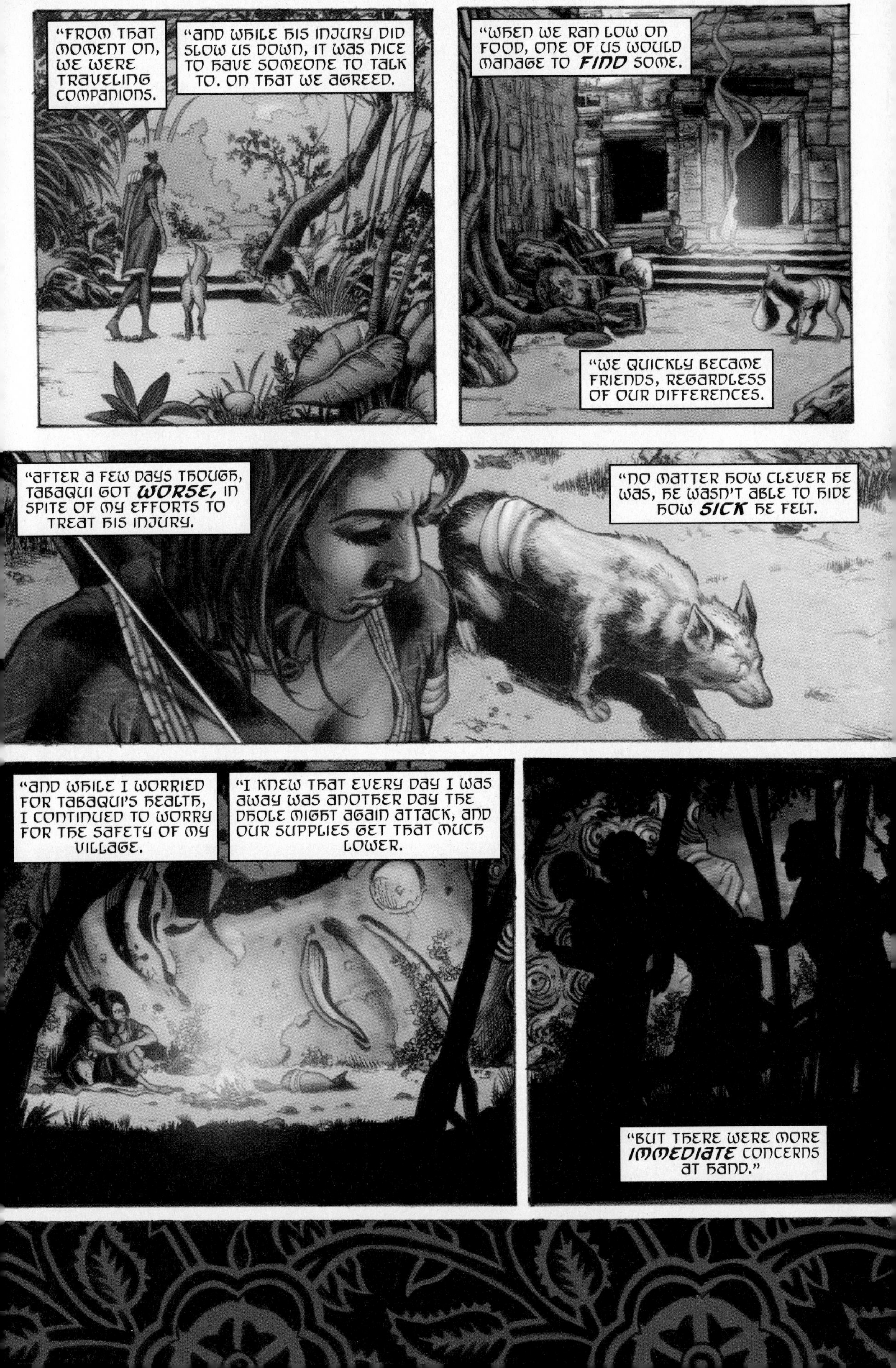

"FROM THAT MOMENT ON, WE WERE TRAVELING COMPANIONS.
"AND WHILE HIS INJURY DID SLOW US DOWN, IT WAS NICE TO HAVE SOMEONE TO TALK TO. ON THAT WE AGREED.
"WHEN WE RAN LOW ON FOOD, ONE OF US WOULD MANAGE TO FIND SOME.
"WE QUICKLY BECAME FRIENDS, REGARDLESS OF OUR DIFFERENCES.
"AFTER A FEW DAYS THOUGH, TABAQUI GOT WORSE, IN SPITE OF MY EFFORTS TO TREAT HIS INJURY.
"NO MATTER HOW CLEVER HE WAS, HE WASN'T ABLE TO HIDE HOW SICK HE FELT.
"AND WHILE I WORRIED FOR TABAQUI'S HEALTH, I CONTINUED TO WORRY FOR THE SAFETY OF MY VILLAGE.
"I KNEW THAT EVERY DAY I WAS AWAY WAS ANOTHER DAY THE DHOLE MIGHT AGAIN ATTACK, AND OUR SUPPLIES GET THAT MUCH LOWER.
"BUT THERE WERE MORE IMMEDIATE CONCERNS AT HAND."

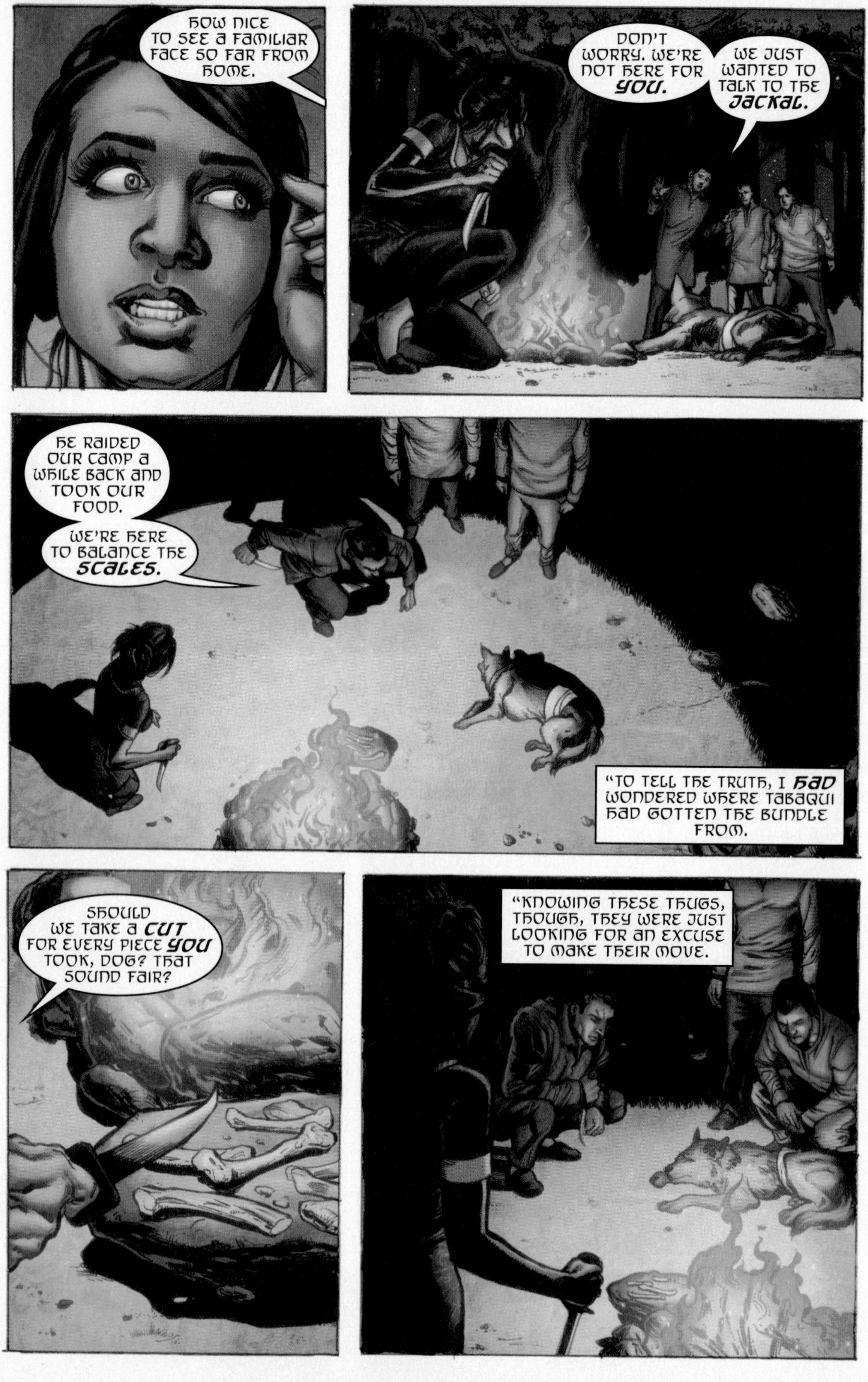
HOW NICE TO SEE A FAMILIAR FACE SO FAR FROM HOME.
DON'T WORRY. WE'RE NOT HERE FOR YOU.
WE JUST WANTED TO TALK TO THE JACKAL.
HE RAIDED OUR CAMP A WHILE BACK AND TOOK OUR FOOD.
WE'RE HERE TO BALANCE THE SCALES.
"TO TELL THE TRUTH, I HAD WONDERED WHERE TABAQUI HAD GOTTEN THE BUNDLE FROM.
SHOULD WE TAKE A CUT FOR EVERY PIECE YOU TOOK, DOG? THAT SOUND FAIR?
"KNOWING THESE THUGS, THOUGH, THEY WERE JUST LOOKING FOR AN EXCUSE TO MAKE THEIR MOVE.

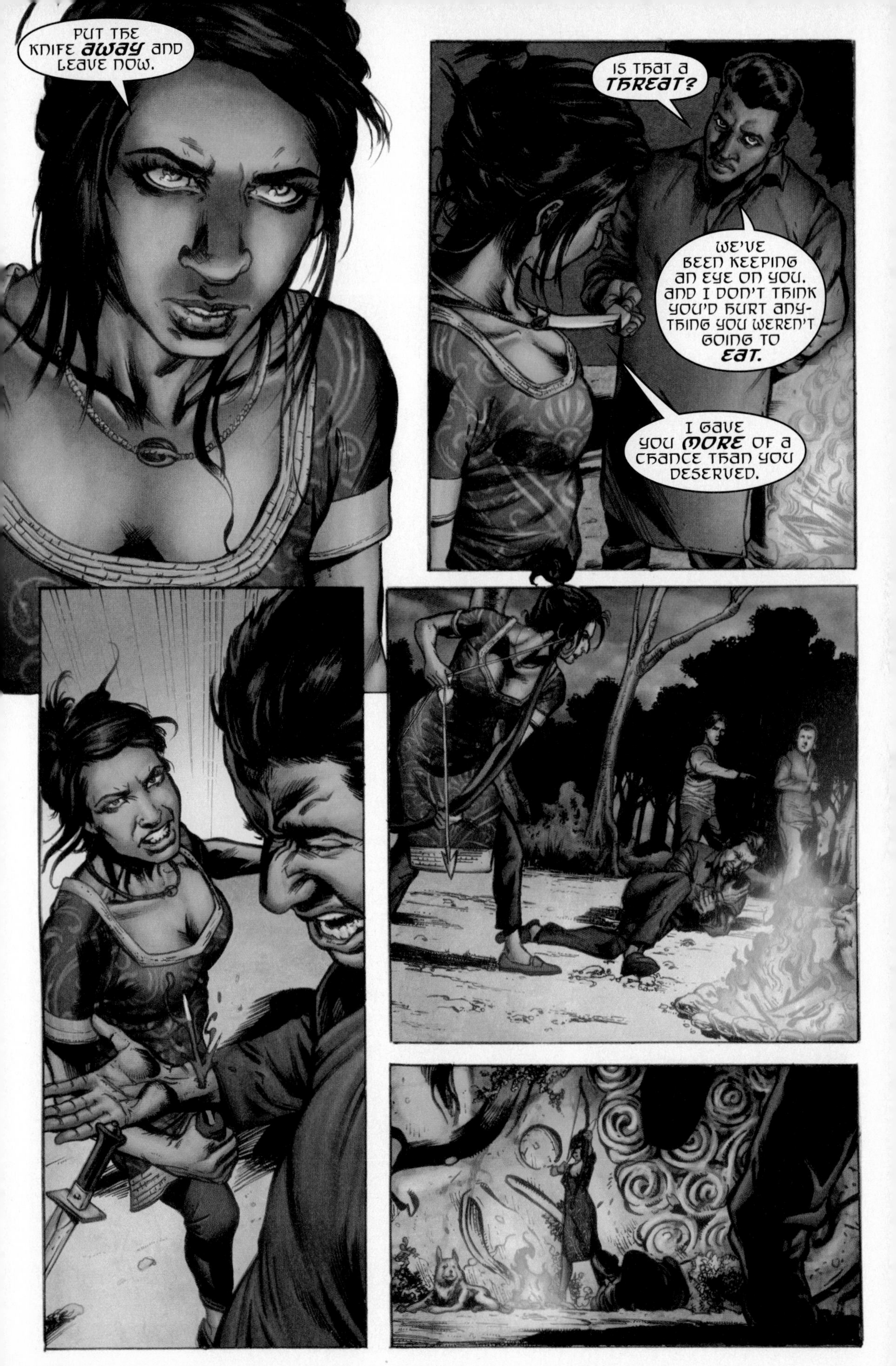
PUT THE KNIFE AWAY AND LEAVE NOW.
IS THAT A THREAT?
WE'VE BEEN KEEPING AN EYE ON YOU, AND I DON'T THINK YOU'D HURT ANY-THING YOU WEREN'T GOING TO EAT.
I GAVE YOU MORE OF A CHANCE THAN YOU DESERVED.

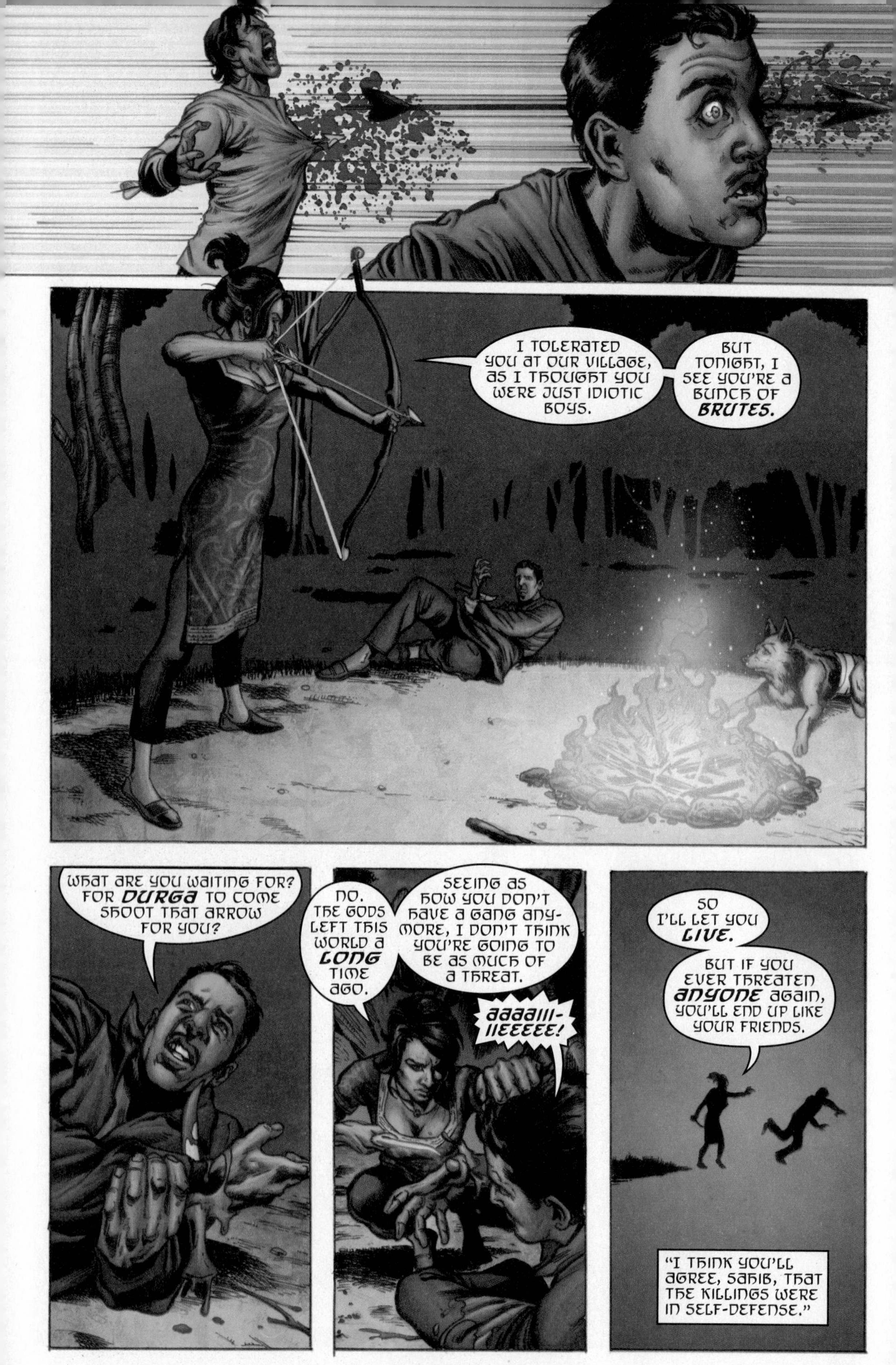

I TOLERATED YOU AT OUR VILLAGE, AS I THOUGHT YOU WERE JUST IDIOTIC BOYS.
BUT TONIGHT, I SEE YOU'RE A BUNCH OF BRUTES.
WHAT ARE YOU WAITING FOR? FOR DURGA TO COME SHOOT THAT ARROW FOR YOU?
NO. THE GODS LEFT THIS WORLD A LONG TIME AGO.
SEEING AS HOW YOU DON'T HAVE A GANG ANY-MORE, I DON'T THINK YOU'RE GOING TO BE AS MUCH OF A THREAT.
AAAAIII-IIEEEEE!
SO I'LL LET YOU LIVE.
BUT IF YOU EVER THREATEN ANYONE AGAIN, YOU'LL END UP LIKE YOUR FRIENDS.
"I THINK YOU'LL AGREE, SAHIB, THAT THE KILLINGS WERE IN SELF-DEFENSE."

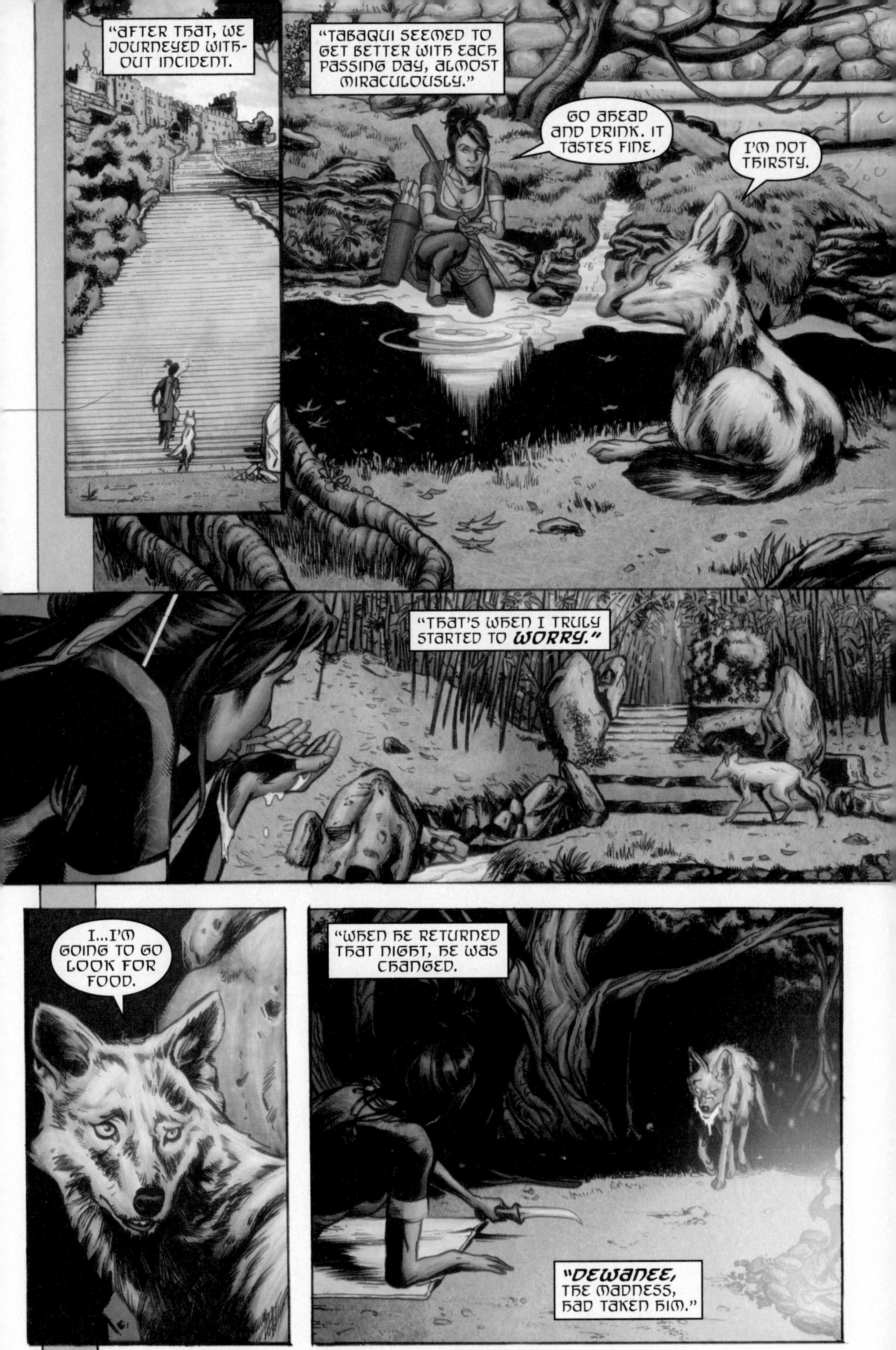
"AFTER THAT, WE JOURNEYED WITHOUT INCIDENT.
"TABAQUI SEEMED TO GET BETTER WITH EACH PASSING DAY, ALMOST MIRACULOUSLY."
GO AHEAD AND DRINK. IT TASTES FINE.
I'M NOT THIRSTY.
"THAT'S WHEN I TRULY STARTED TO WORRY."
I...I'M GOING TO GO LOOK FOR FOOD.
"WHEN HE RETURNED THAT NIGHT, HE WAS CHANGED.
"DEWANEE, THE MADNESS, HAD TAKEN HIM."

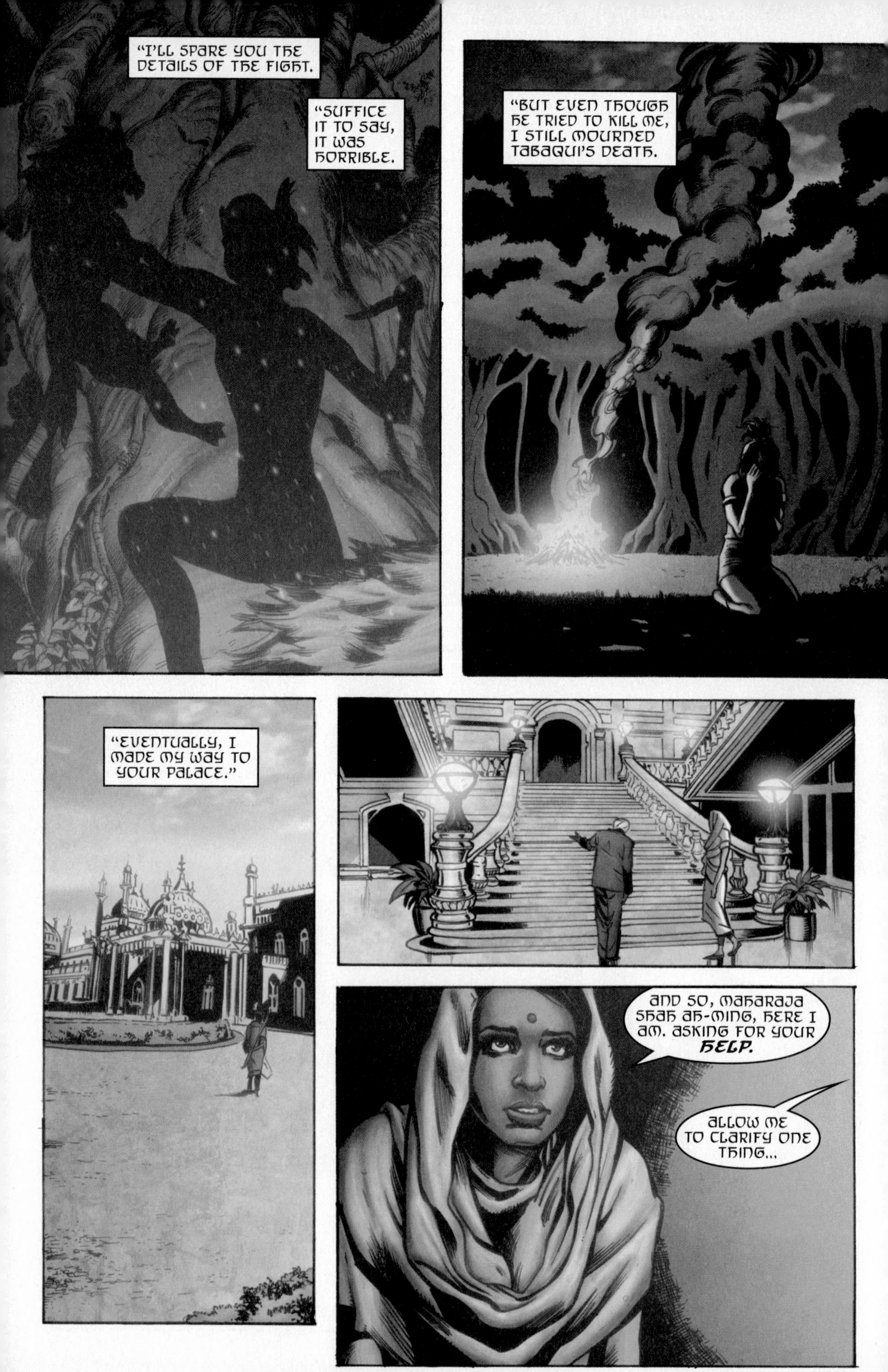
"I'LL SPARE YOU THE DETAILS OF THE FIGHT.
"SUFFICE IT TO SAY, IT WAS HORRIBLE.
"BUT EVEN THOUGH HE TRIED TO KILL ME, I STILL MOURNED TABAQUI'S DEATH.
"EVENTUALLY, I MADE MY WAY TO YOUR PALACE."
AND SO, MAHARAJA SHAH AH-MING, HERE I AM. ASKING FOR YOUR HELP.
ALLOW ME TO CLARIFY ONE THING...

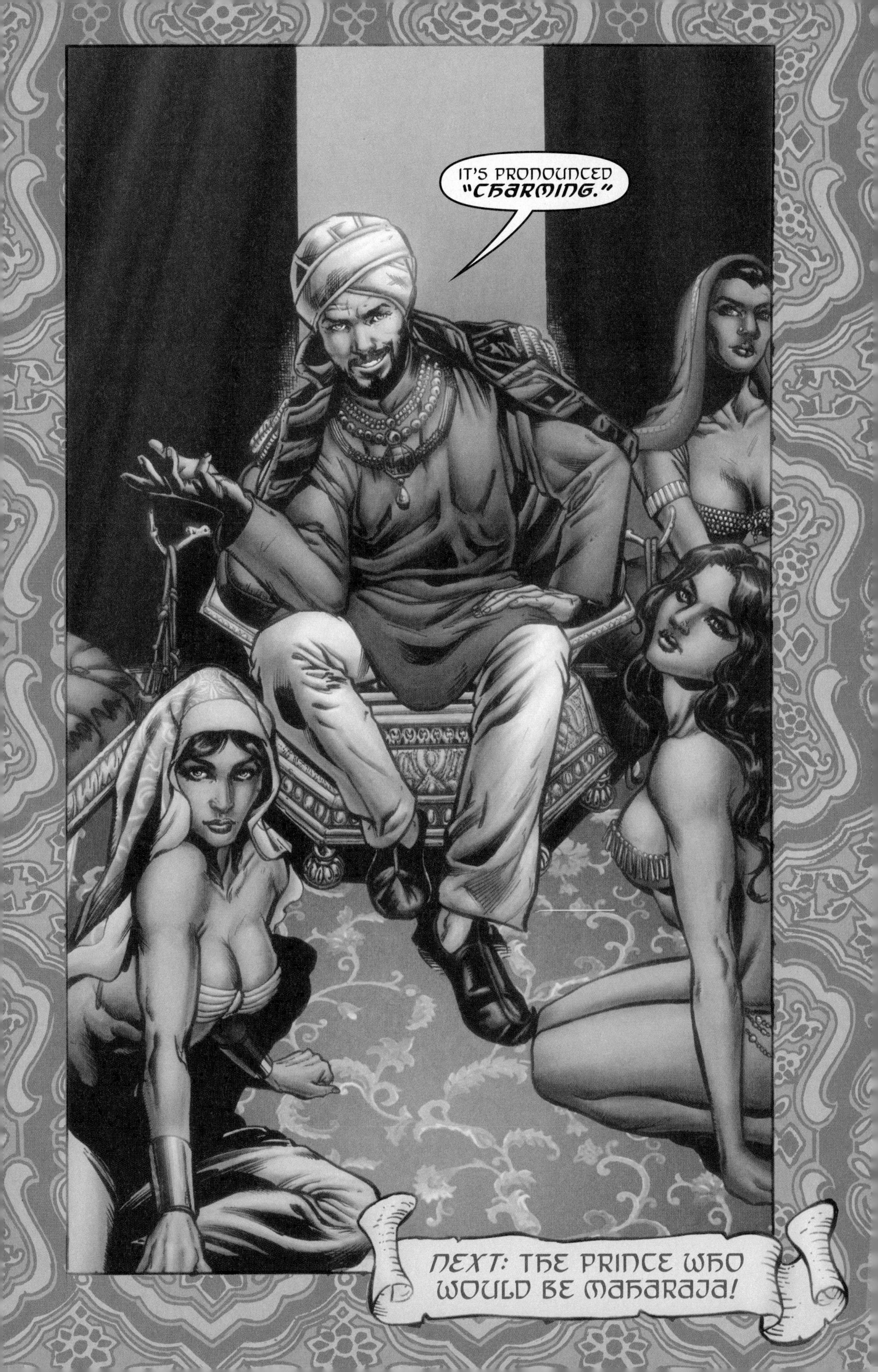
IT'S PRONOUNCED "CHARMING."
NEXT: THE PRINCE WHO WOULD BE MAHARAJA!

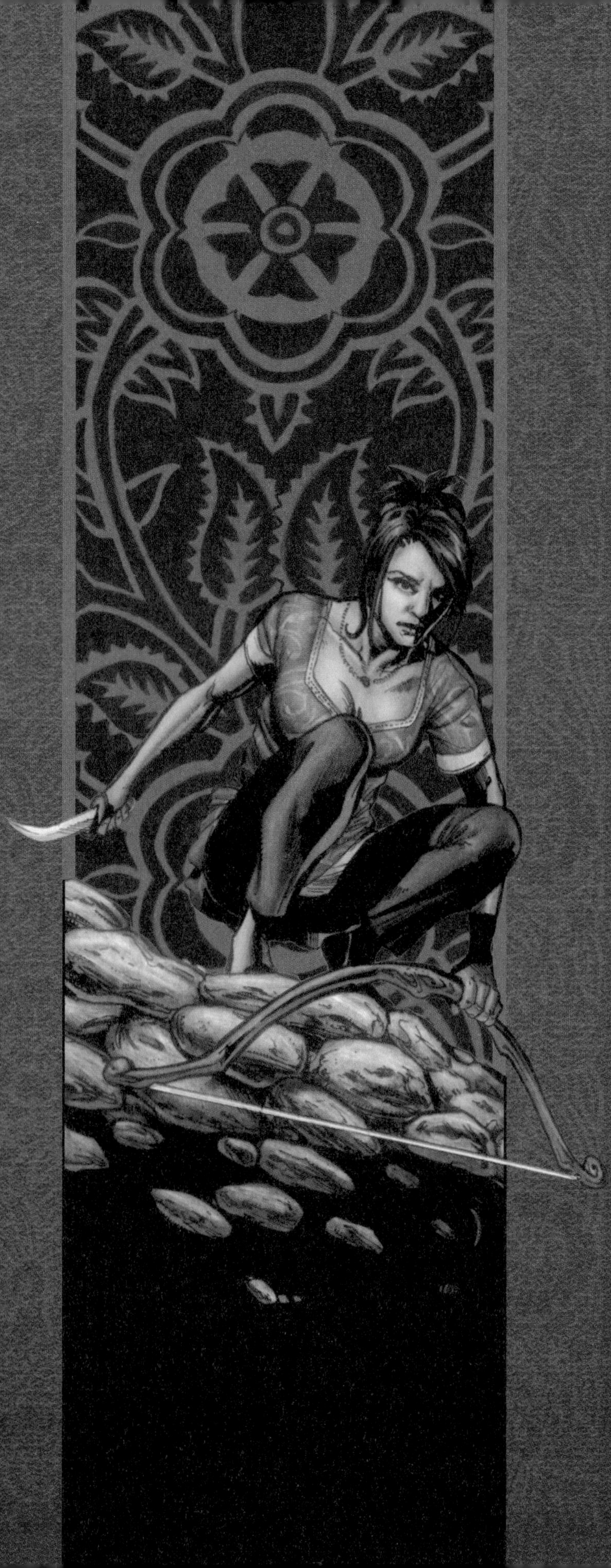

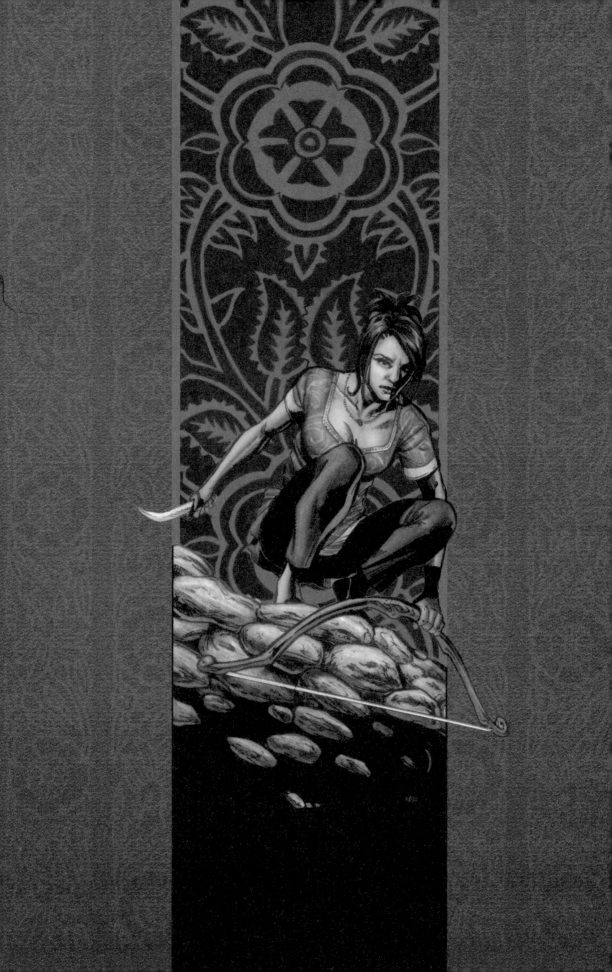

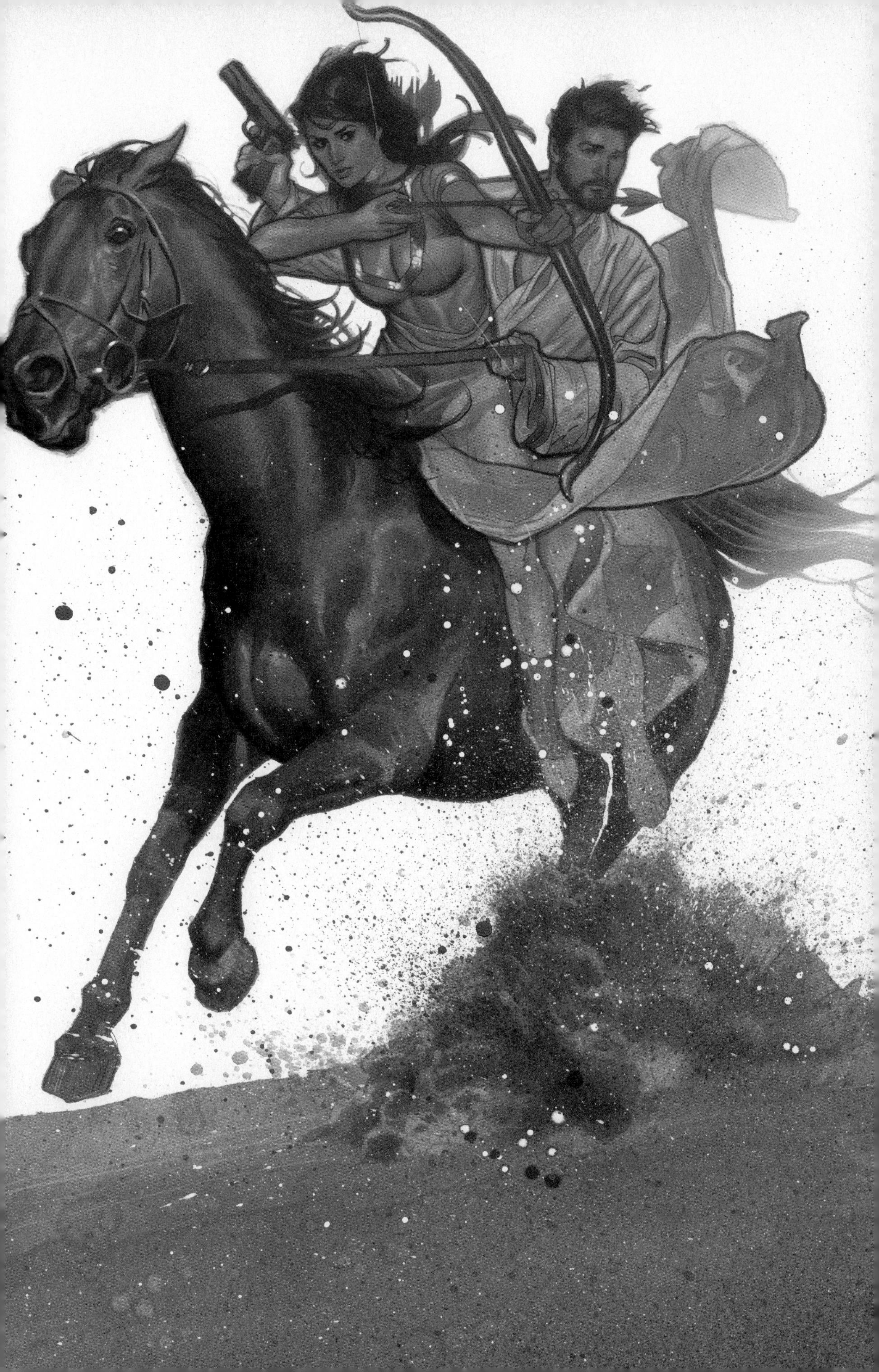

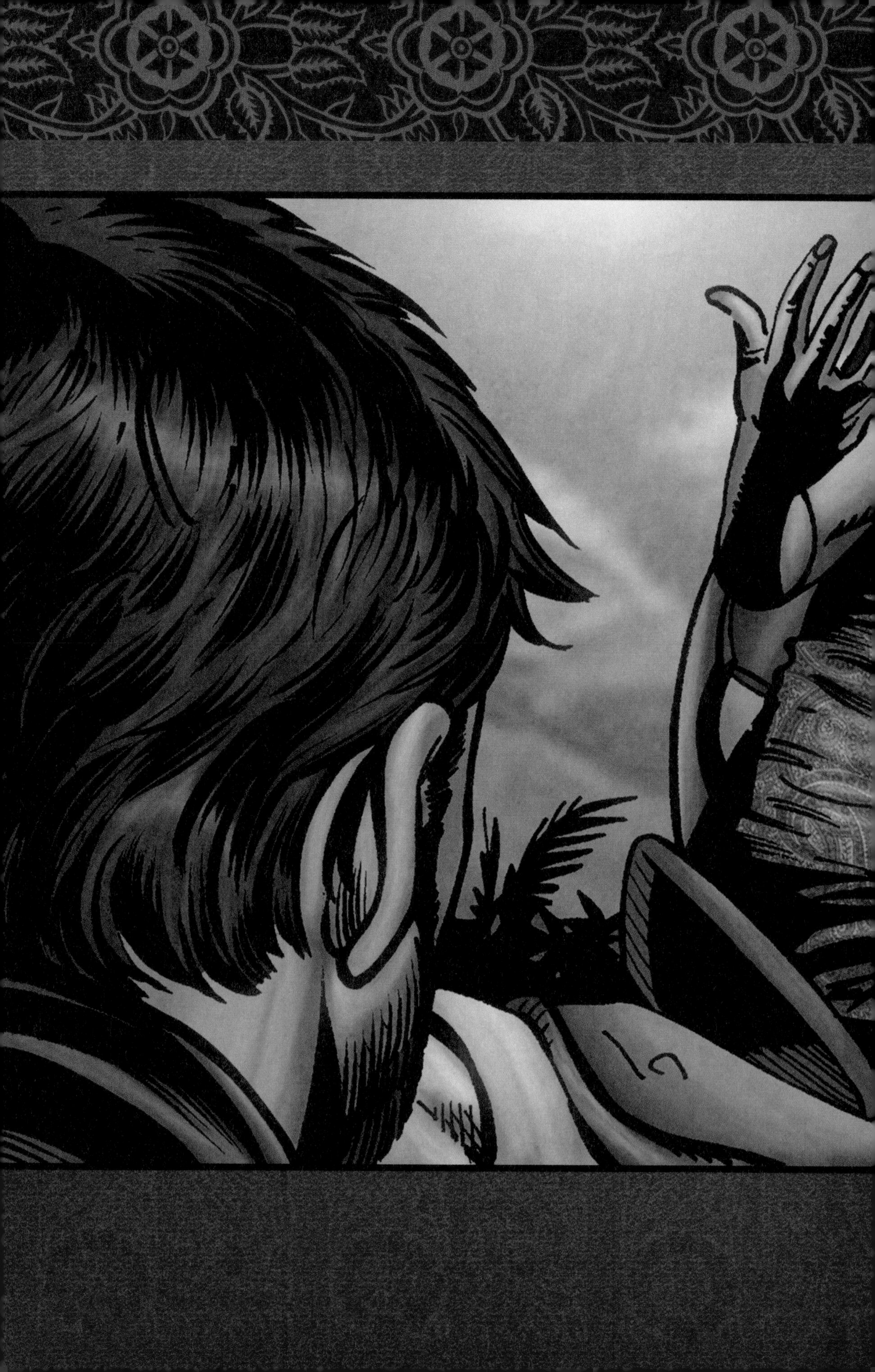

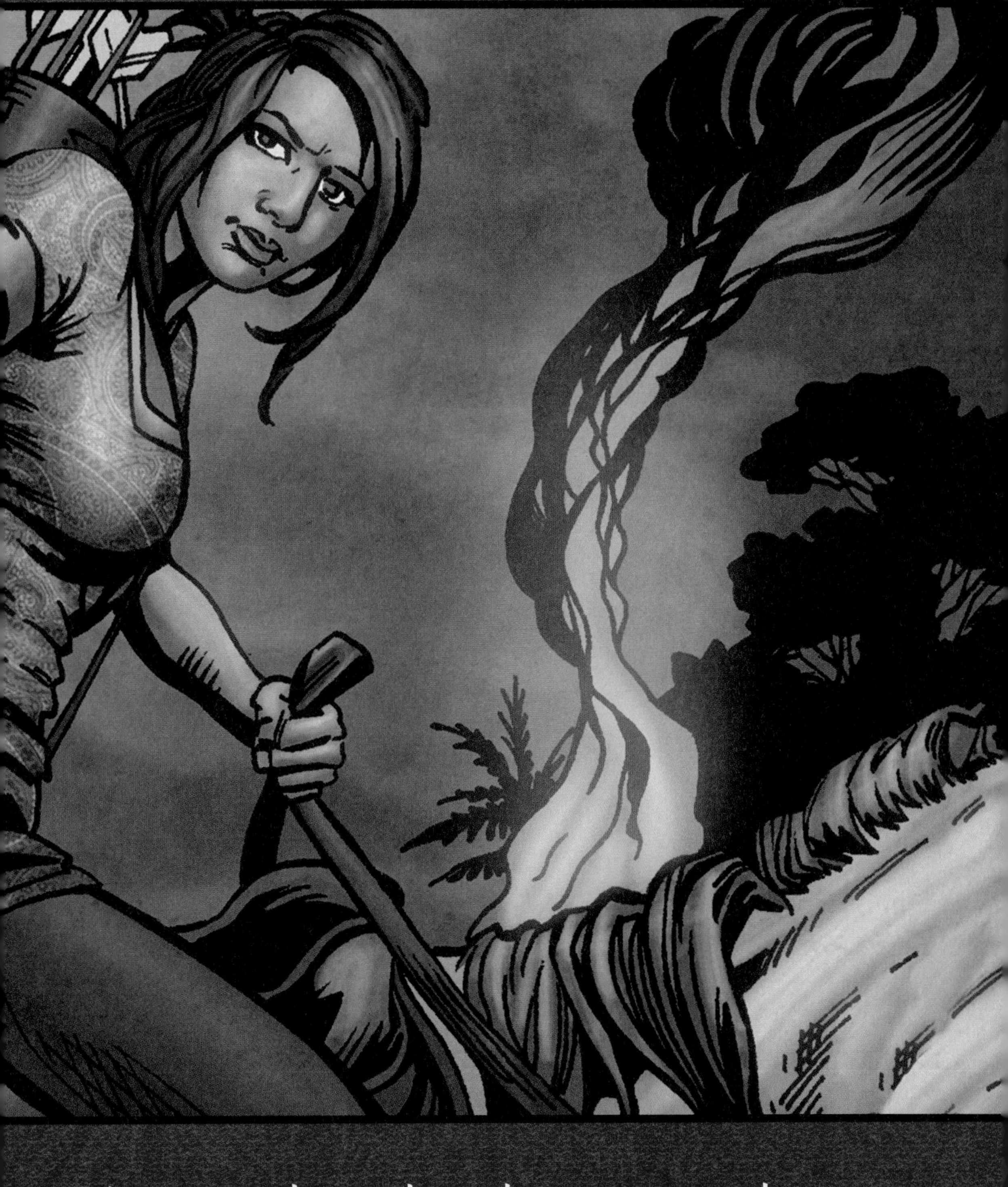

"You can either ride with me or try to keep up.
It's up to you."

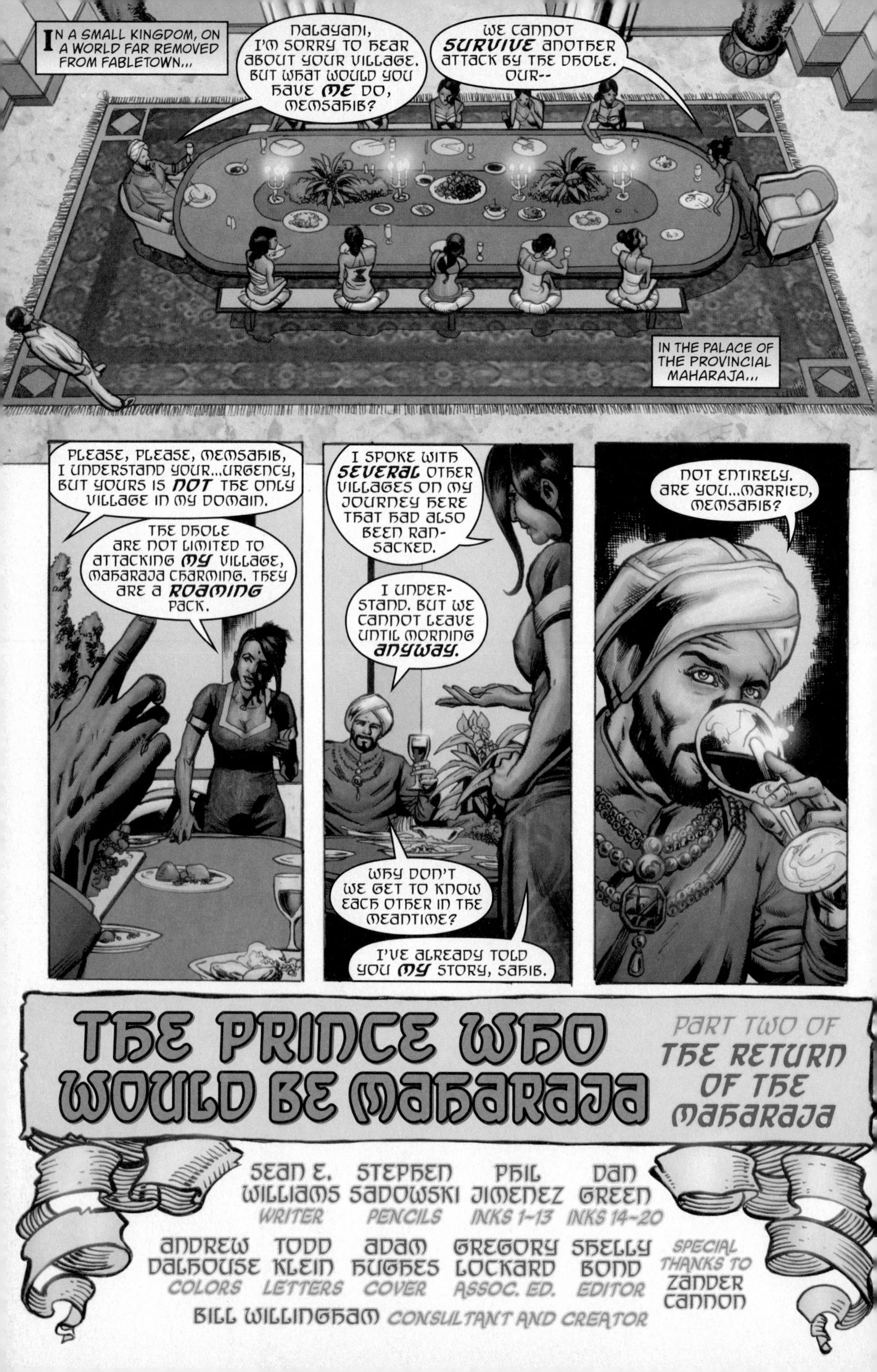
IN A SMALL KINGDOM, ON A WORLD FAR REMOVED FROM FABLETOWN...
NALAYANI, I'M SORRY TO HEAR ABOUT YOUR VILLAGE. BUT WHAT WOULD YOU HAVE ME DO, MEMSAHIB?
WE CANNOT SURVIVE ANOTHER ATTACK BY THE DHOLE. OUR--
IN THE PALACE OF THE PROVINCIAL MAHARAJA...
PLEASE, PLEASE, MEMSAHIB, I UNDERSTAND YOUR...URGENCY, BUT YOURS IS NOT THE ONLY VILLAGE IN MY DOMAIN.
THE DHOLE ARE NOT LIMITED TO ATTACKING MY VILLAGE, MAHARAJA CHARMING. THEY ARE A ROAMING PACK.
I SPOKE WITH SEVERAL OTHER VILLAGES ON MY JOURNEY HERE THAT HAD ALSO BEEN RANSACKED.
I UNDERSTAND. BUT WE CANNOT LEAVE UNTIL MORNING ANYWAY.
WHY DON'T WE GET TO KNOW EACH OTHER IN THE MEANTIME?
I'VE ALREADY TOLD YOU MY STORY, SAHIB.
NOT ENTIRELY. ARE YOU...MARRIED, MEMSAHIB?
THE PRINCE WHO WOULD BE MAHARAJA
PART TWO OF THE RETURN OF THE MAHARAJA
SEAN E. WILLIAMS WRITER
STEPHEN SADOWSKI PENCILS
PHIL JIMENEZ INKS 1-13
DAN GREEN INKS 14-20
ANDREW DALHOUSE COLORS
TODD KLEIN LETTERS
ADAM HUGHES COVER
GREGORY LOCKARD ASSOC. ED.
SHELLY BOND EDITOR
SPECIAL THANKS TO ZANDER CANNON
BILL WILLINGHAM CONSULTANT AND CREATOR

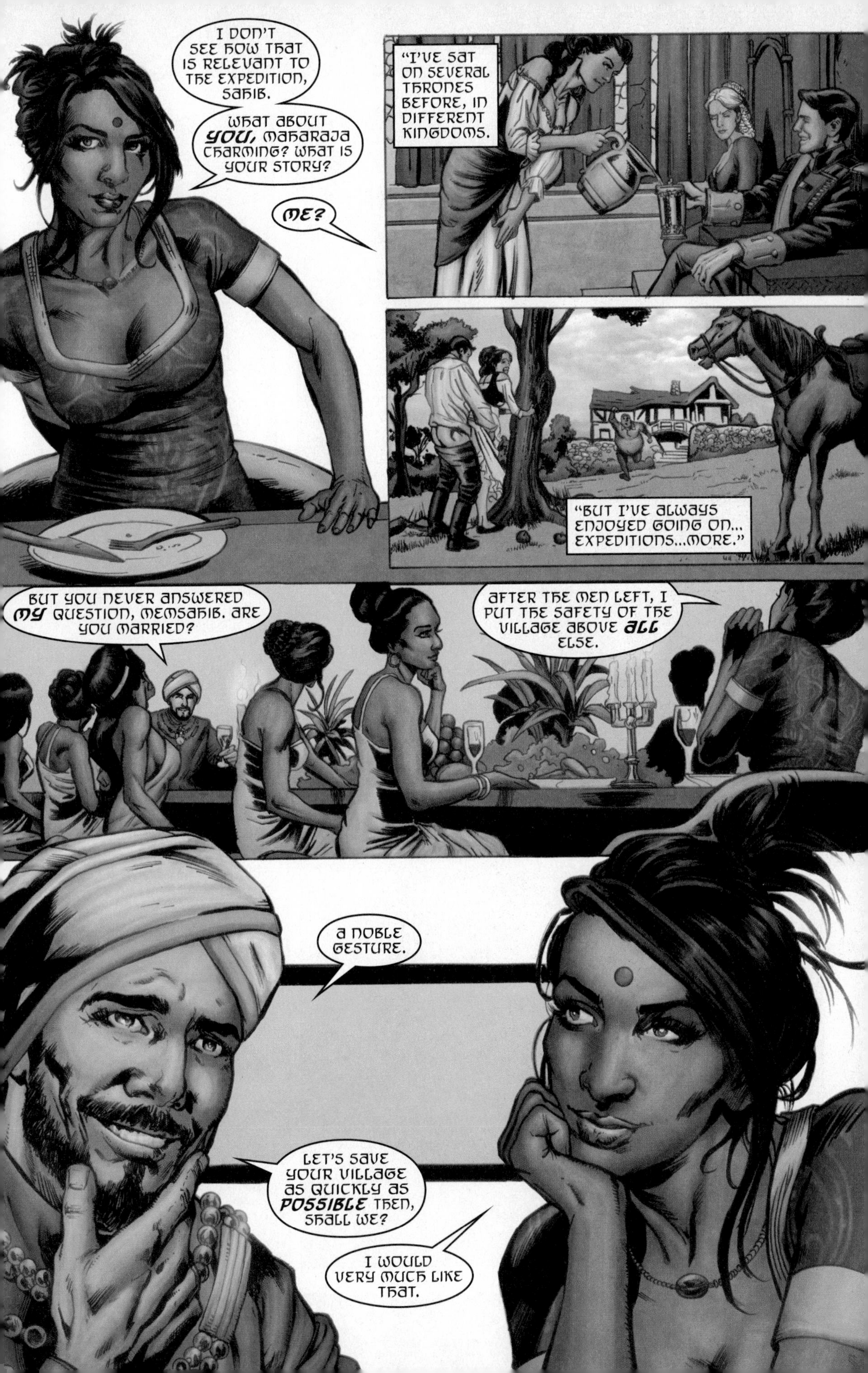
I DON'T SEE HOW THAT IS RELEVANT TO THE EXPEDITION, SAHIB.
WHAT ABOUT YOU, MAHARAJA CHARMING? WHAT IS YOUR STORY?
ME?
"I'VE SAT ON SEVERAL THRONES BEFORE, IN DIFFERENT KINGDOMS.
"BUT I'VE ALWAYS ENJOYED GOING ON... EXPEDITIONS...MORE."
BUT YOU NEVER ANSWERED MY QUESTION, MEMSAHIB. ARE YOU MARRIED?
AFTER THE MEN LEFT, I PUT THE SAFETY OF THE VILLAGE ABOVE ALL ELSE.
A NOBLE GESTURE.
LET'S SAVE YOUR VILLAGE AS QUICKLY AS POSSIBLE THEN, SHALL WE?
I WOULD VERY MUCH LIKE THAT.

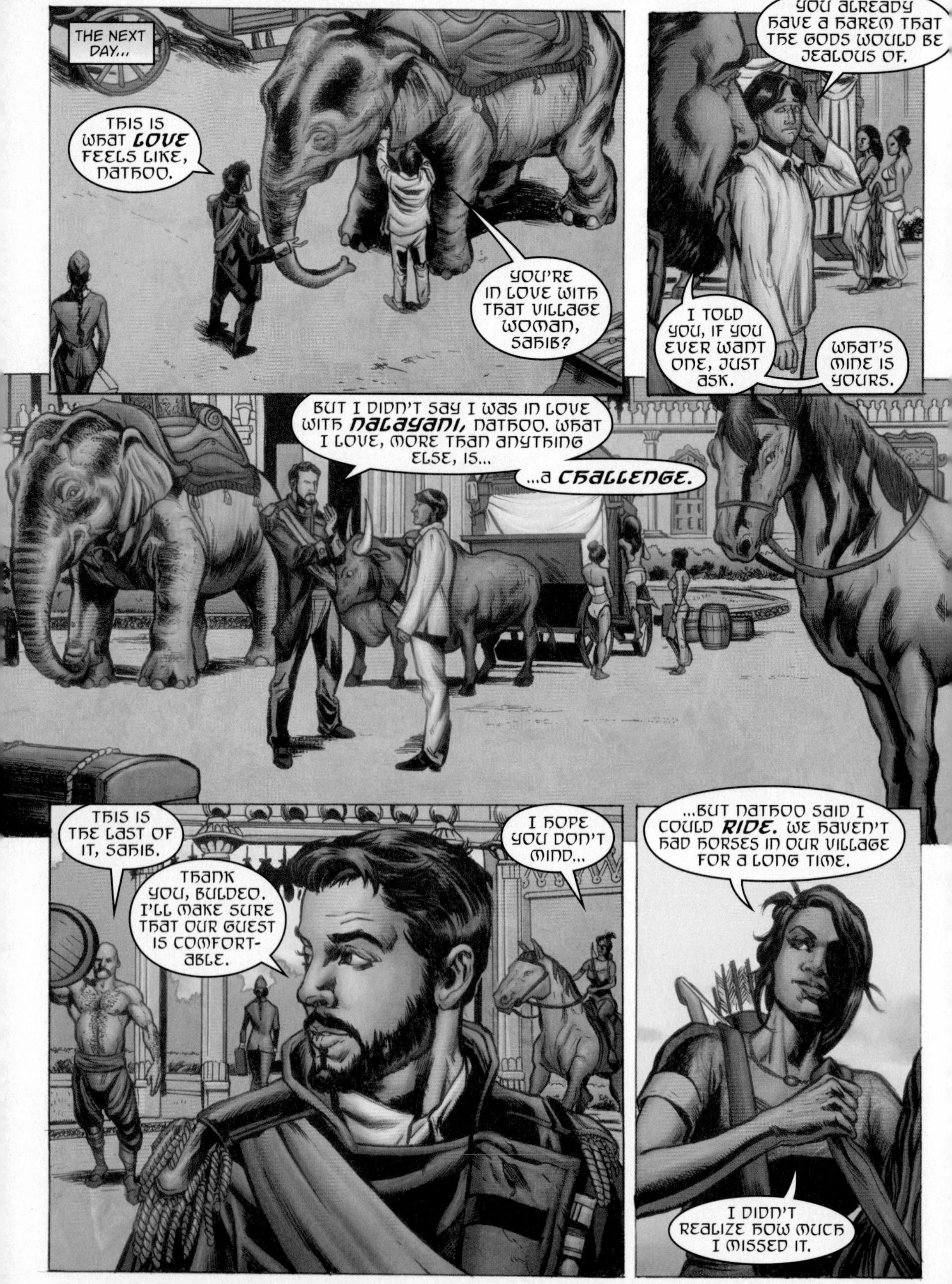
THE NEXT DAY...
THIS IS WHAT LOVE FEELS LIKE, NATHOO.
YOU'RE IN LOVE WITH THAT VILLAGE WOMAN, SAHIB?
YOU ALREADY HAVE A HAREM THAT THE GODS WOULD BE JEALOUS OF.
I TOLD YOU, IF YOU EVER WANT ONE, JUST ASK.
WHAT'S MINE IS YOURS.
BUT I DIDN'T SAY I WAS IN LOVE WITH NALAYANI, NATHOO. WHAT I LOVE, MORE THAN ANYTHING ELSE, IS...
...A CHALLENGE.
THIS IS THE LAST OF IT, SAHIB.
THANK YOU, BULDEO. I'LL MAKE SURE THAT OUR GUEST IS COMFORT-ABLE.
I HOPE YOU DON'T MIND...
...BUT NATHOO SAID I COULD RIDE. WE HAVEN'T HAD HORSES IN OUR VILLAGE FOR A LONG TIME.
I DIDN'T REALIZE HOW MUCH I MISSED IT.

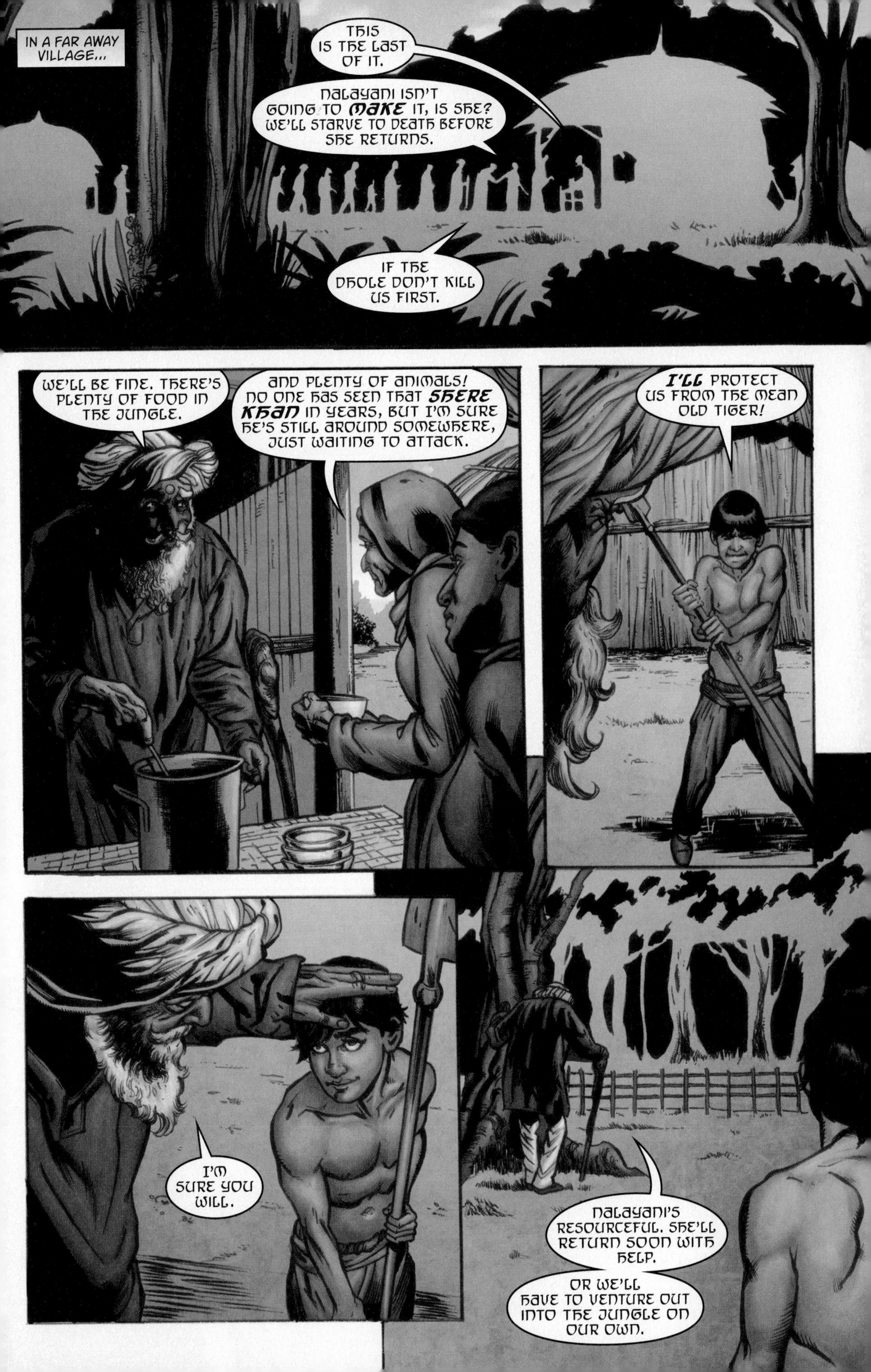
IN A FAR AWAY VILLAGE...
THIS IS THE LAST OF IT.
NALAYANI ISN'T GOING TO MAKE IT, IS SHE? WE'LL STARVE TO DEATH BEFORE SHE RETURNS.
IF THE DHOLE DON'T KILL US FIRST.
WE'LL BE FINE. THERE'S PLENTY OF FOOD IN THE JUNGLE.
AND PLENTY OF ANIMALS! NO ONE HAS SEEN THAT SHERE KHAN IN YEARS, BUT I'M SURE HE'S STILL AROUND SOMEWHERE, JUST WAITING TO ATTACK.
I'LL PROTECT US FROM THE MEAN OLD TIGER!
I'M SURE YOU WILL.
NALAYANI'S RESOURCEFUL. SHE'LL RETURN SOON WITH HELP.
OR WE'LL HAVE TO VENTURE OUT INTO THE JUNGLE ON OUR OWN.

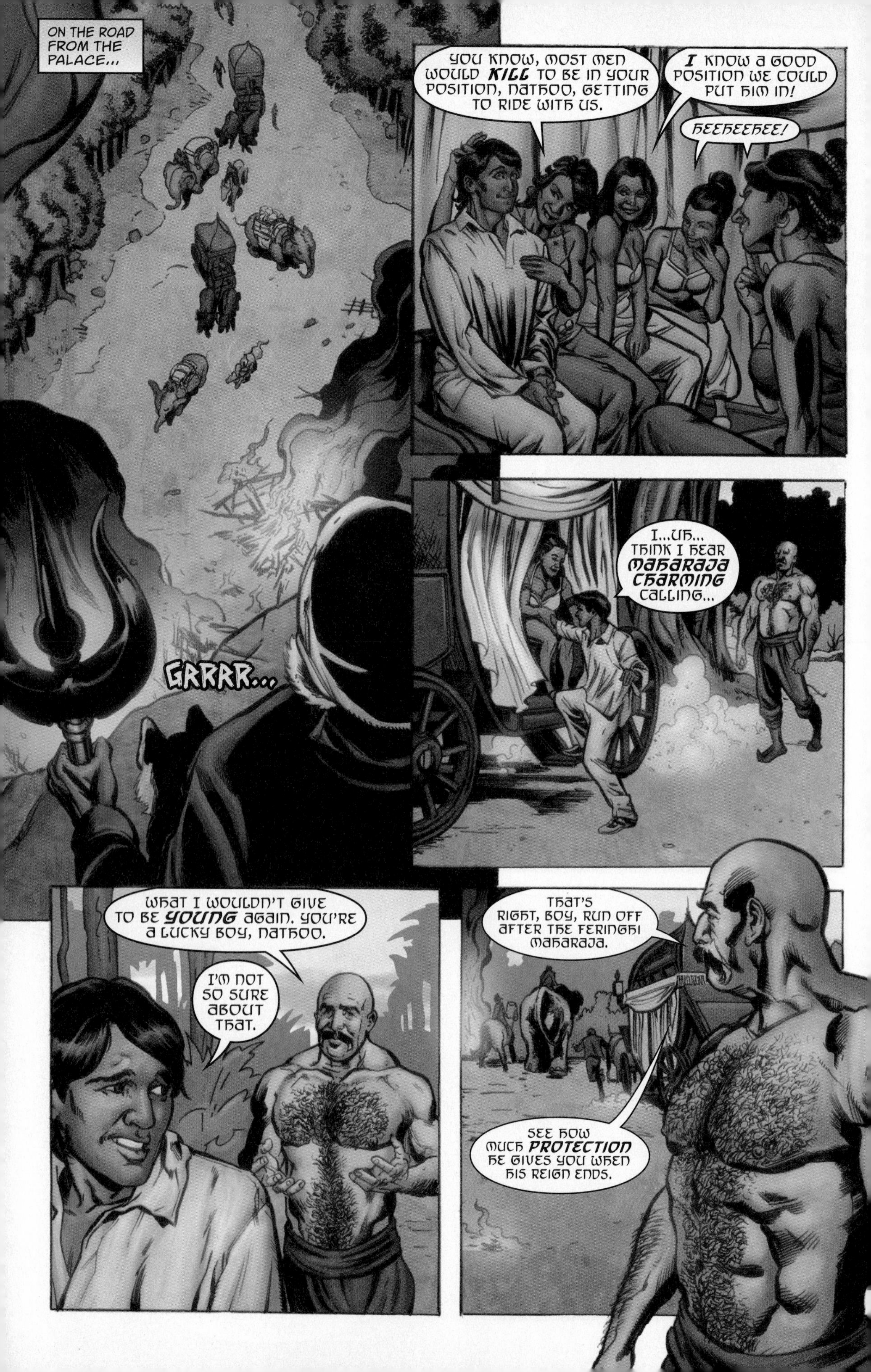
ON THE ROAD FROM THE PALACE...
YOU KNOW, MOST MEN WOULD KILL TO BE IN YOUR POSITION, NATHOO, GETTING TO RIDE WITH US.
I KNOW A GOOD POSITION WE COULD PUT HIM IN!
HEEHEEHEE!
GRRRR...
I...UH... THINK I HEAR MAHARAJA CHARMING CALLING...
WHAT I WOULDN'T GIVE TO BE YOUNG AGAIN. YOU'RE A LUCKY BOY, NATHOO.
I'M NOT SO SURE ABOUT THAT.
THAT'S RIGHT, BOY, RUN OFF AFTER THE FERINGHI MAHARAJA.
SEE HOW MUCH PROTECTION HE GIVES YOU WHEN HIS REIGN ENDS.

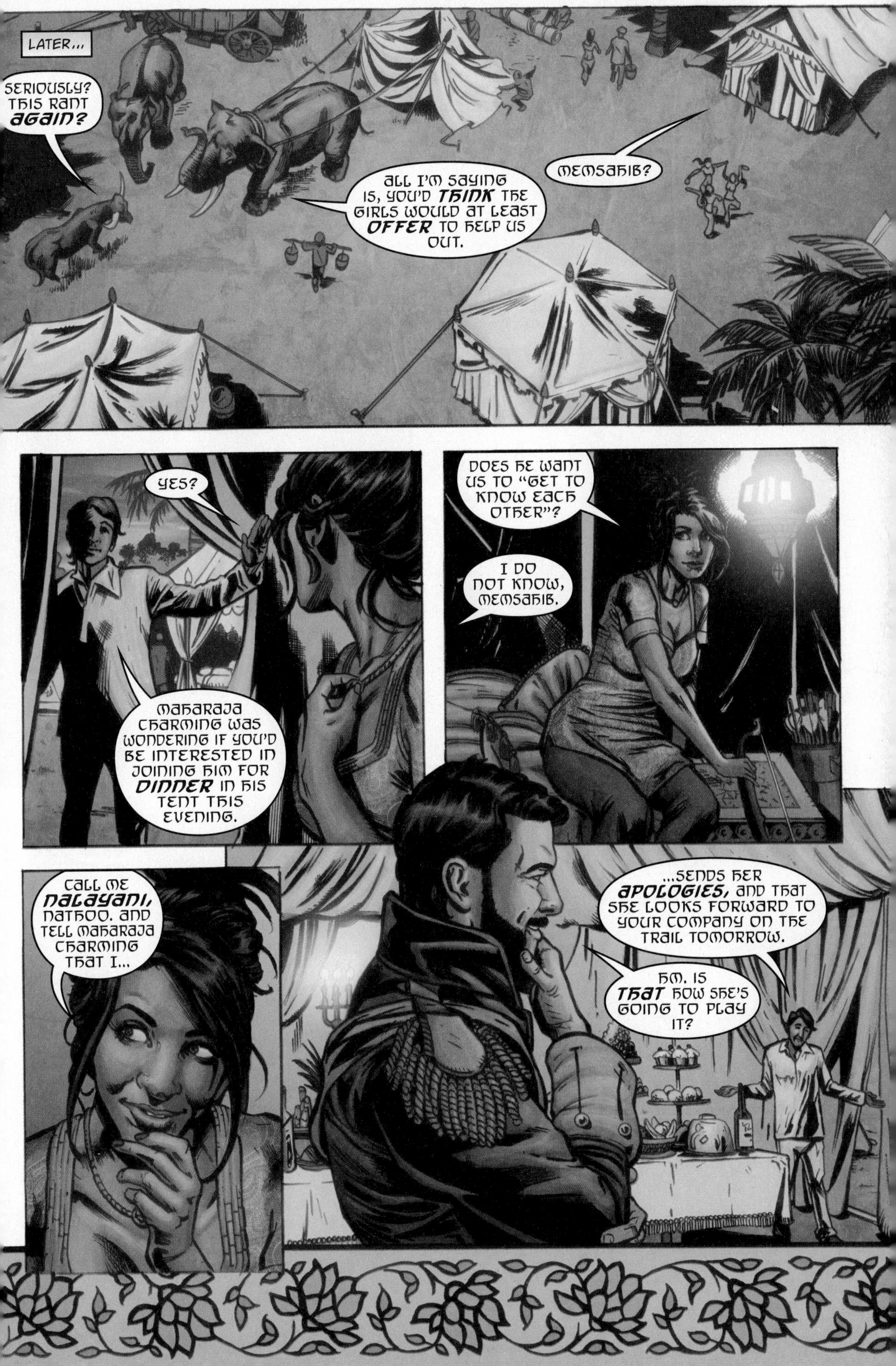
LATER...
SERIOUSLY? THIS RANT AGAIN?
ALL I'M SAYING IS, YOU'D THINK THE GIRLS WOULD AT LEAST OFFER TO HELP US OUT.
MEMSAHIB?
YES?
MAHARAJA CHARMING WAS WONDERING IF YOU'D BE INTERESTED IN JOINING HIM FOR DINNER IN HIS TENT THIS EVENING.
DOES HE WANT US TO "GET TO KNOW EACH OTHER"?
I DO NOT KNOW, MEMSAHIB.
CALL ME NALAYANI, NATHOO. AND TELL MAHARAJA CHARMING THAT I...
...SENDS HER APOLOGIES, AND THAT SHE LOOKS FORWARD TO YOUR COMPANY ON THE TRAIL TOMORROW.
HM. IS THAT HOW SHE'S GOING TO PLAY IT?

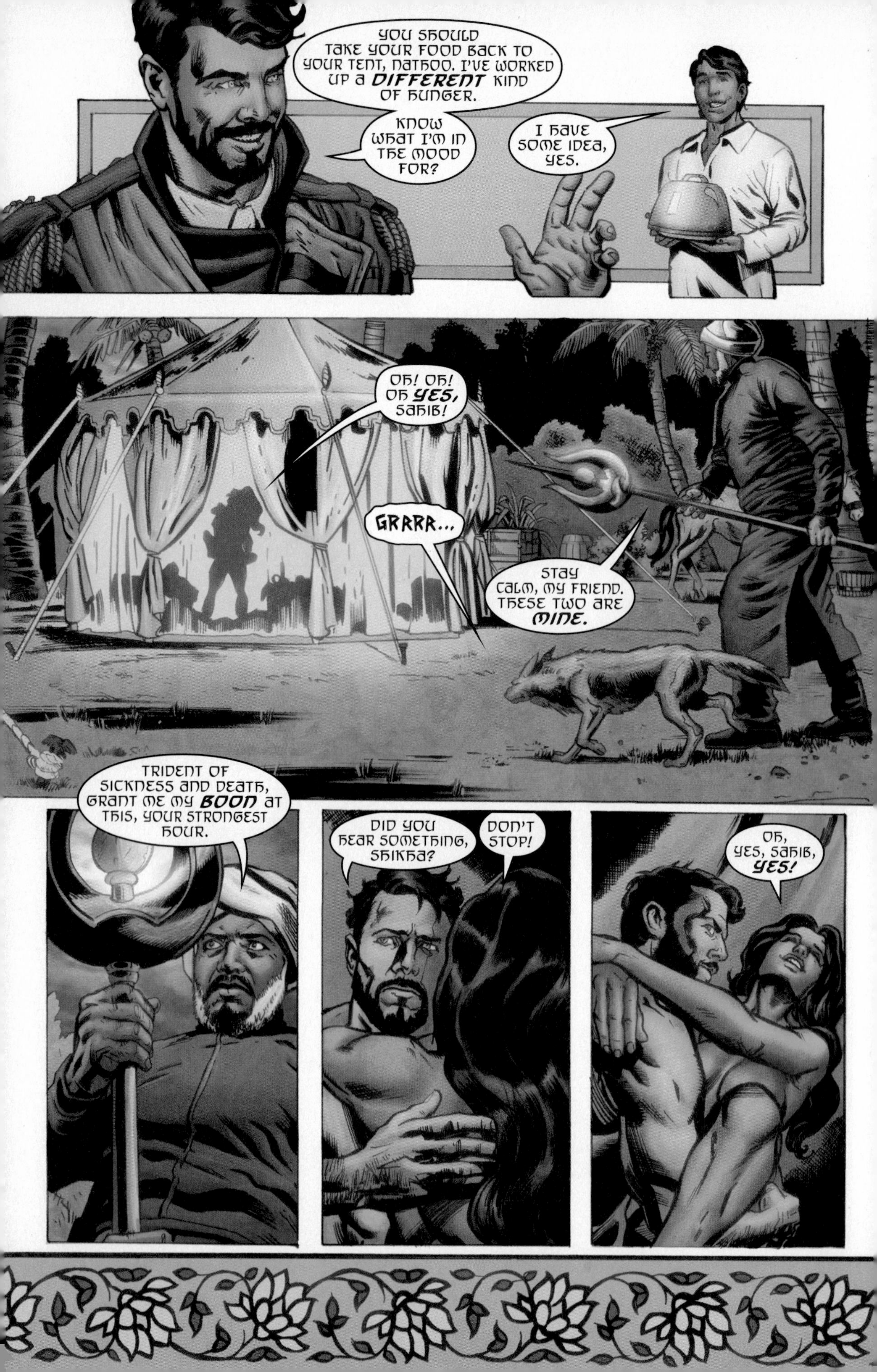
YOU SHOULD TAKE YOUR FOOD BACK TO YOUR TENT, NATHOO. I'VE WORKED UP A DIFFERENT KIND OF HUNGER.
KNOW WHAT I'M IN THE MOOD FOR?
I HAVE SOME IDEA, YES.
OH! OH! OH YES, SAHIB!
GRRRR...
STAY CALM, MY FRIEND. THESE TWO ARE MINE.
TRIDENT OF SICKNESS AND DEATH, GRANT ME MY BOON AT THIS, YOUR STRONGEST HOUR.
DID YOU HEAR SOMETHING, SHIKHA?
DON'T STOP!
OH, YES, SAHIB, YES!

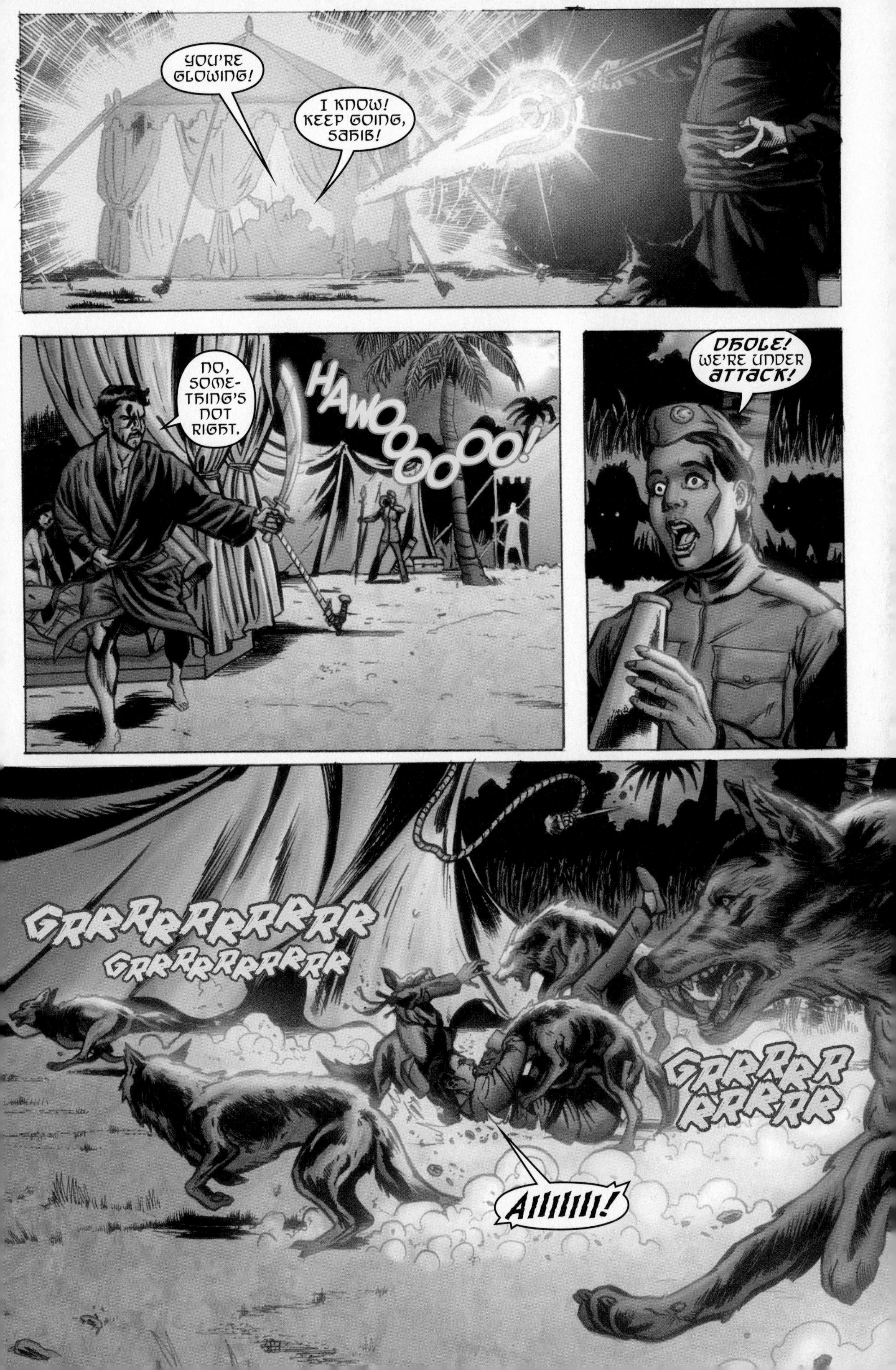
YOU'RE GLOWING!
I KNOW! KEEP GOING, SAHIB!
NO, SOME-THING'S NOT RIGHT.
HAWOOOOOOO!
DHOLE! WE'RE UNDER ATTACK!
GRRRRRRRRRR
GRRRRRRRRRR
GRRRRR RRRRR
AIIIIIII!

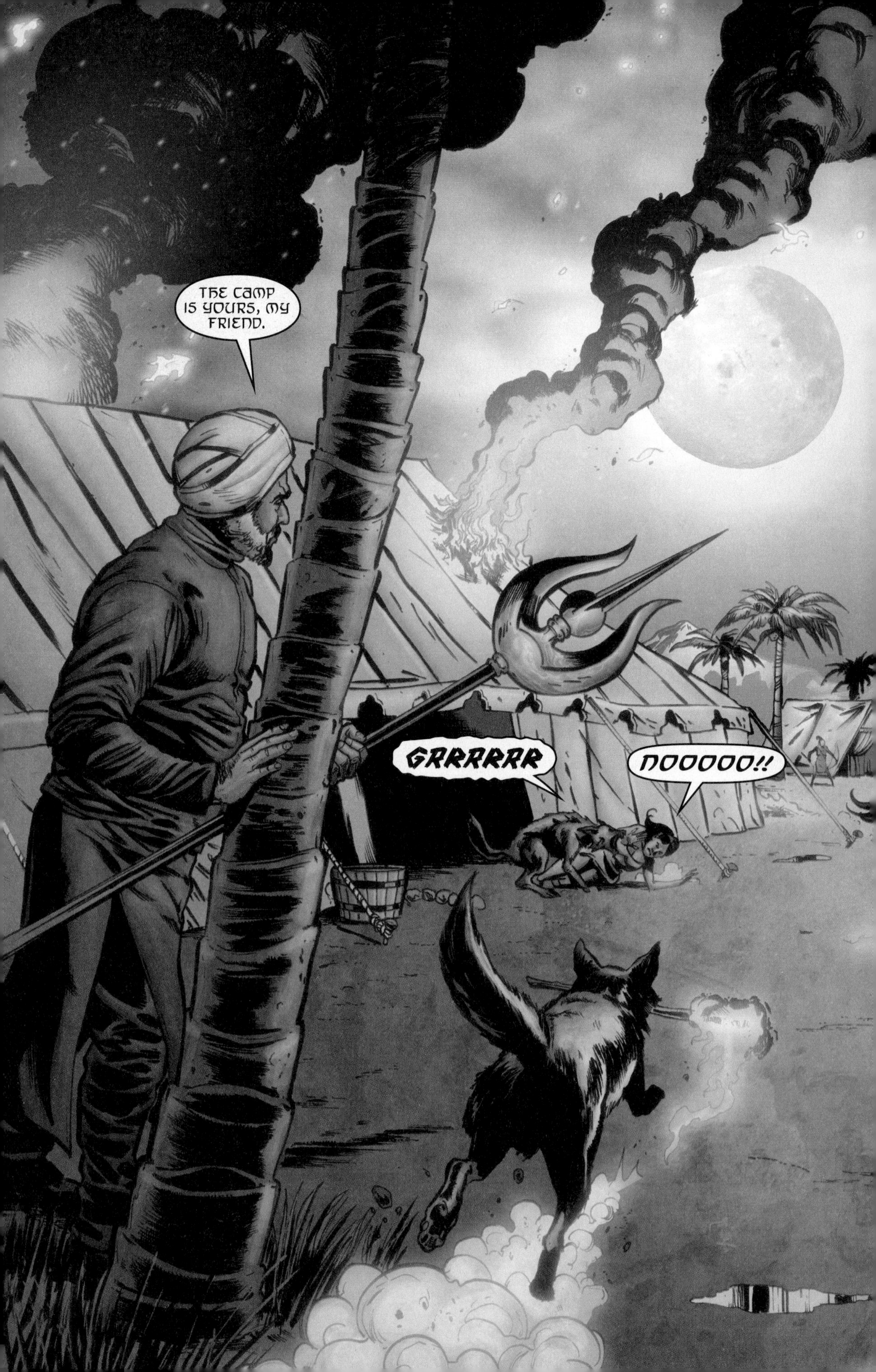
THE CAMP IS YOURS, MY FRIEND.
GRRRRRR
NOOOOO!!

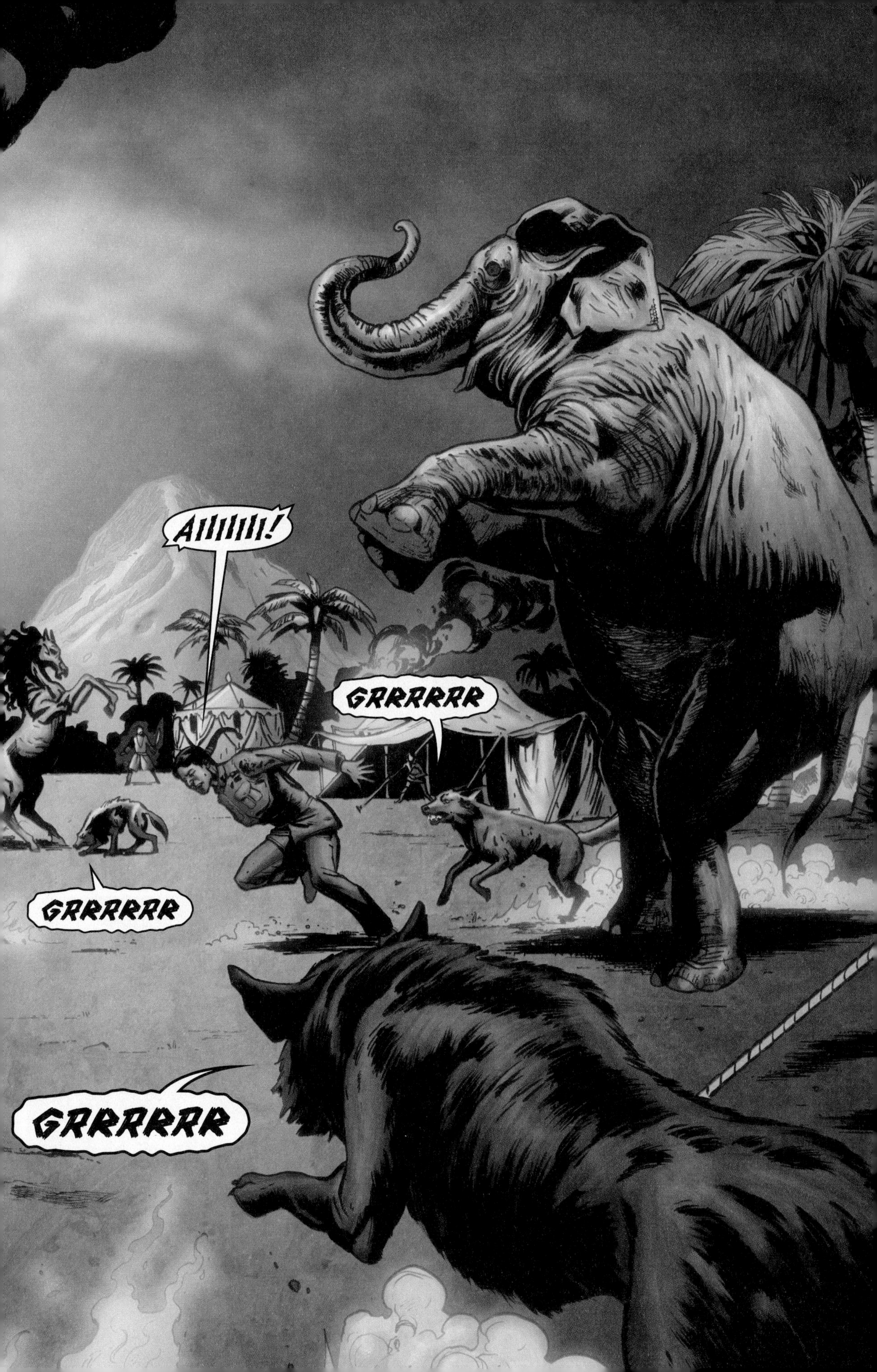
AIIIIIII!
GRRRRRR
GRRRRRR
GRRRRRR

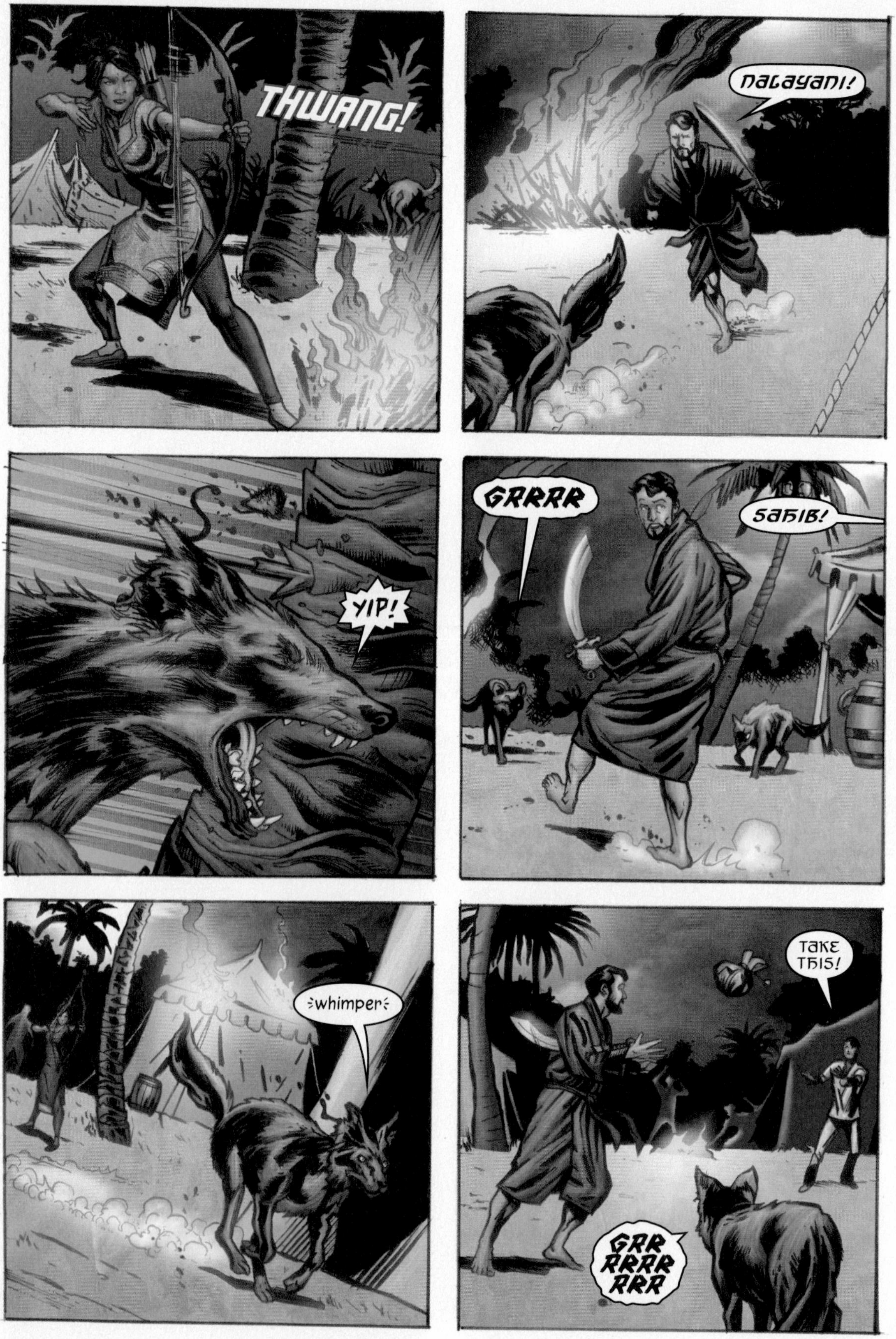
THWANG!
NALAYANI!
YIP!
GRRRR
SAHIB!
whimper
TAKE THIS!
GRR RRRR RRR

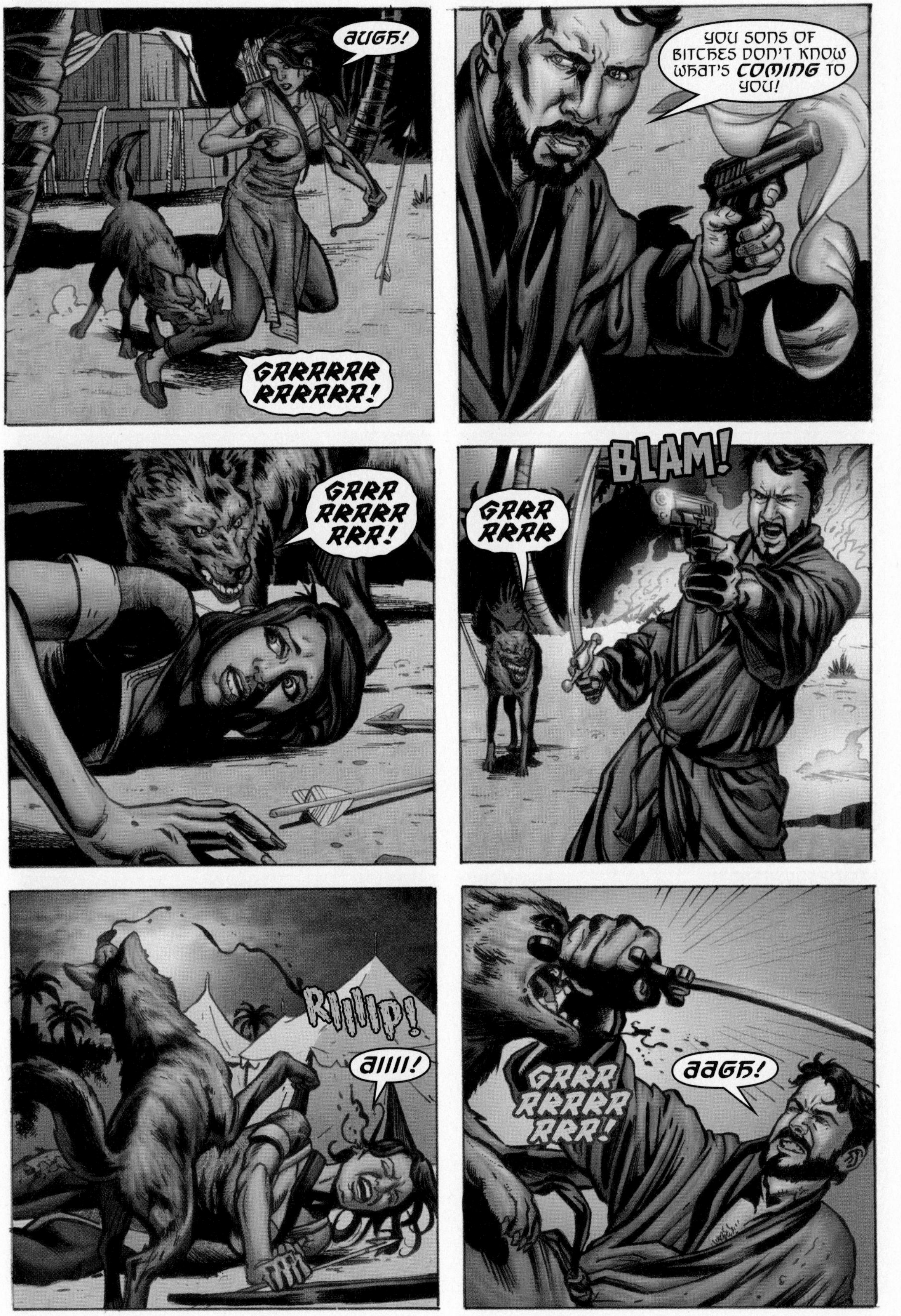
AUGH!
GRRRRRR RRRRRR!
YOU SONS OF BITCHES DON'T KNOW WHAT'S COMING TO YOU!
GRRR RRRRR RRR!
BLAM!
GRRR RRRR
RIIIIP!
AIIII!
GRRR RRRRR RRR!
AAGH!

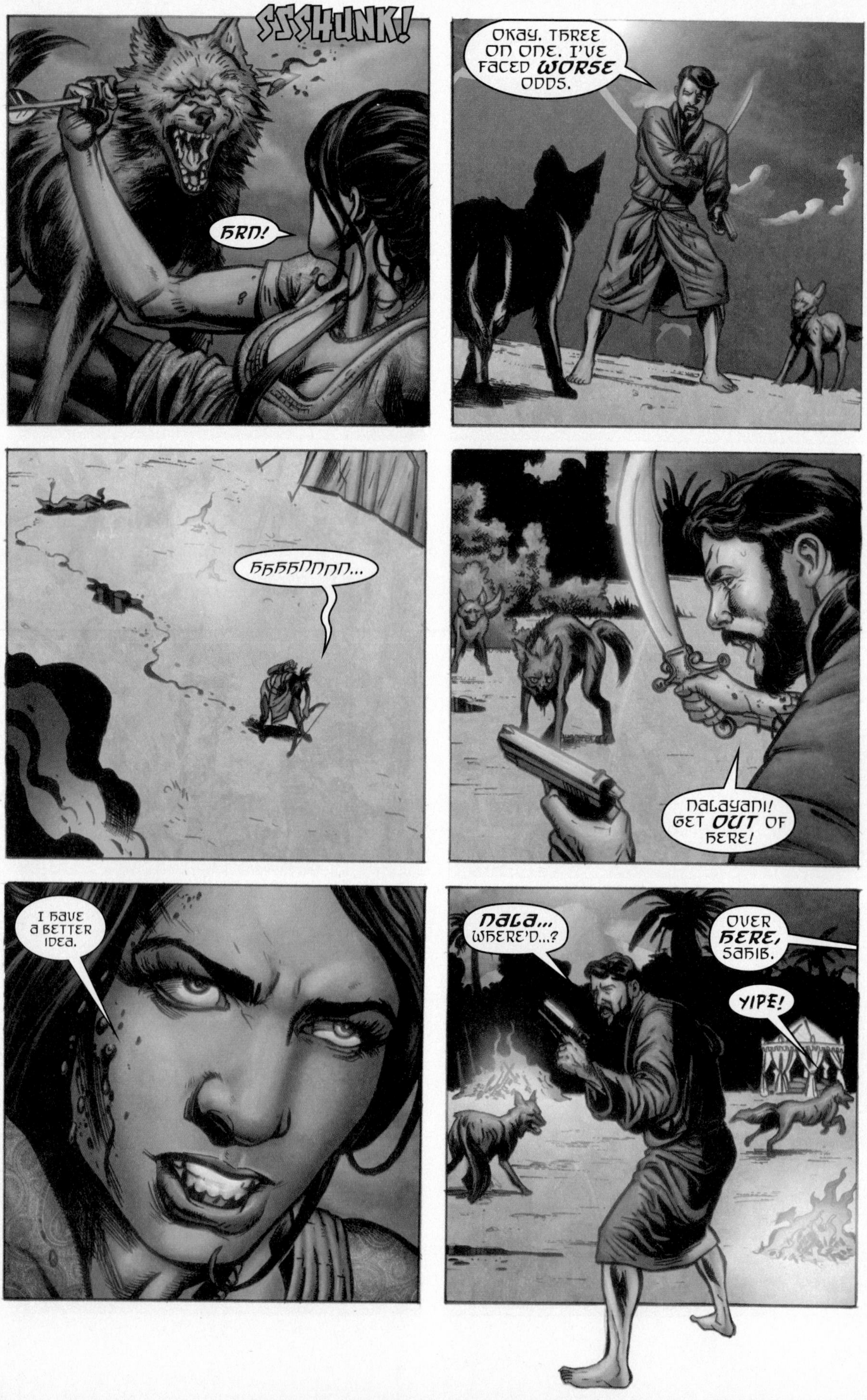
SSSHUNK!
HRN!
OKAY. THREE ON ONE. I'VE FACED WORSE ODDS.
HHHHNNNN...
NALAYANI! GET OUT OF HERE!
I HAVE A BETTER IDEA.
NALA... WHERE'D...?
OVER HERE, SAHIB.
YIPE!

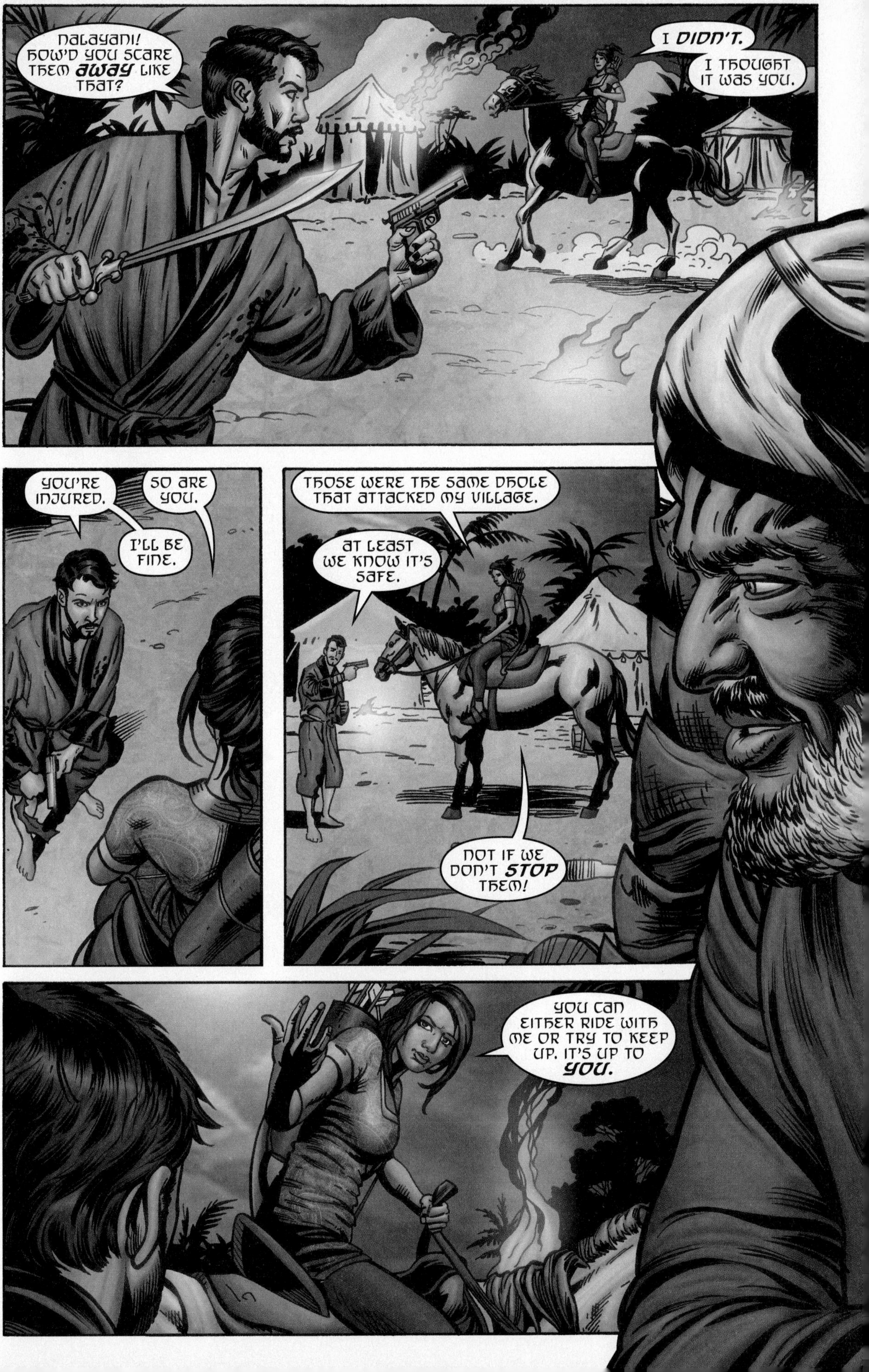
NALAYANI! HOW'D YOU SCARE THEM AWAY LIKE THAT?
I DIDN'T.
I THOUGHT IT WAS YOU.
YOU'RE INJURED.
SO ARE YOU.
I'LL BE FINE.
THOSE WERE THE SAME DHOLE THAT ATTACKED MY VILLAGE.
AT LEAST WE KNOW IT'S SAFE.
NOT IF WE DON'T STOP THEM!
YOU CAN EITHER RIDE WITH ME OR TRY TO KEEP UP. IT'S UP TO YOU.

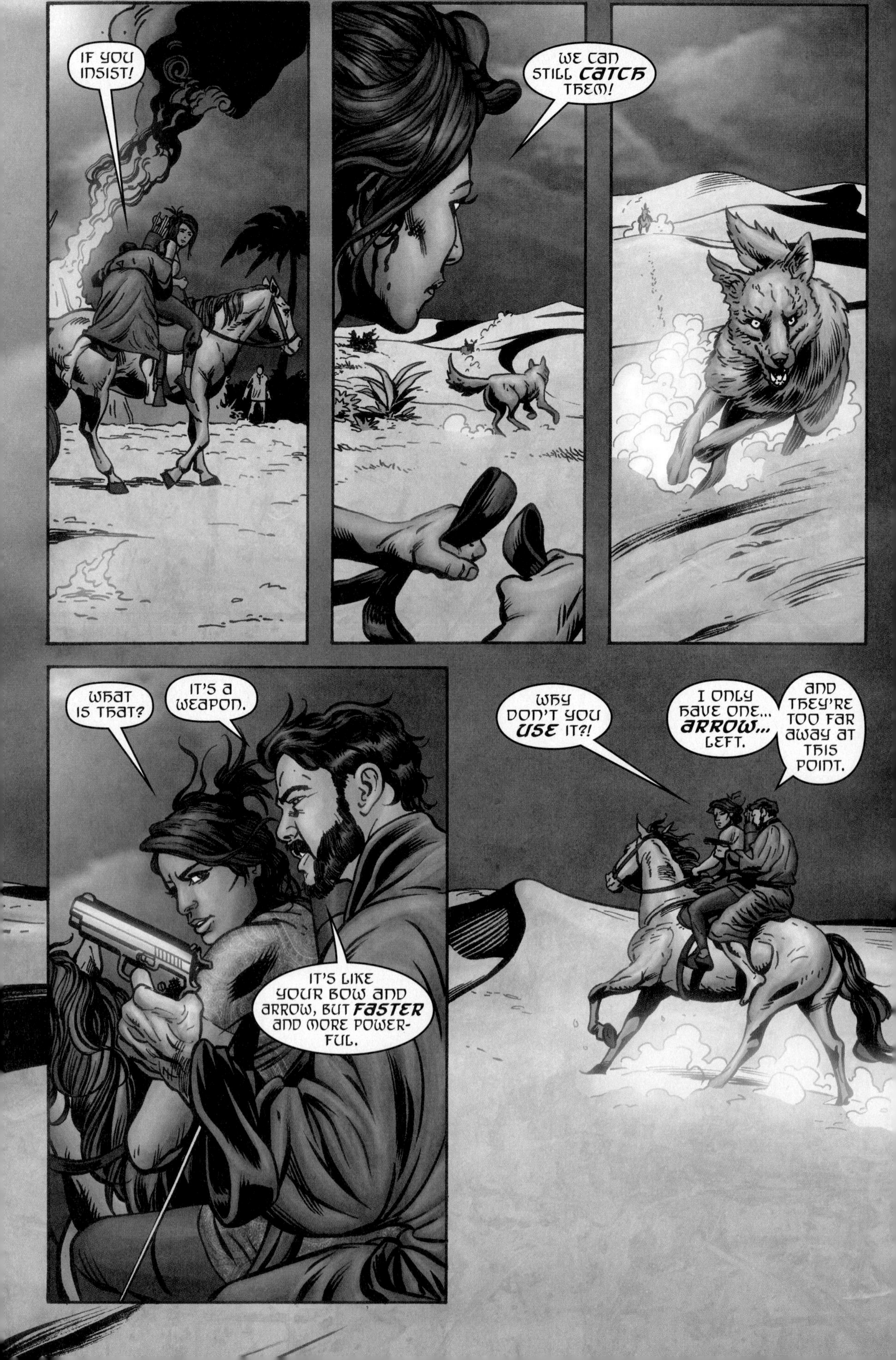
IF YOU INSIST!
WE CAN STILL CATCH THEM!
WHAT IS THAT?
IT'S A WEAPON.
IT'S LIKE YOUR BOW AND ARROW, BUT FASTER AND MORE POWER-FUL.
WHY DON'T YOU USE IT?!
I ONLY HAVE ONE... ARROW... LEFT.
AND THEY'RE TOO FAR AWAY AT THIS POINT.

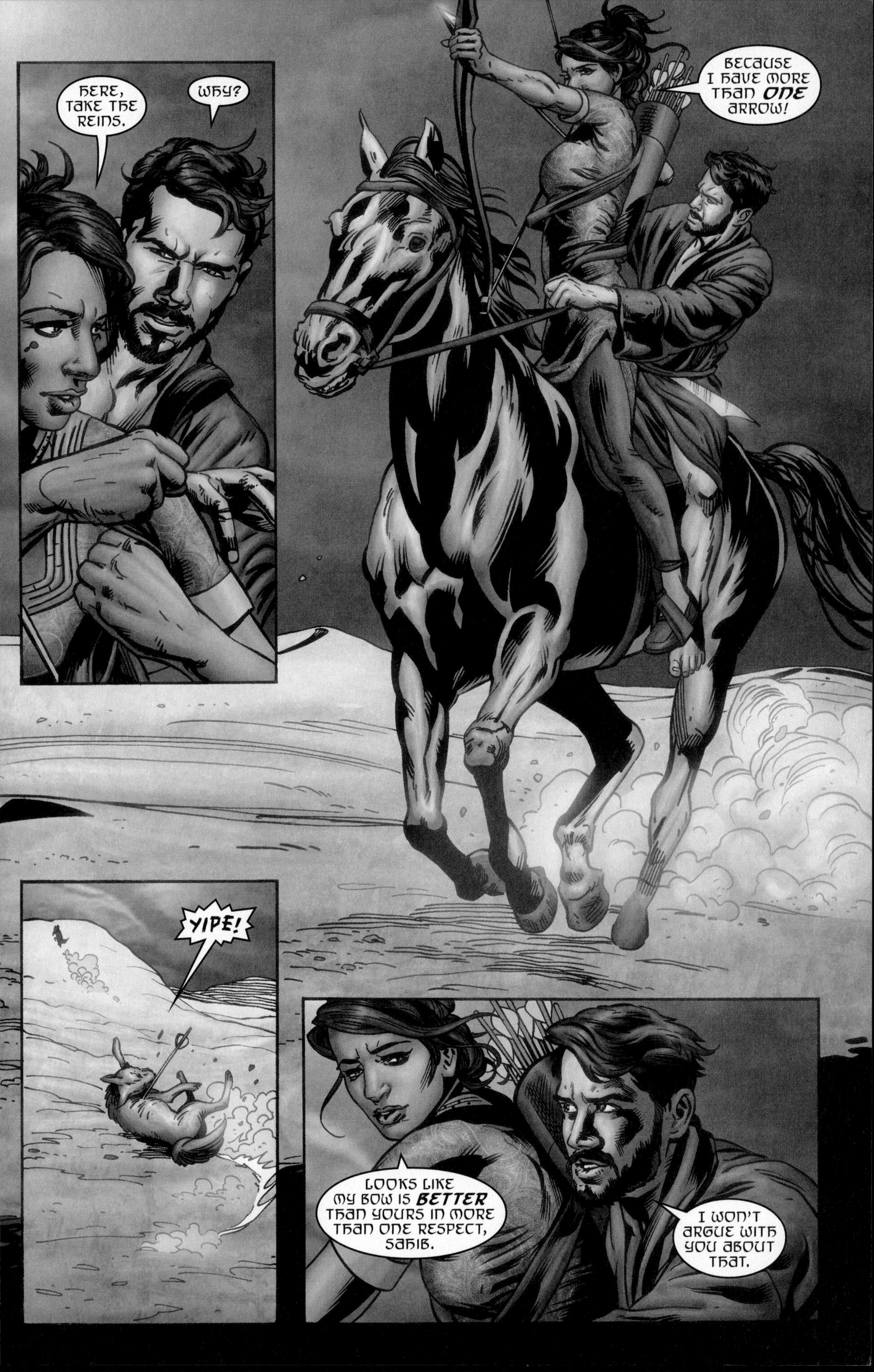
HERE, TAKE THE REINS.
WHY?
BECAUSE I HAVE MORE THAN ONE ARROW!
YIPE!
LOOKS LIKE MY BOW IS BETTER THAN YOURS IN MORE THAN ONE RESPECT, SAHIB.
I WON'T ARGUE WITH YOU ABOUT THAT.

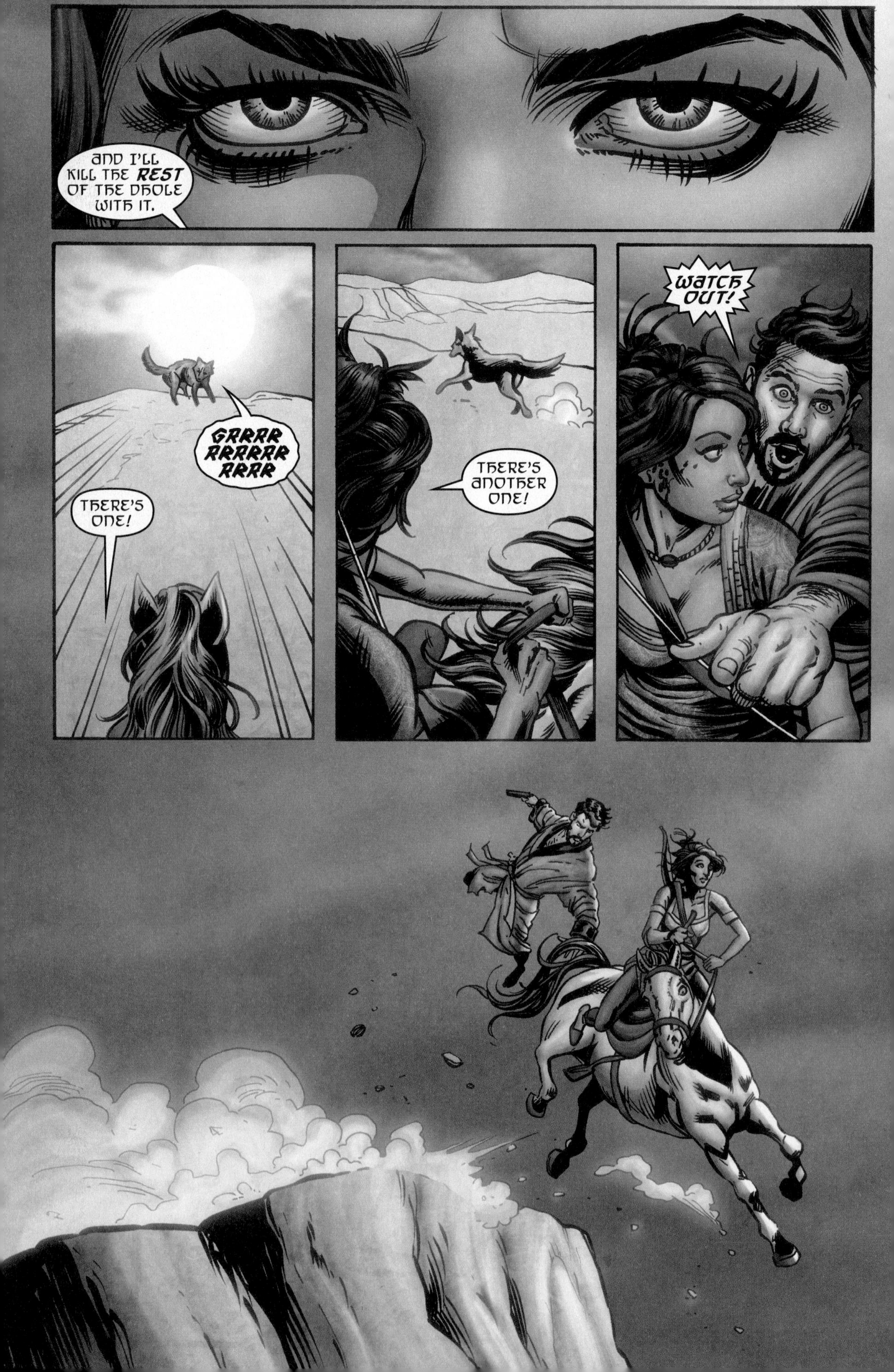
AND I'LL KILL THE REST OF THE DHOLE WITH IT.
GRRRR RRRRRR RRRR
THERE'S ONE!
THERE'S ANOTHER ONE!
WATCH OUT!

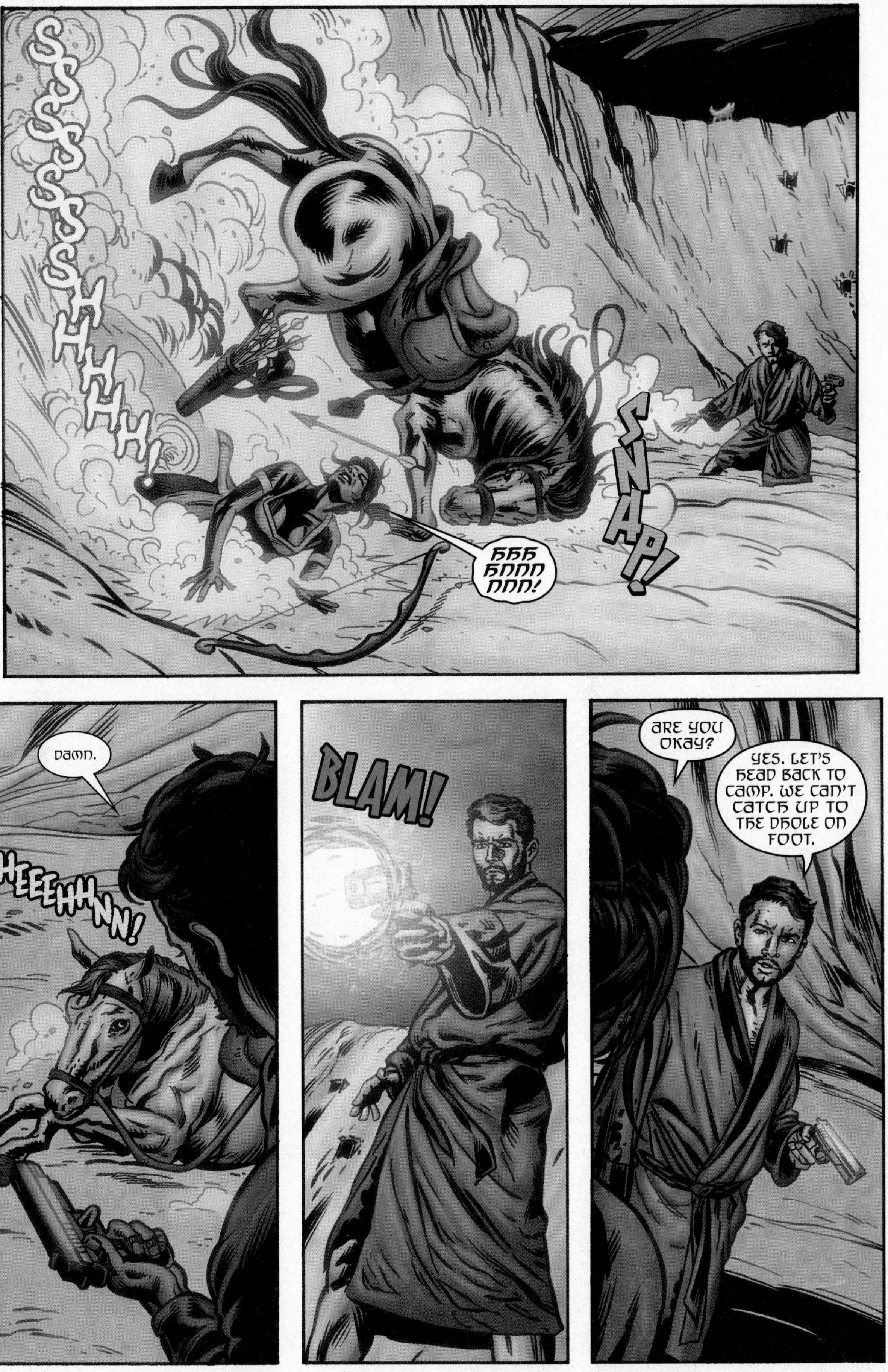

SSSSSSHHHHH!
GGG GNNN NNN!
SNAP!
DAMN.
HEEEHHNN!
BLAM!
ARE YOU OKAY?
YES. LET'S HEAD BACK TO CAMP. WE CAN'T CATCH UP TO THE DHOLE ON FOOT.

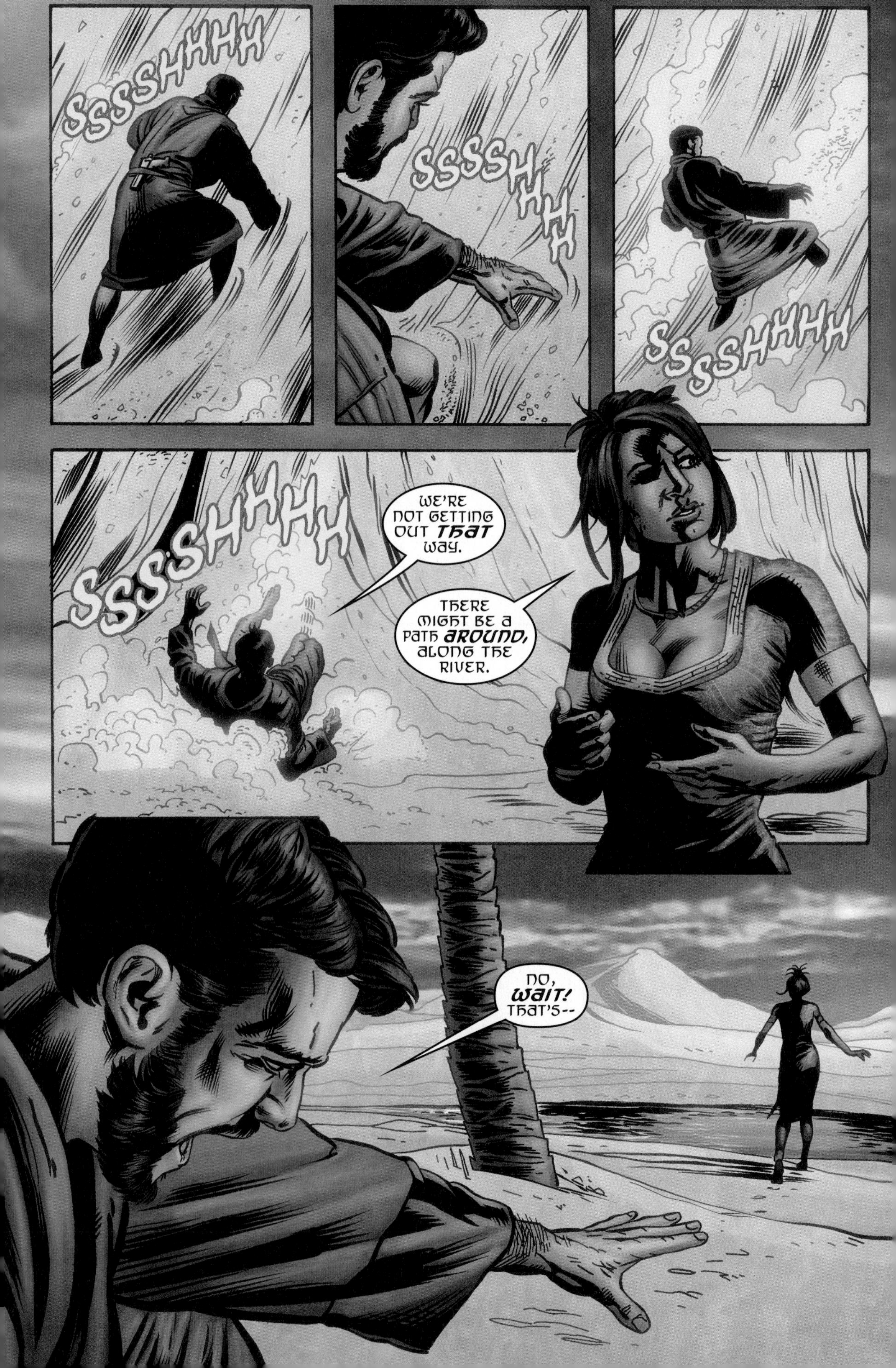
SSSSHHHH
SSSSHHHH
SSSSHHHH
SSSSHHHH
WE'RE NOT GETTING OUT THAT WAY.
THERE MIGHT BE A PATH AROUND, ALONG THE RIVER.
NO, WAIT! THAT'S--

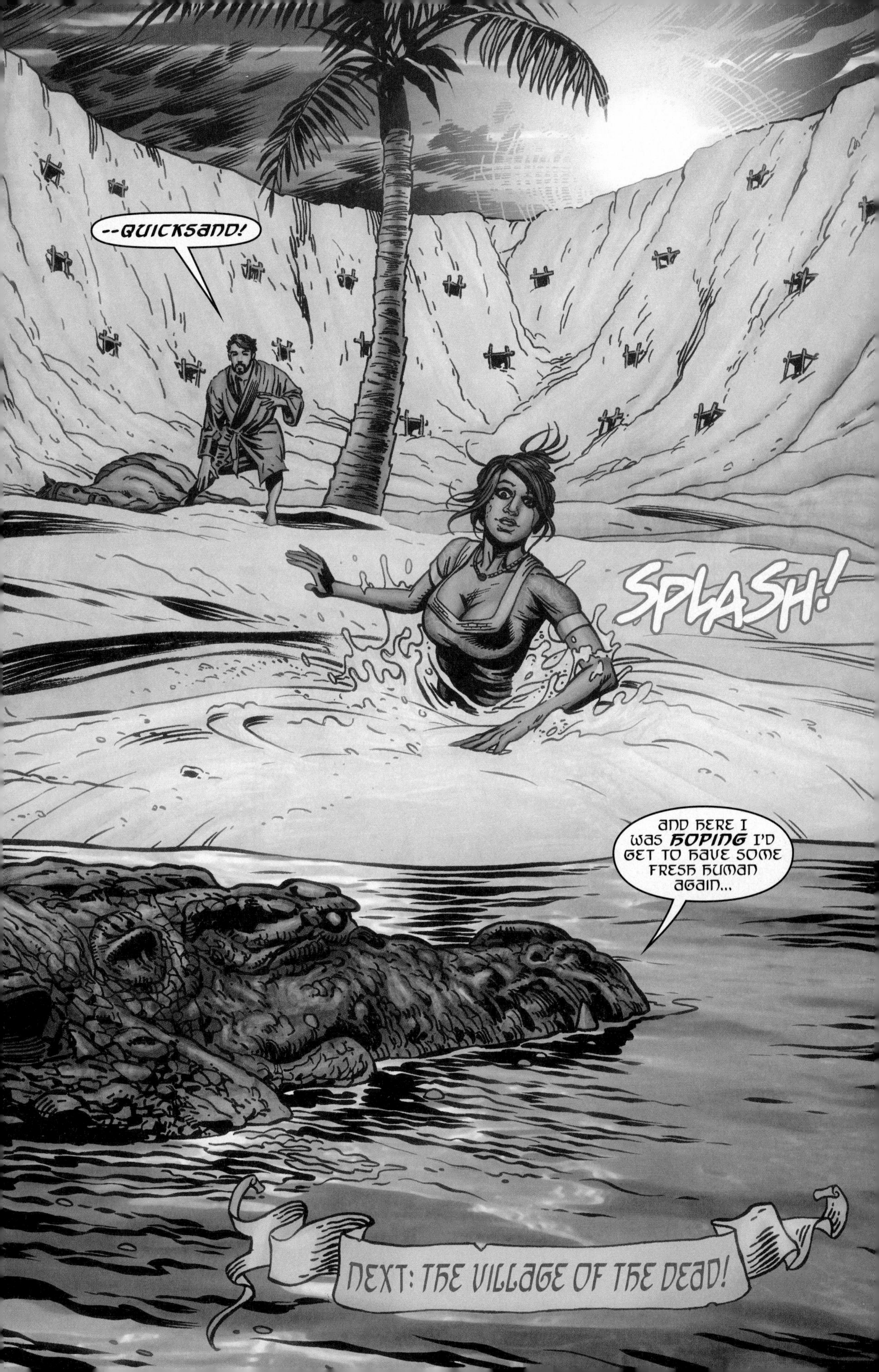
--QUICKSAND!
SPLASH!
AND HERE I WAS HOPING I'D GET TO HAVE SOME FRESH HUMAN AGAIN...
NEXT: THE VILLAGE OF THE DEAD!

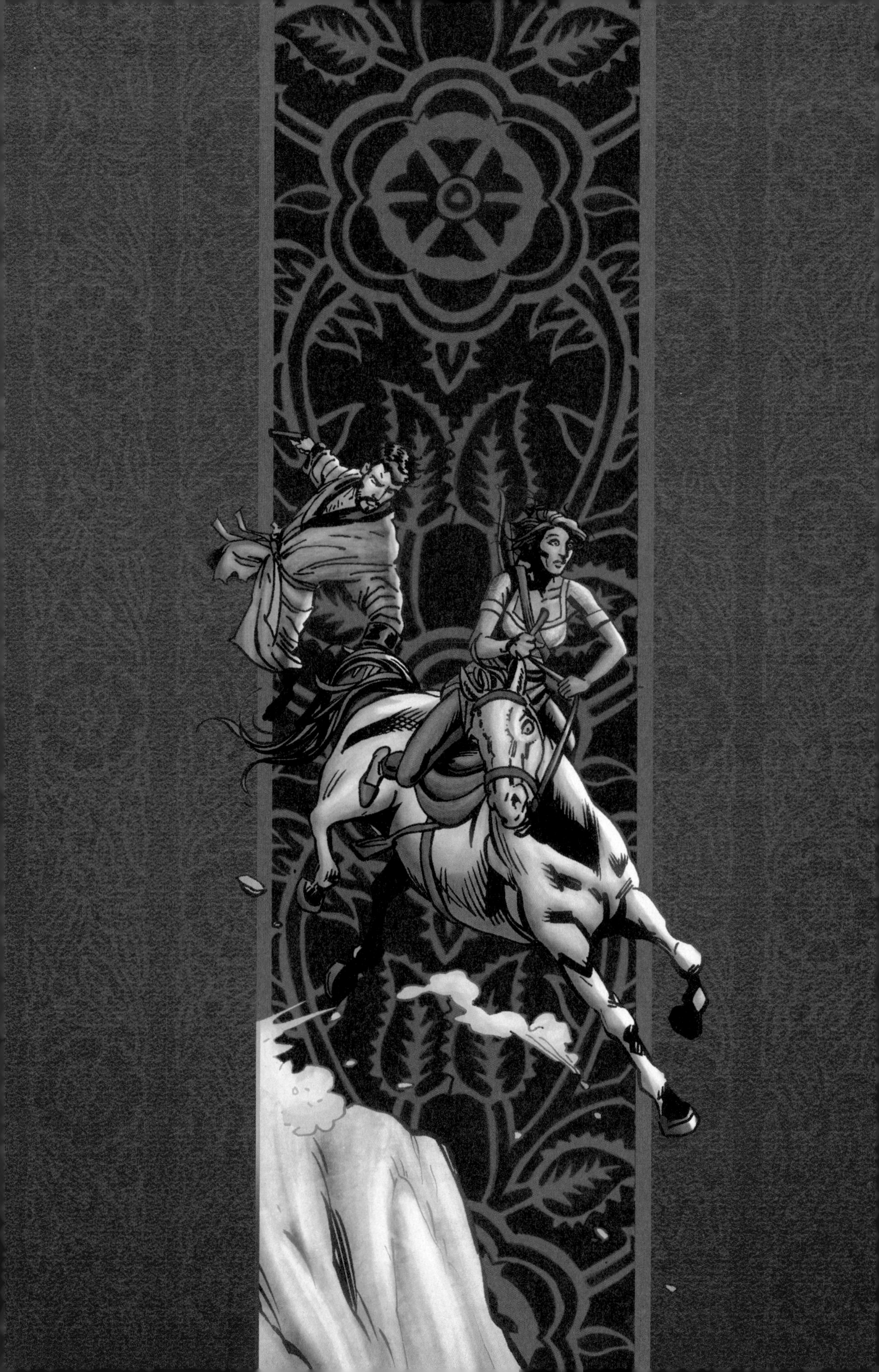

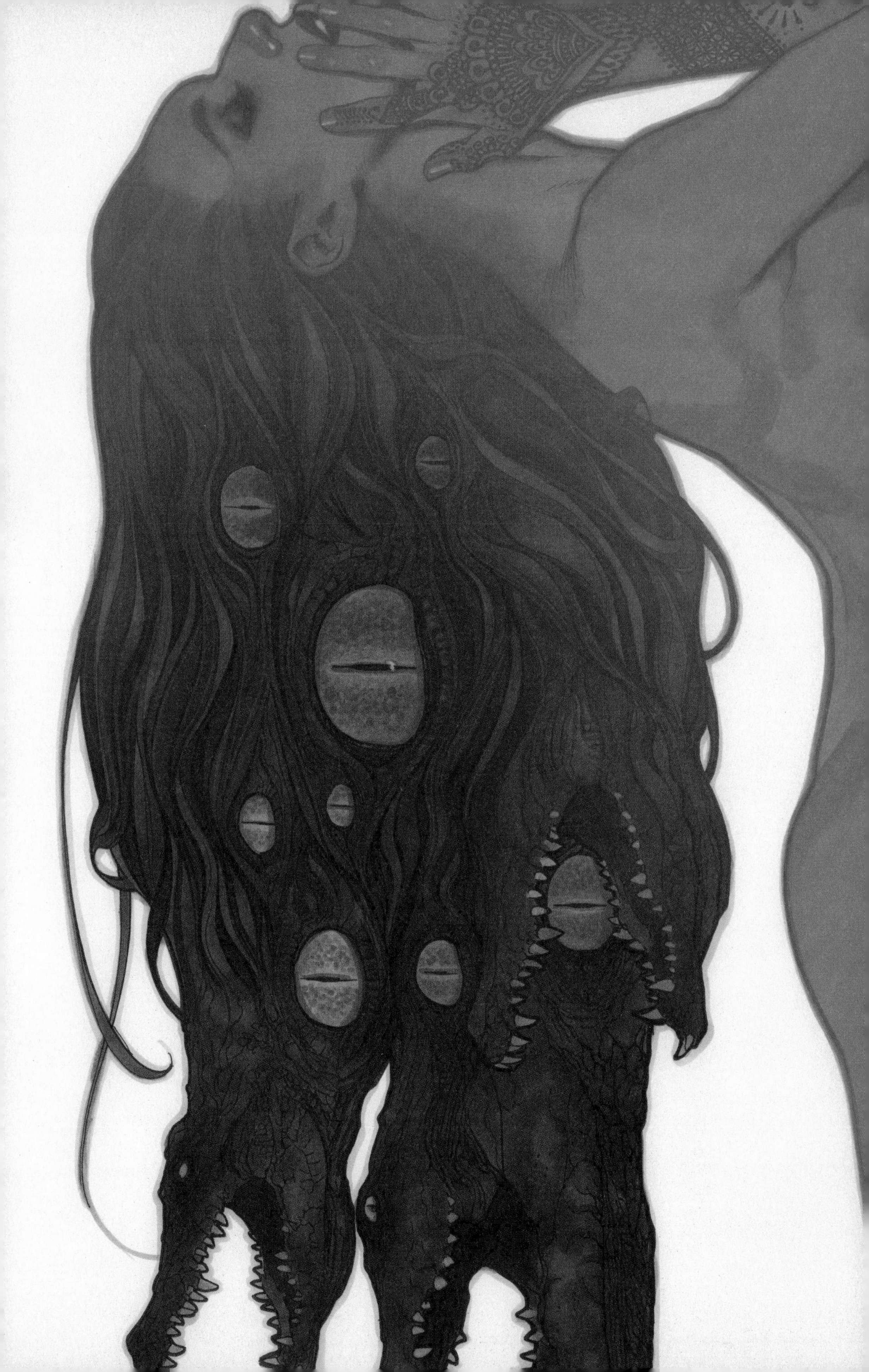

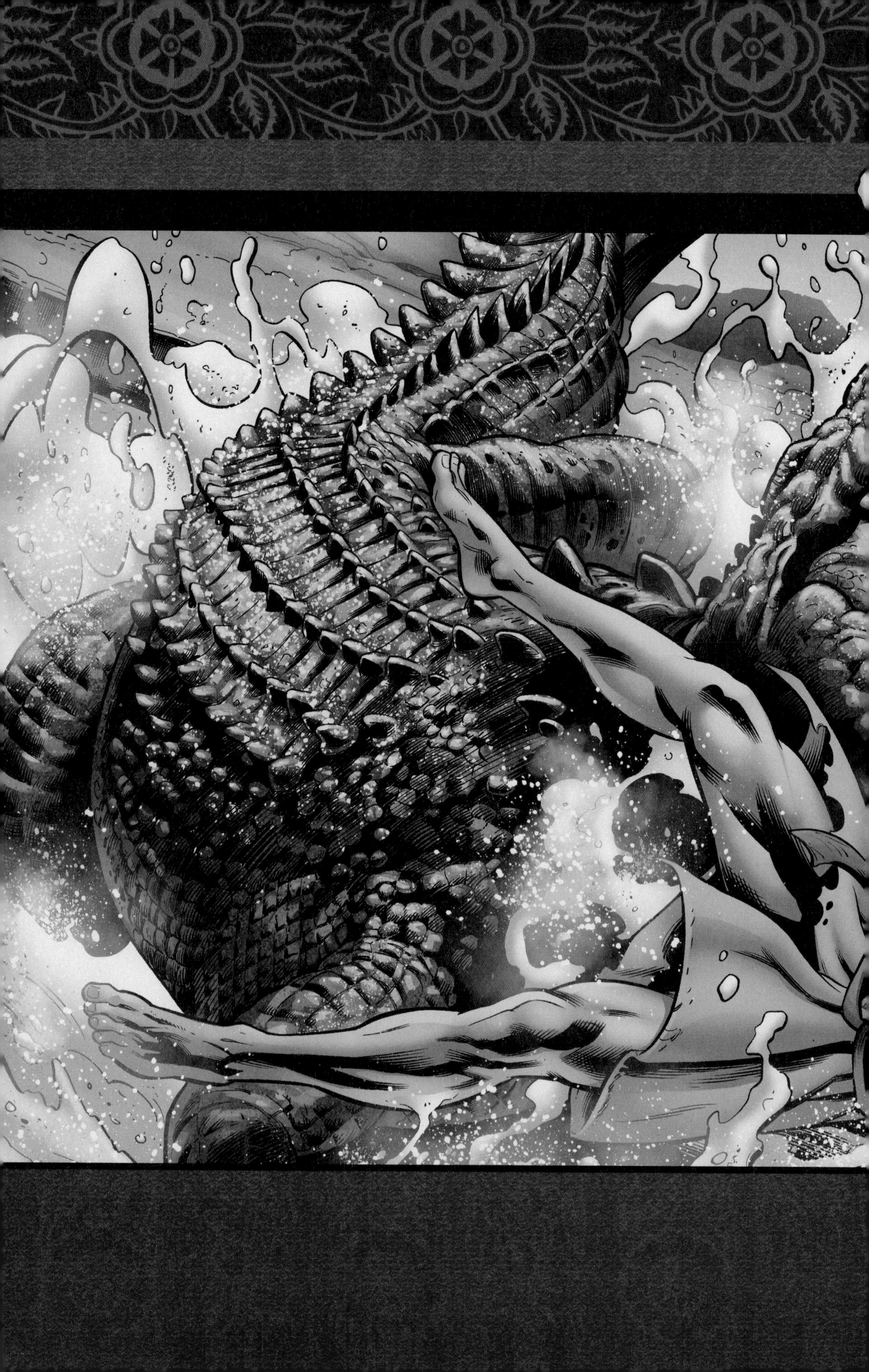

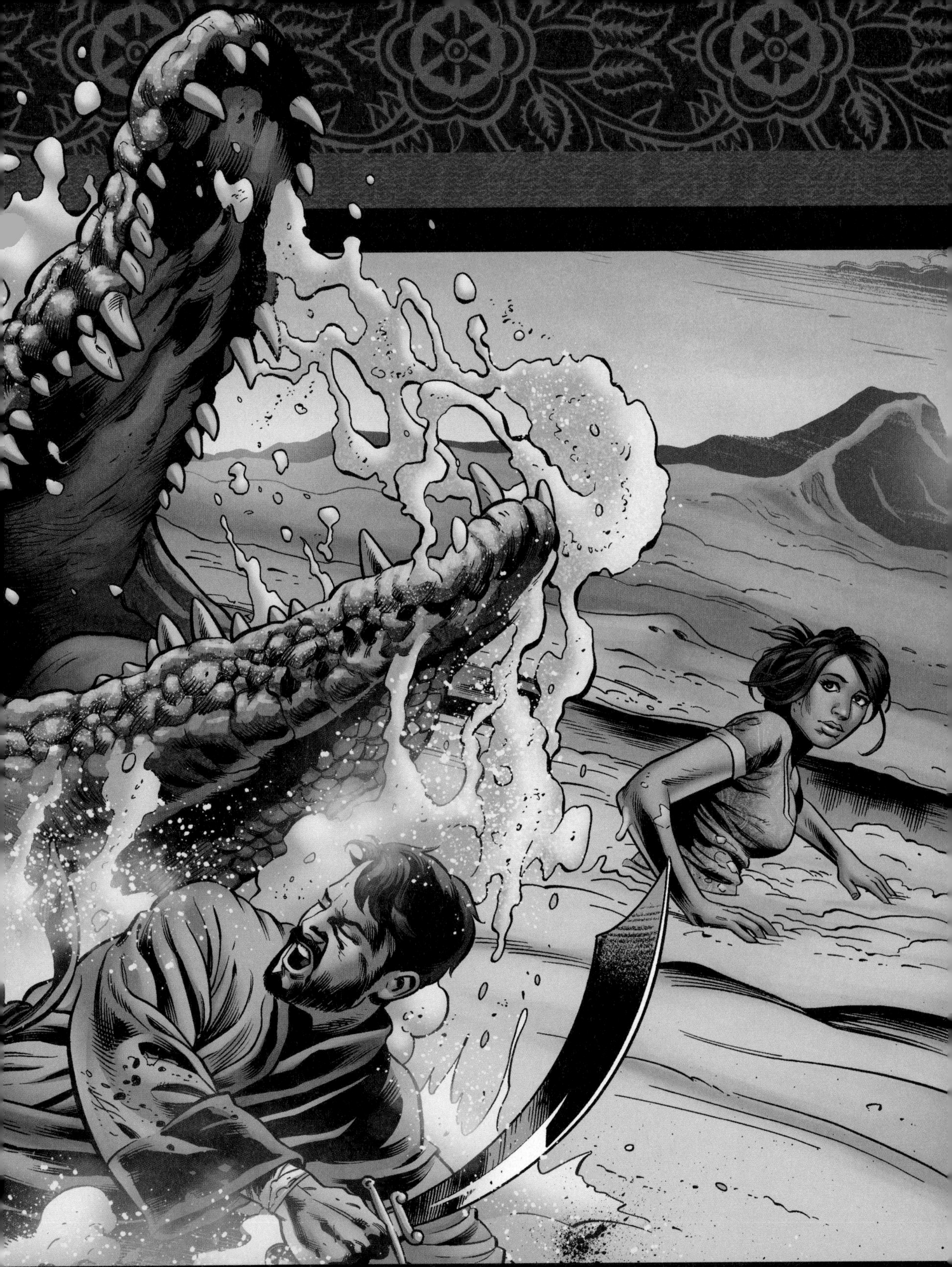

"No one lasts long in the village of the dead."

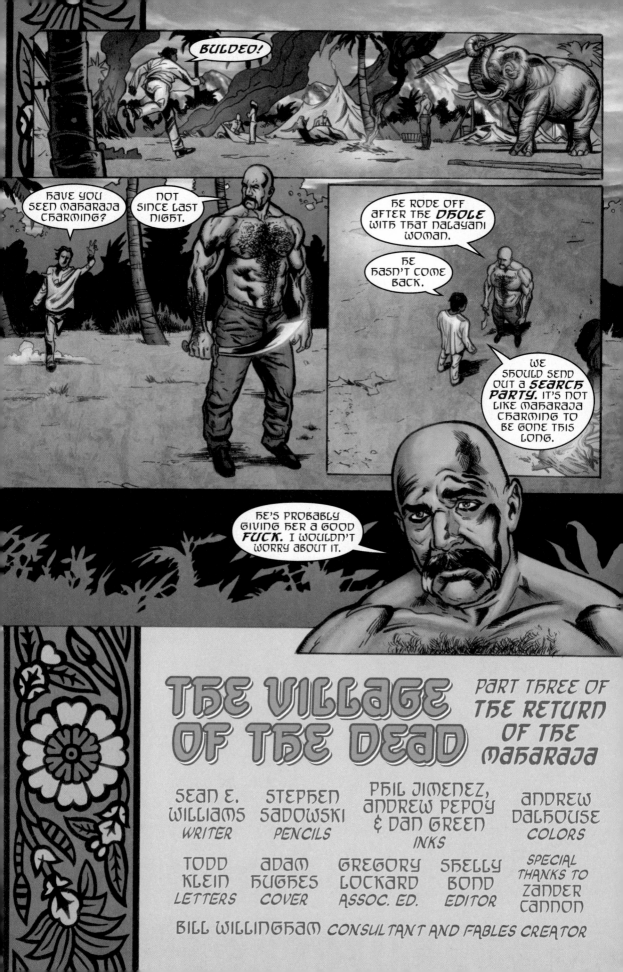

BULDEO!

HAVE YOU SEEN MAHARAJA CHARMING?

NOT SINCE LAST NIGHT.

HE RODE OFF AFTER THE *DHOLE* WITH THAT NALAYANI WOMAN.

HE HASN'T COME BACK.

WE SHOULD SEND OUT A *SEARCH PARTY.* IT'S NOT LIKE MAHARAJA CHARMING TO BE GONE THIS LONG.

HE'S PROBABLY GIVING HER A GOOD *FUCK.* I WOULDN'T WORRY ABOUT IT.

THE VILLAGE OF THE DEAD

PART THREE OF
THE RETURN OF THE MAHARAJA

SEAN E. WILLIAMS
WRITER

STEPHEN SADOWSKI
PENCILS

PHIL JIMENEZ, ANDREW PEPOY & DAN GREEN
INKS

ANDREW DALHOUSE
COLORS

TODD KLEIN
LETTERS

ADAM HUGHES
COVER

GREGORY LOCKARD
ASSOC. ED.

SHELLY BOND
EDITOR

SPECIAL THANKS TO ZANDER CANNON

BILL WILLINGHAM CONSULTANT AND FABLES CREATOR

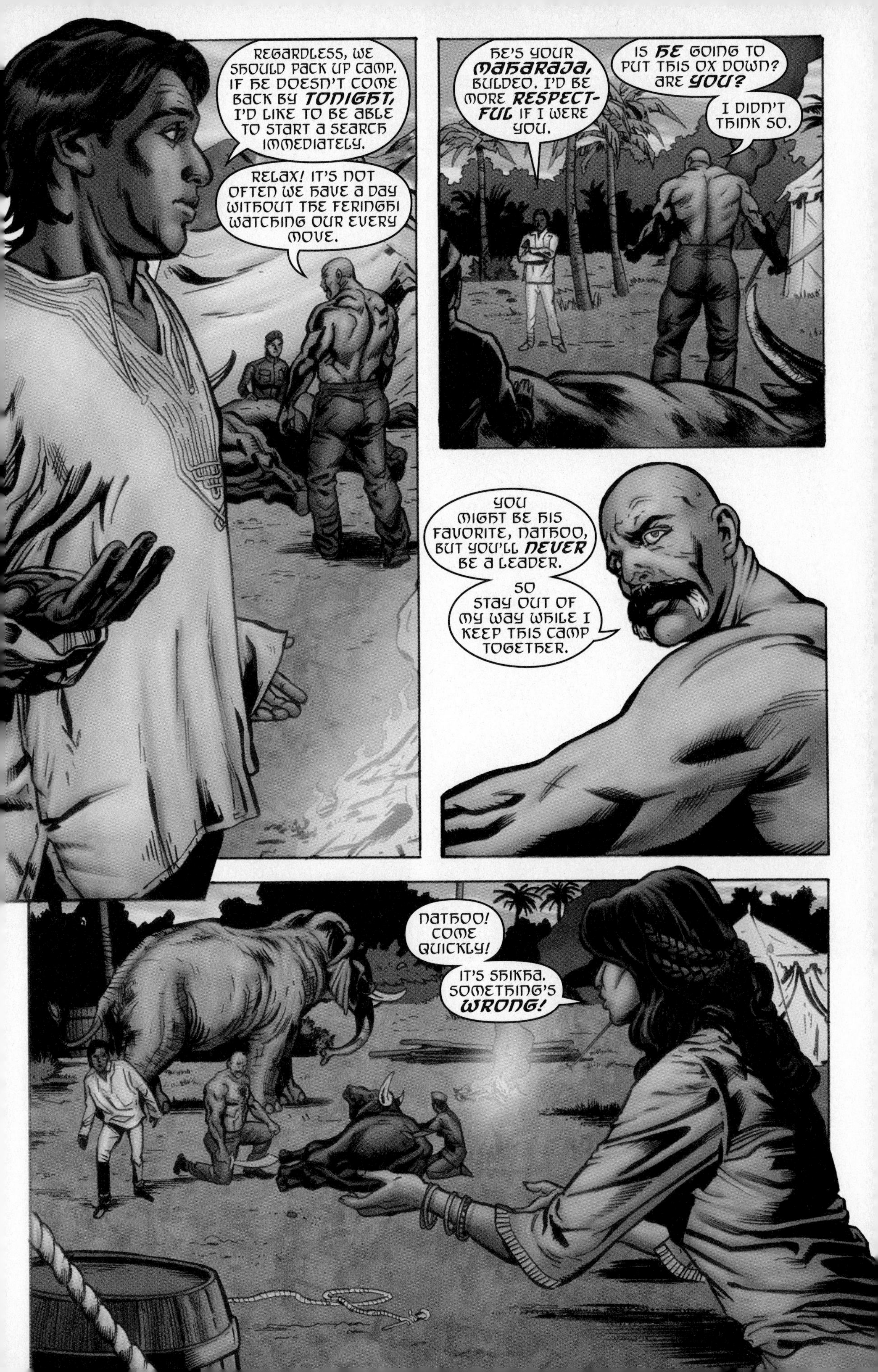
REGARDLESS, WE SHOULD PACK UP CAMP. IF HE DOESN'T COME BACK BY TONIGHT, I'D LIKE TO BE ABLE TO START A SEARCH IMMEDIATELY.
RELAX! IT'S NOT OFTEN WE HAVE A DAY WITHOUT THE FERINGHI WATCHING OUR EVERY MOVE.
HE'S YOUR MAHARAJA, BULDEO. I'D BE MORE RESPECTFUL IF I WERE YOU.
IS HE GOING TO PUT THIS OX DOWN? ARE YOU?
I DIDN'T THINK SO.
YOU MIGHT BE HIS FAVORITE, NATHOO, BUT YOU'LL NEVER BE A LEADER.
SO STAY OUT OF MY WAY WHILE I KEEP THIS CAMP TOGETHER.
NATHOO! COME QUICKLY!
IT'S SHIKHA. SOMETHING'S WRONG!

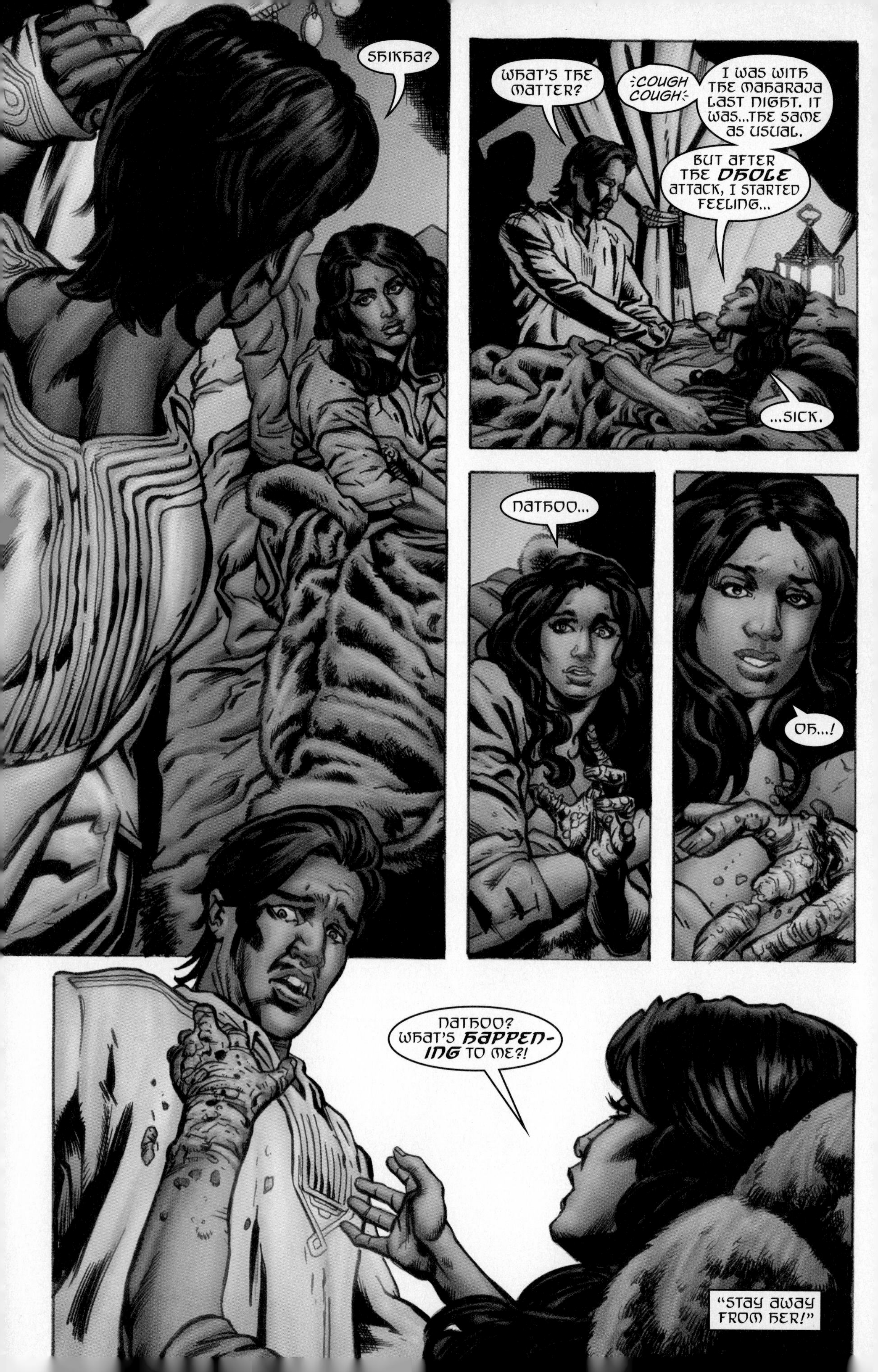
SHIKHA?
WHAT'S THE MATTER?
COUGH COUGH
I WAS WITH THE MAHARAJA LAST NIGHT. IT WAS...THE SAME AS USUAL.
BUT AFTER THE DHOLE ATTACK, I STARTED FEELING...
...SICK.
NATHOO...
OH...!
NATHOO? WHAT'S HAPPEN-ING TO ME?!
"STAY AWAY FROM HER!"

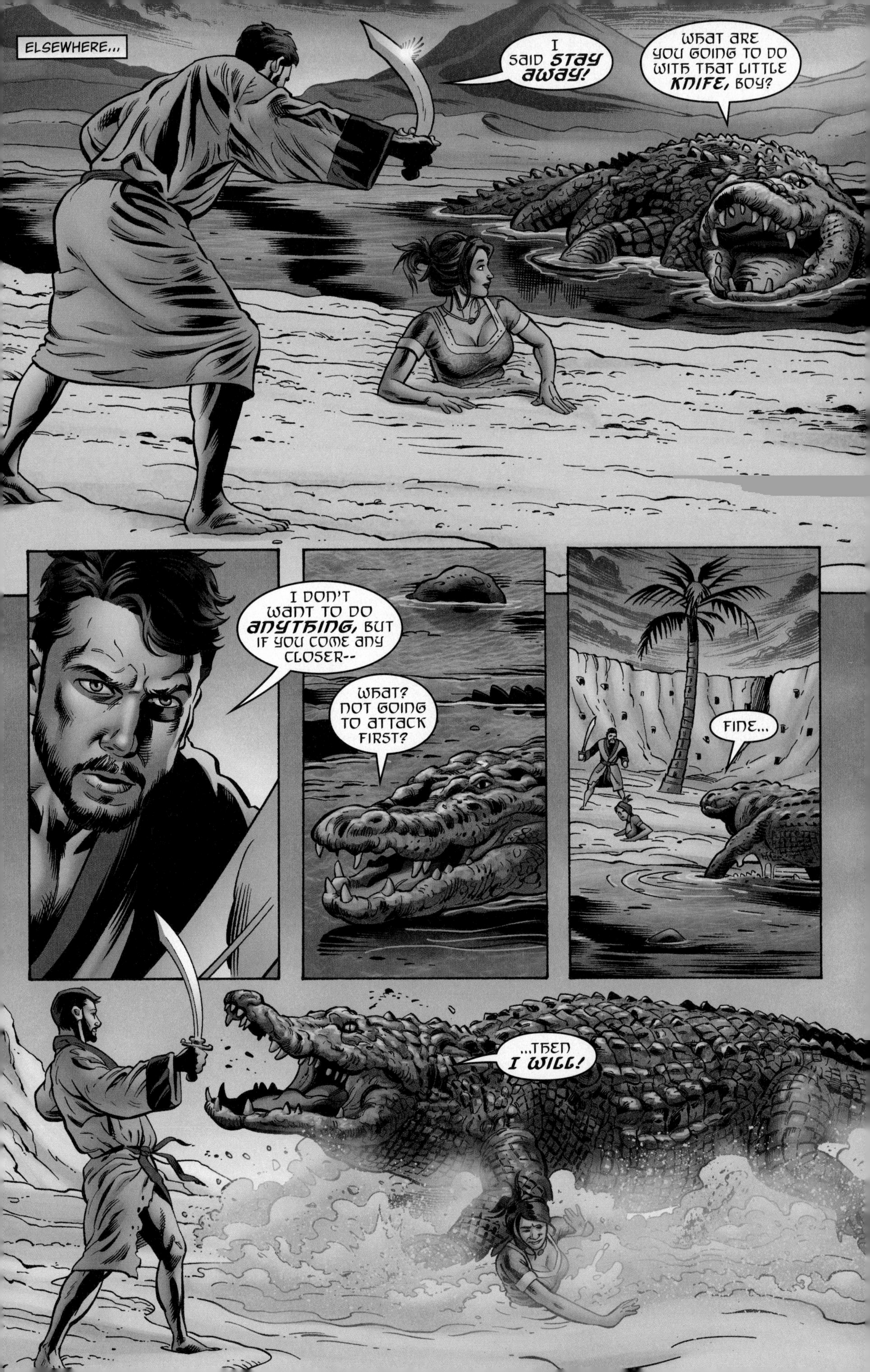
ELSEWHERE...
I said STAY away!
WHAT ARE YOU GOING TO DO WITH THAT LITTLE KNIFE, BOY?
I DON'T WANT TO DO ANYTHING, BUT IF YOU COME ANY CLOSER--
WHAT? NOT GOING TO ATTACK FIRST?
FINE...
...THEN I WILL!

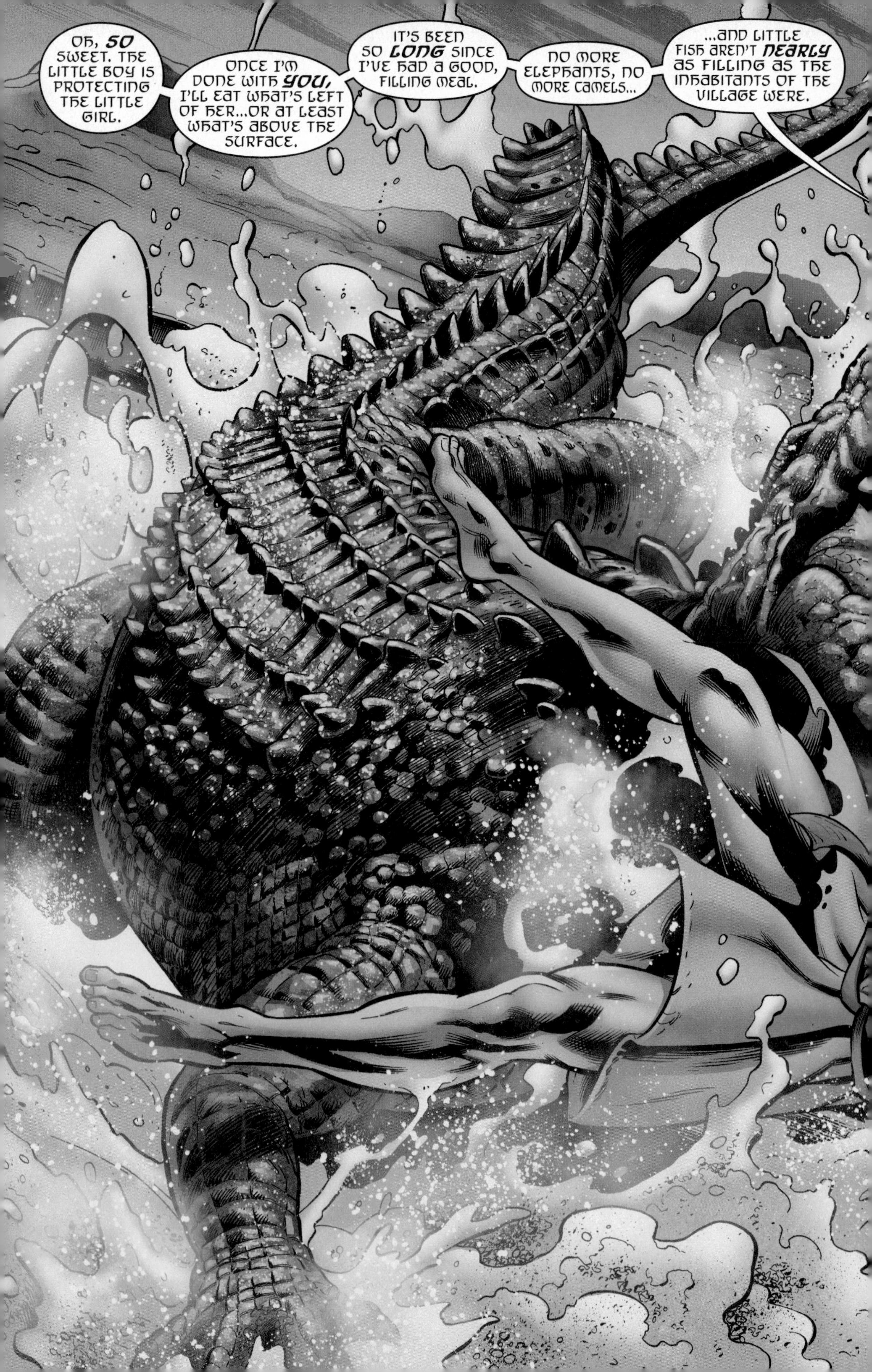
OH, SO SWEET. THE LITTLE BOY IS PROTECTING THE LITTLE GIRL.
ONCE I'M DONE WITH YOU, I'LL EAT WHAT'S LEFT OF HER...OR AT LEAST WHAT'S ABOVE THE SURFACE.
IT'S BEEN SO LONG SINCE I'VE HAD A GOOD, FILLING MEAL.
NO MORE ELEPHANTS, NO MORE CAMELS...
...AND LITTLE FISH AREN'T NEARLY AS FILLING AS THE INHABITANTS OF THE VILLAGE WERE.

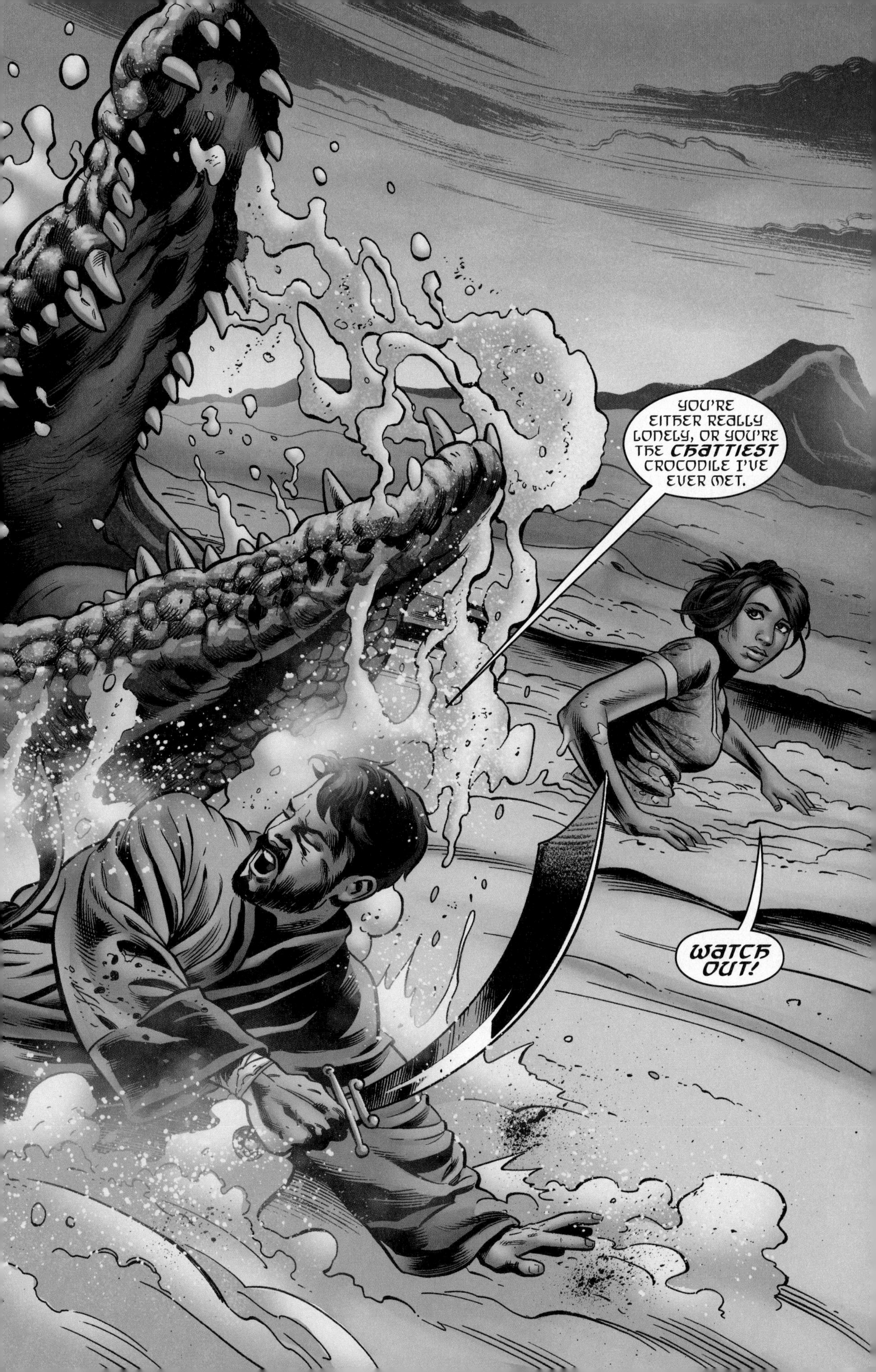
YOU'RE EITHER REALLY LONELY, OR YOU'RE THE CHATTIEST CROCODILE I'VE EVER MET.
WATCH OUT!

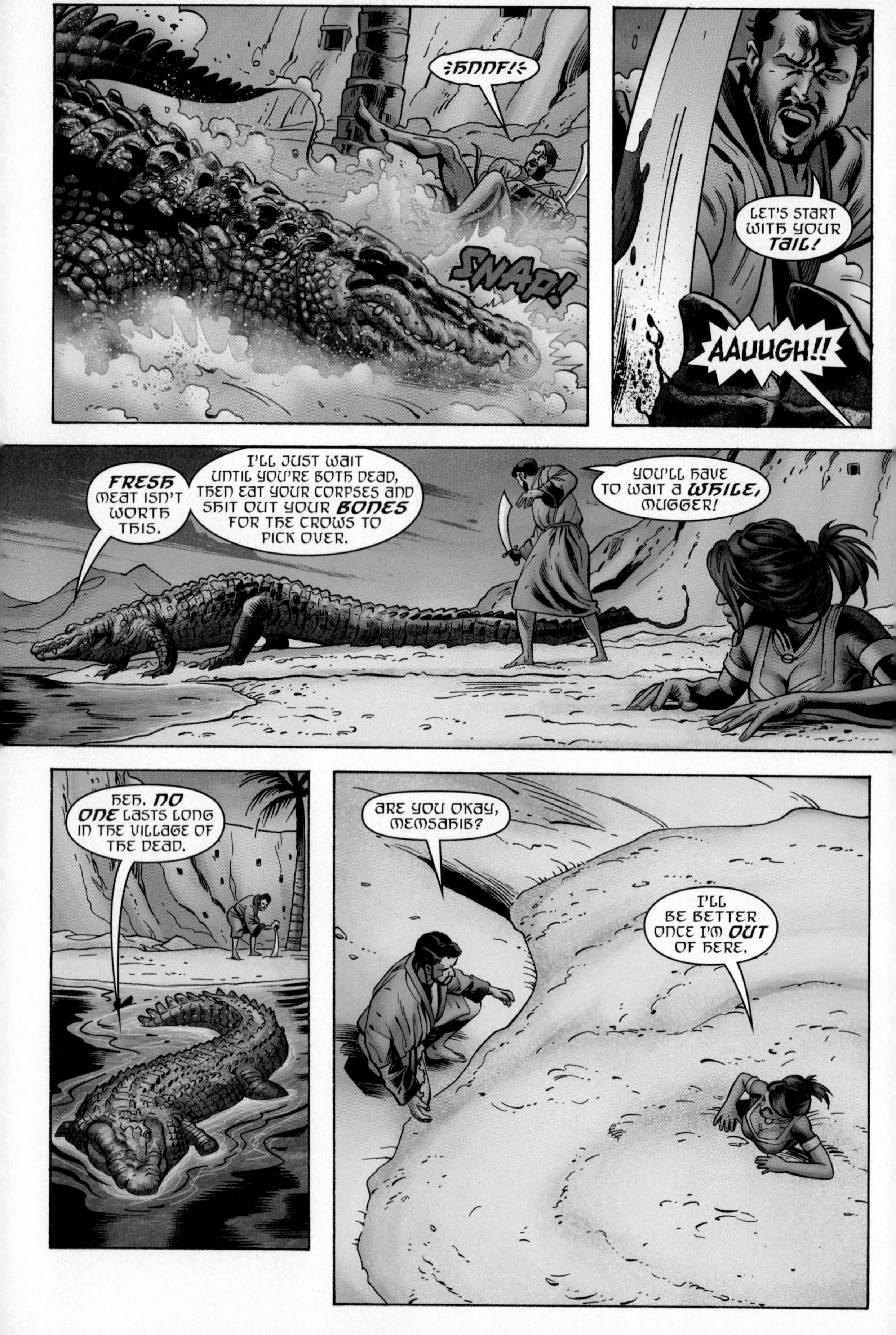
HNNF!
SNAP!
LET'S START WITH YOUR TAIL!
AAUUGH!!
FRESH MEAT ISN'T WORTH THIS.
I'LL JUST WAIT UNTIL YOU'RE BOTH DEAD, THEN EAT YOUR CORPSES AND SHIT OUT YOUR BONES FOR THE CROWS TO PICK OVER.
YOU'LL HAVE TO WAIT A WHILE, MUGGER!
HEH. NO ONE LASTS LONG IN THE VILLAGE OF THE DEAD.
ARE YOU OKAY, MEMSAHIB?
I'LL BE BETTER ONCE I'M OUT OF HERE.

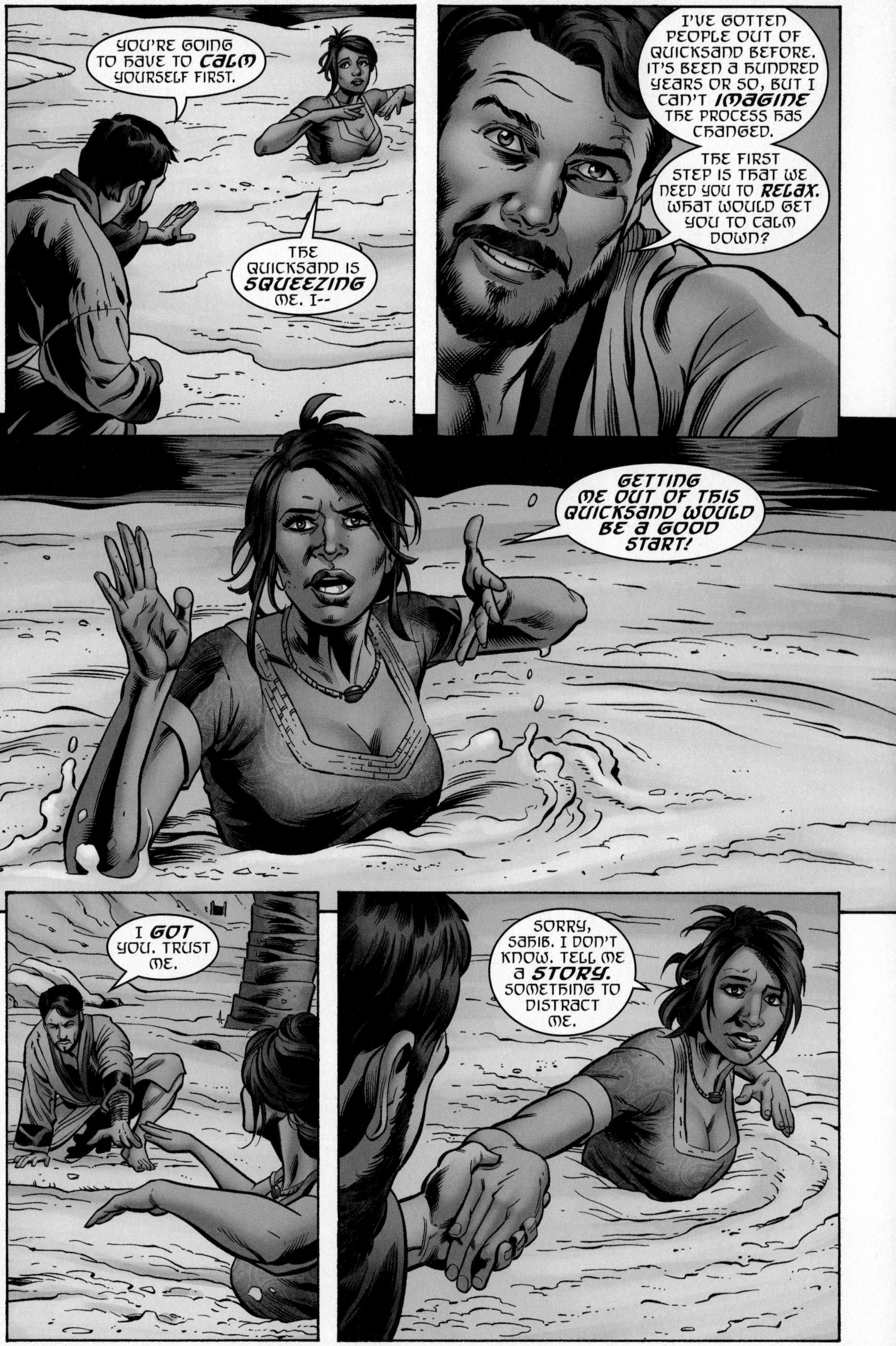
YOU'RE GOING TO HAVE TO CALM YOURSELF FIRST.
THE QUICKSAND IS SQUEEZING ME. I--
I'VE GOTTEN PEOPLE OUT OF QUICKSAND BEFORE. IT'S BEEN A HUNDRED YEARS OR SO, BUT I CAN'T IMAGINE THE PROCESS HAS CHANGED.
THE FIRST STEP IS THAT WE NEED YOU TO RELAX. WHAT WOULD GET YOU TO CALM DOWN?
GETTING ME OUT OF THIS QUICKSAND WOULD BE A GOOD START!
I GOT YOU. TRUST ME.
SORRY, SAHIB. I DON'T KNOW. TELL ME A STORY. SOMETHING TO DISTRACT ME.

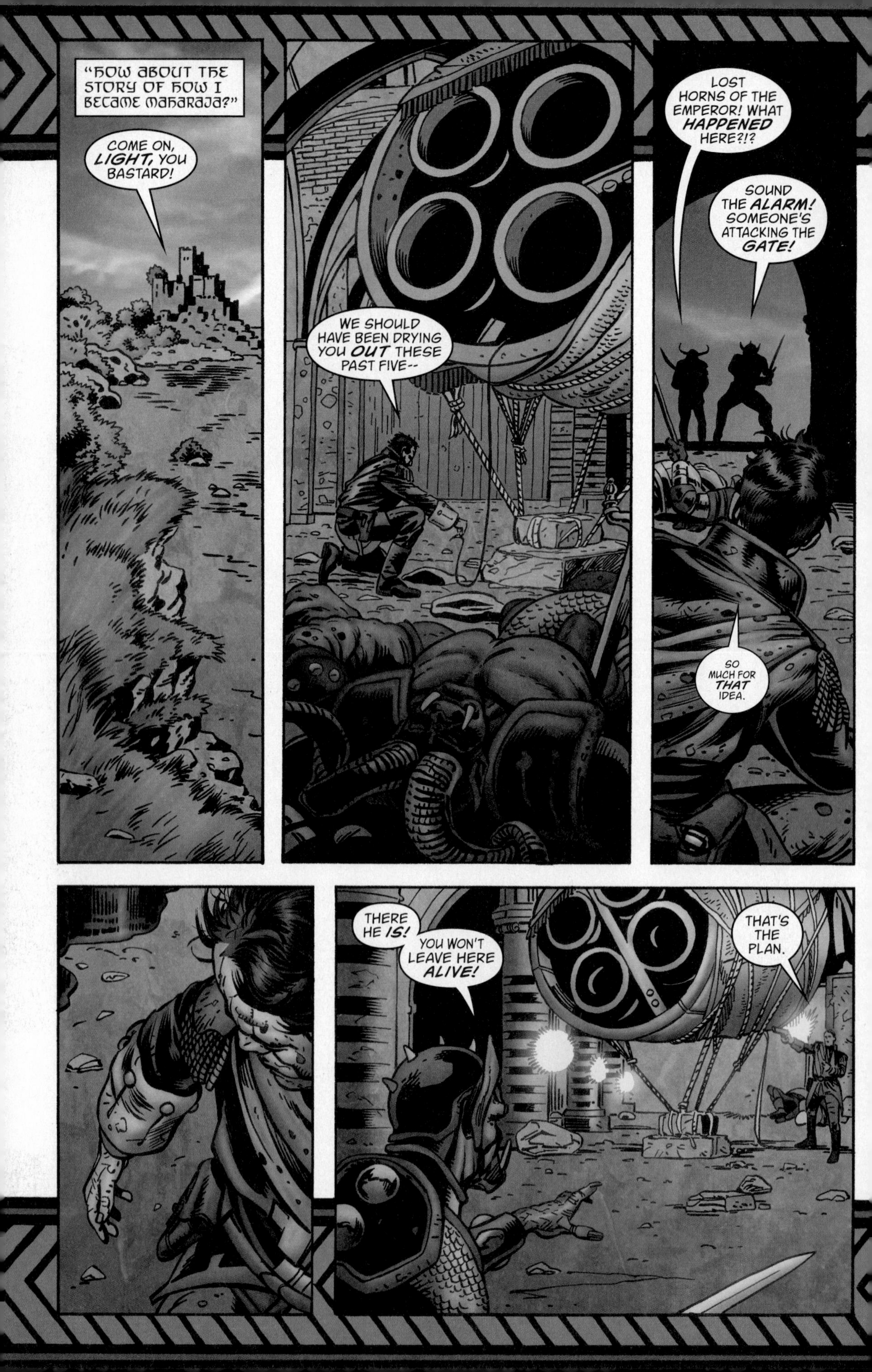
"HOW ABOUT THE STORY OF HOW I BECAME MAHARAJA?"
COME ON, LIGHT, YOU BASTARD!
WE SHOULD HAVE BEEN DRYING YOU OUT THESE PAST FIVE--
LOST HORNS OF THE EMPEROR! WHAT HAPPENED HERE?!?
SOUND THE ALARM! SOMEONE'S ATTACKING THE GATE!
SO MUCH FOR THAT IDEA.
THERE HE IS!
YOU WON'T LEAVE HERE ALIVE!
THAT'S THE PLAN.

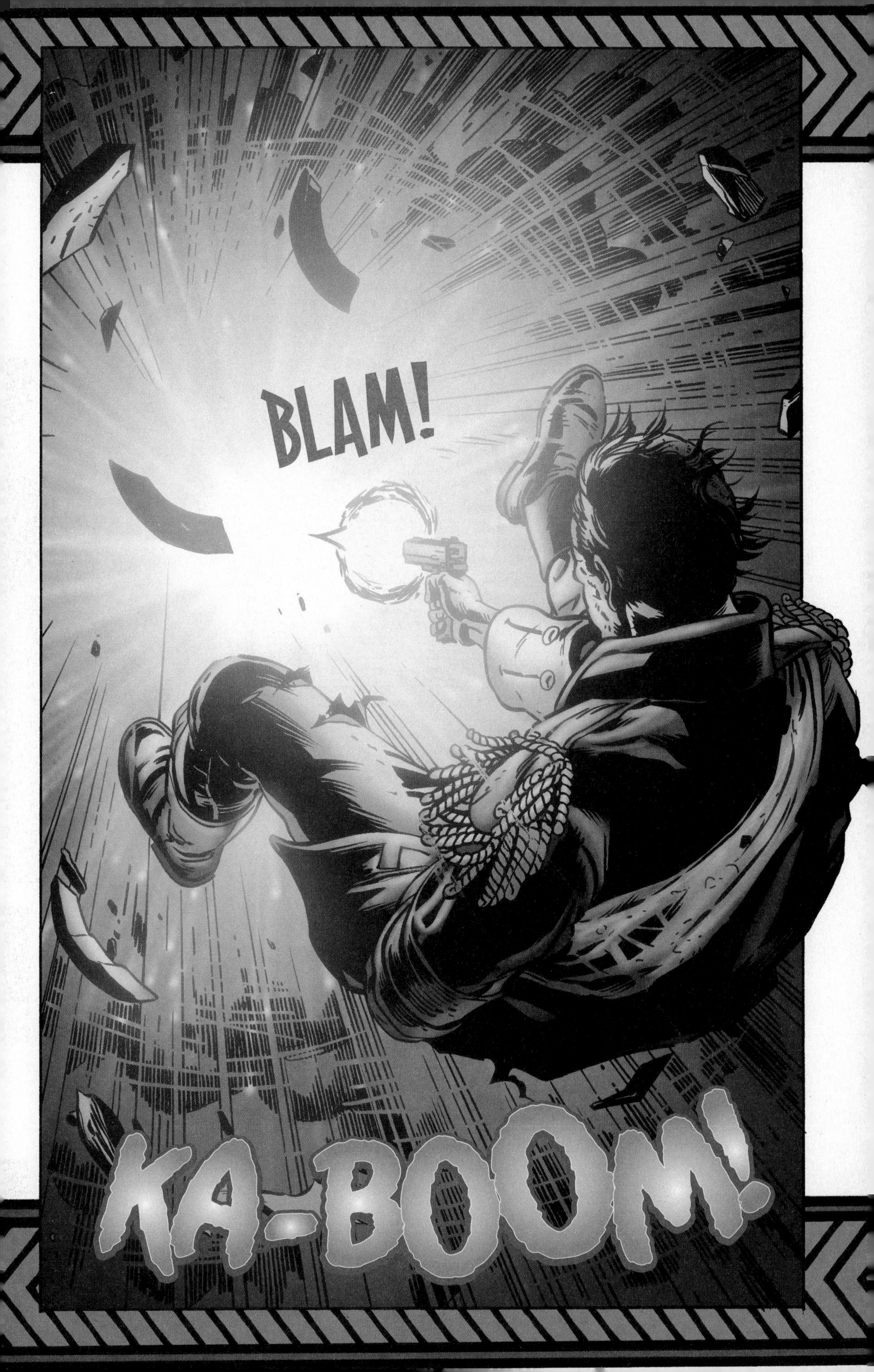
BLAM!
KA-BOOM!

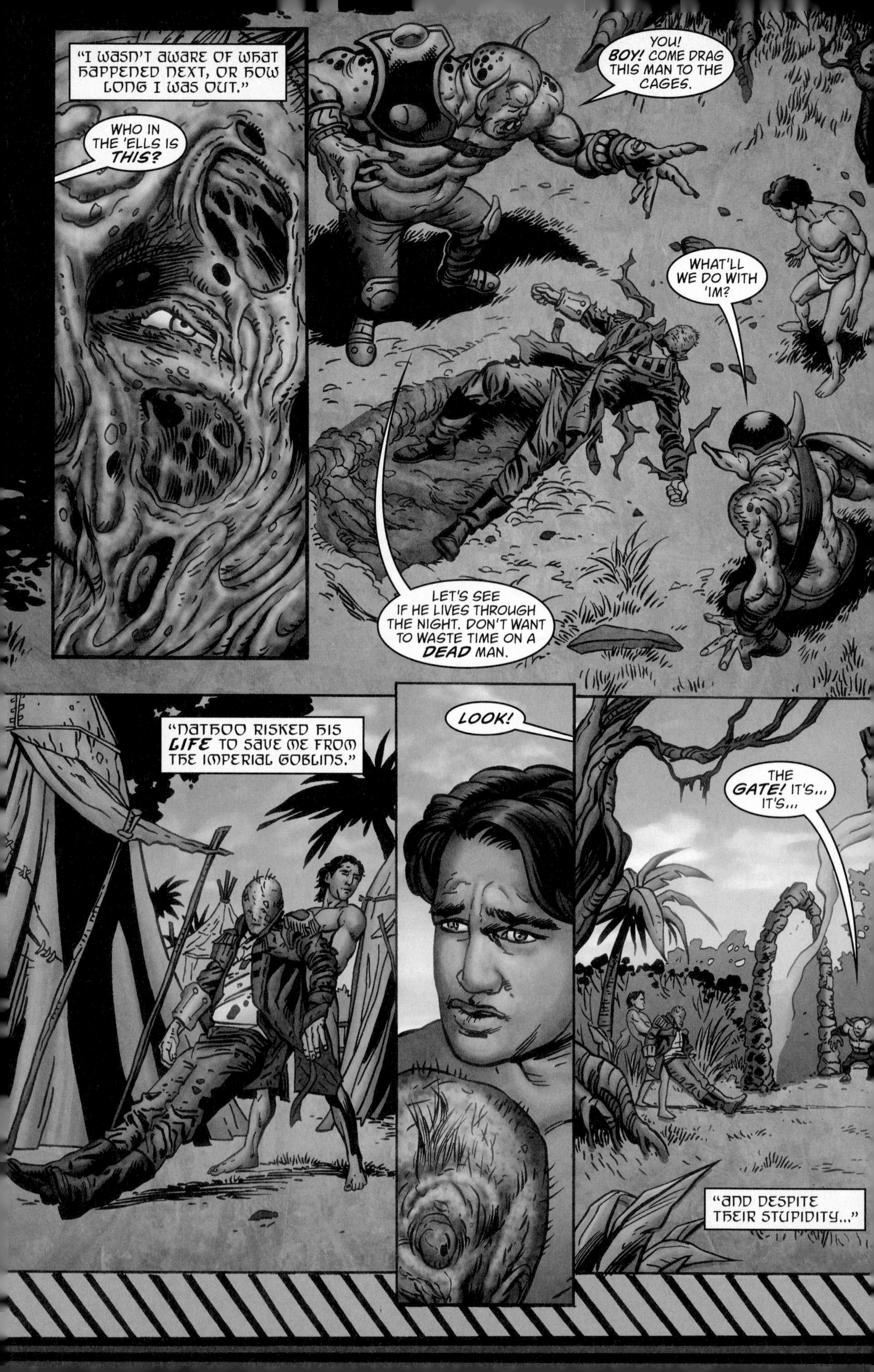
"I WASN'T AWARE OF WHAT HAPPENED NEXT, OR HOW LONG I WAS OUT."
WHO IN THE 'ELLS IS THIS?
YOU! BOY! COME DRAG THIS MAN TO THE CAGES.
WHAT'LL WE DO WITH 'IM?
LET'S SEE IF HE LIVES THROUGH THE NIGHT. DON'T WANT TO WASTE TIME ON A DEAD MAN.
"NATHOO RISKED HIS LIFE TO SAVE ME FROM THE IMPERIAL GOBLINS."
LOOK!
THE GATE! IT'S... IT'S...
"AND DESPITE THEIR STUPIDITY..."

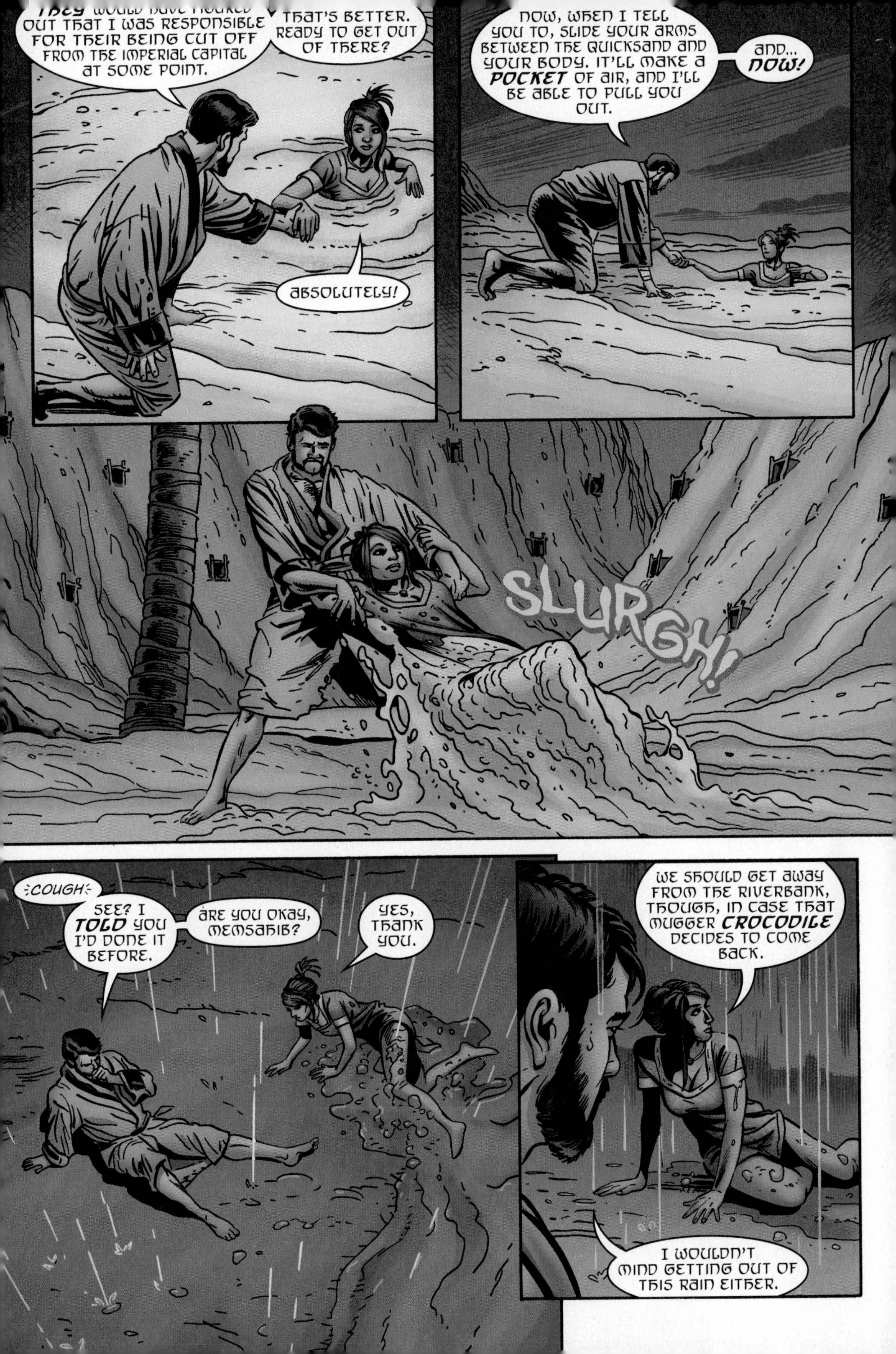

OUT THAT I WAS RESPONSIBLE FOR THEIR BEING CUT OFF FROM THE IMPERIAL CAPITAL AT SOME POINT.
THAT'S BETTER. READY TO GET OUT OF THERE?
ABSOLUTELY!
NOW, WHEN I TELL YOU TO, SLIDE YOUR ARMS BETWEEN THE QUICKSAND AND YOUR BODY. IT'LL MAKE A POCKET OF AIR, AND I'LL BE ABLE TO PULL YOU OUT.
AND... NOW!
SLURGH!
COUGH
SEE? I TOLD YOU I'D DONE IT BEFORE.
ARE YOU OKAY, MEMSAHIB?
YES, THANK YOU.
WE SHOULD GET AWAY FROM THE RIVERBANK, THOUGH, IN CASE THAT MUGGER CROCODILE DECIDES TO COME BACK.
I WOULDN'T MIND GETTING OUT OF THIS RAIN EITHER.

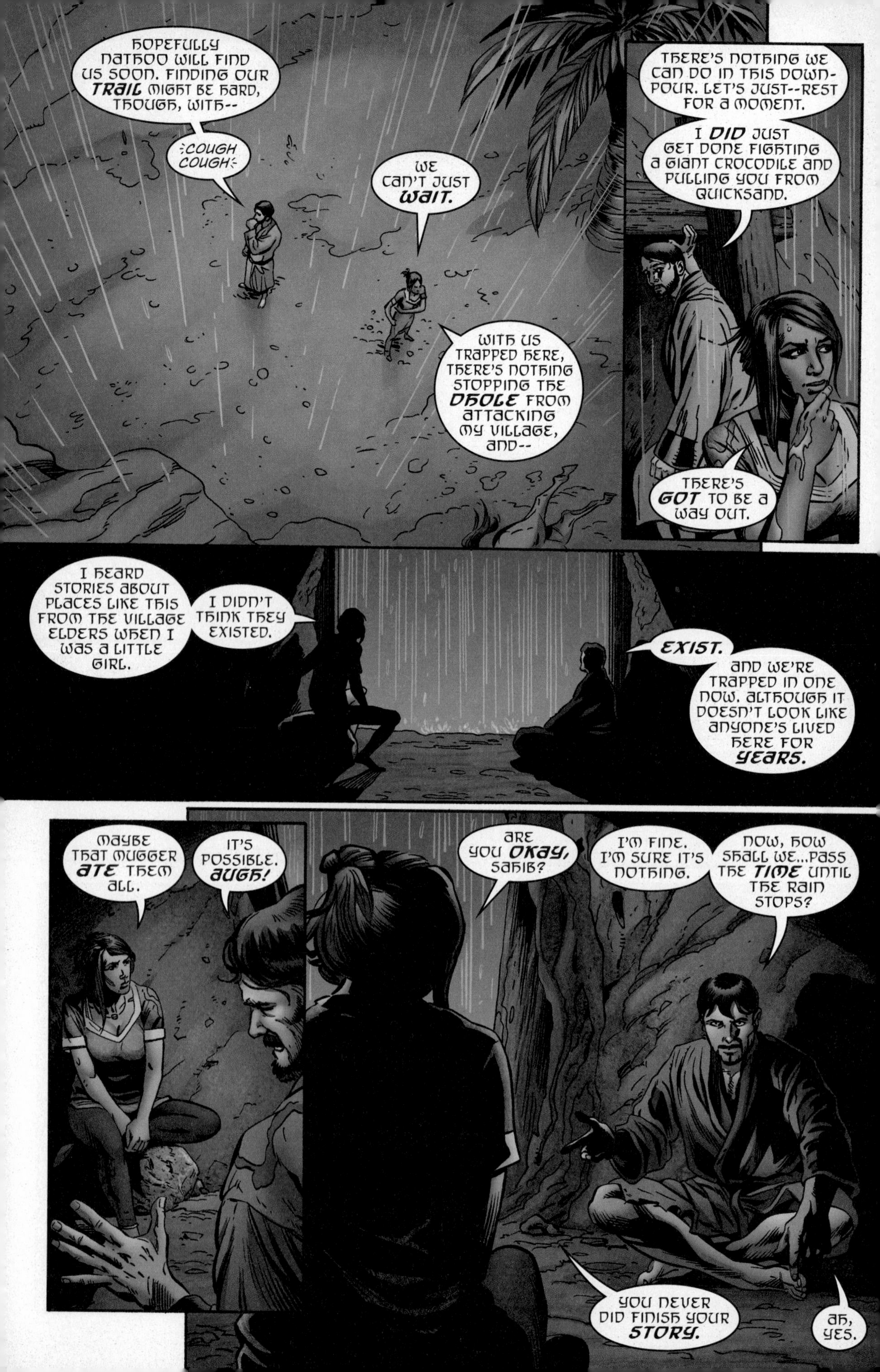
HOPEFULLY NATHOO WILL FIND US SOON. FINDING OUR TRAIL MIGHT BE HARD, THOUGH, WITH--
COUGH COUGH
WE CAN'T JUST WAIT.
WITH US TRAPPED HERE, THERE'S NOTHING STOPPING THE DHOLE FROM ATTACKING MY VILLAGE, AND--
THERE'S NOTHING WE CAN DO IN THIS DOWN-POUR. LET'S JUST--REST FOR A MOMENT.
I DID JUST GET DONE FIGHTING A GIANT CROCODILE AND PULLING YOU FROM QUICKSAND.
THERE'S GOT TO BE A WAY OUT.
I HEARD STORIES ABOUT PLACES LIKE THIS FROM THE VILLAGE ELDERS WHEN I WAS A LITTLE GIRL.
I DIDN'T THINK THEY EXISTED.
EXIST.
AND WE'RE TRAPPED IN ONE NOW. ALTHOUGH IT DOESN'T LOOK LIKE ANYONE'S LIVED HERE FOR YEARS.
MAYBE THAT MUGGER ATE THEM ALL.
IT'S POSSIBLE. AUGH!
ARE YOU OKAY, SAHIB?
I'M FINE. I'M SURE IT'S NOTHING.
NOW, HOW SHALL WE...PASS THE TIME UNTIL THE RAIN STOPS?
YOU NEVER DID FINISH YOUR STORY.
AH, YES.

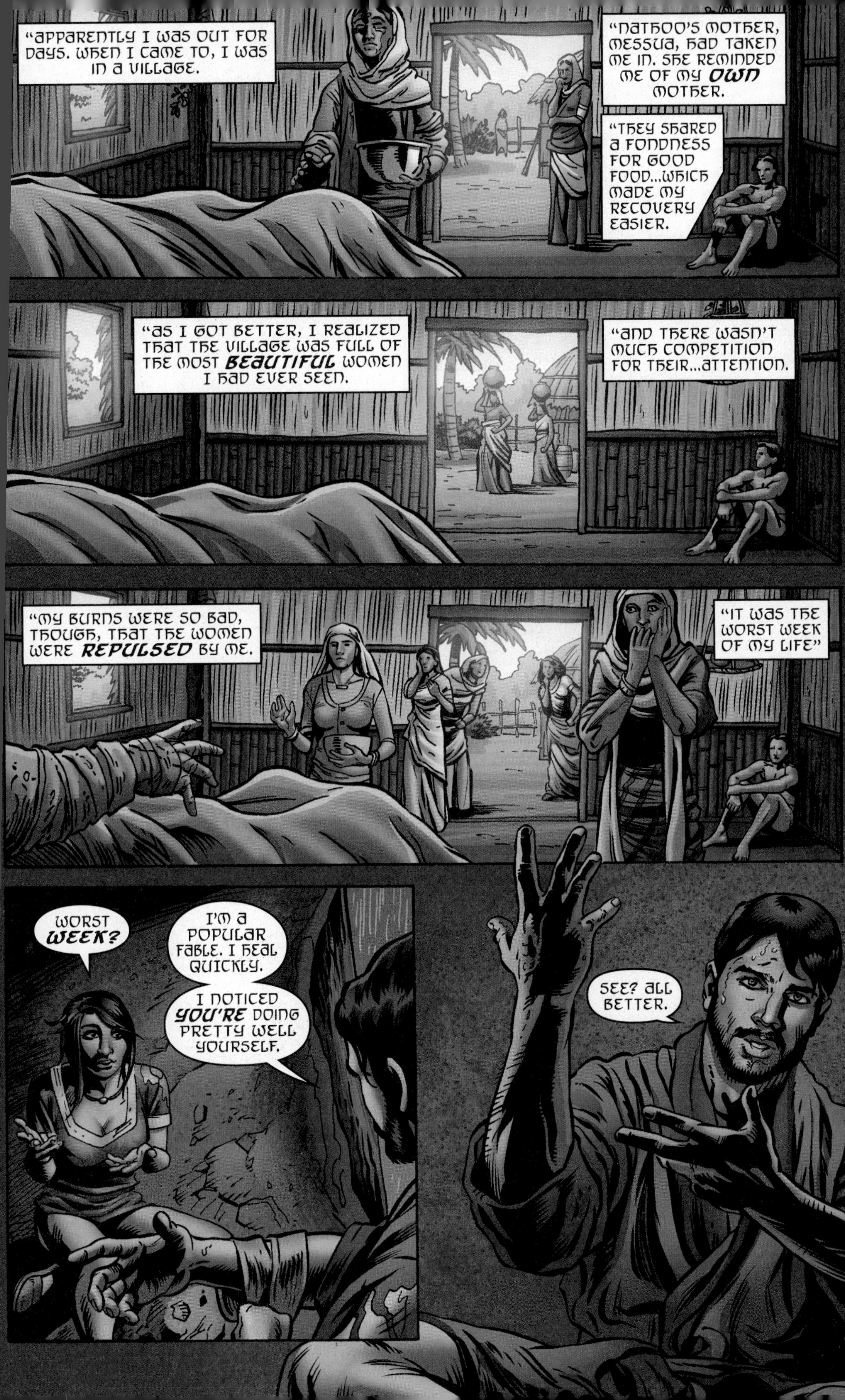
"APPARENTLY I WAS OUT FOR DAYS. WHEN I CAME TO, I WAS IN A VILLAGE.
"NATHOO'S MOTHER, MESSUA, HAD TAKEN ME IN. SHE REMINDED ME OF MY OWN MOTHER.
"THEY SHARED A FONDNESS FOR GOOD FOOD...WHICH MADE MY RECOVERY EASIER.
"AS I GOT BETTER, I REALIZED THAT THE VILLAGE WAS FULL OF THE MOST BEAUTIFUL WOMEN I HAD EVER SEEN.
"AND THERE WASN'T MUCH COMPETITION FOR THEIR...ATTENTION.
"MY BURNS WERE SO BAD, THOUGH, THAT THE WOMEN WERE REPULSED BY ME.
"IT WAS THE WORST WEEK OF MY LIFE"
WORST WEEK?
I'M A POPULAR FABLE. I HEAL QUICKLY.
I NOTICED YOU'RE DOING PRETTY WELL YOURSELF.
SEE? ALL BETTER.

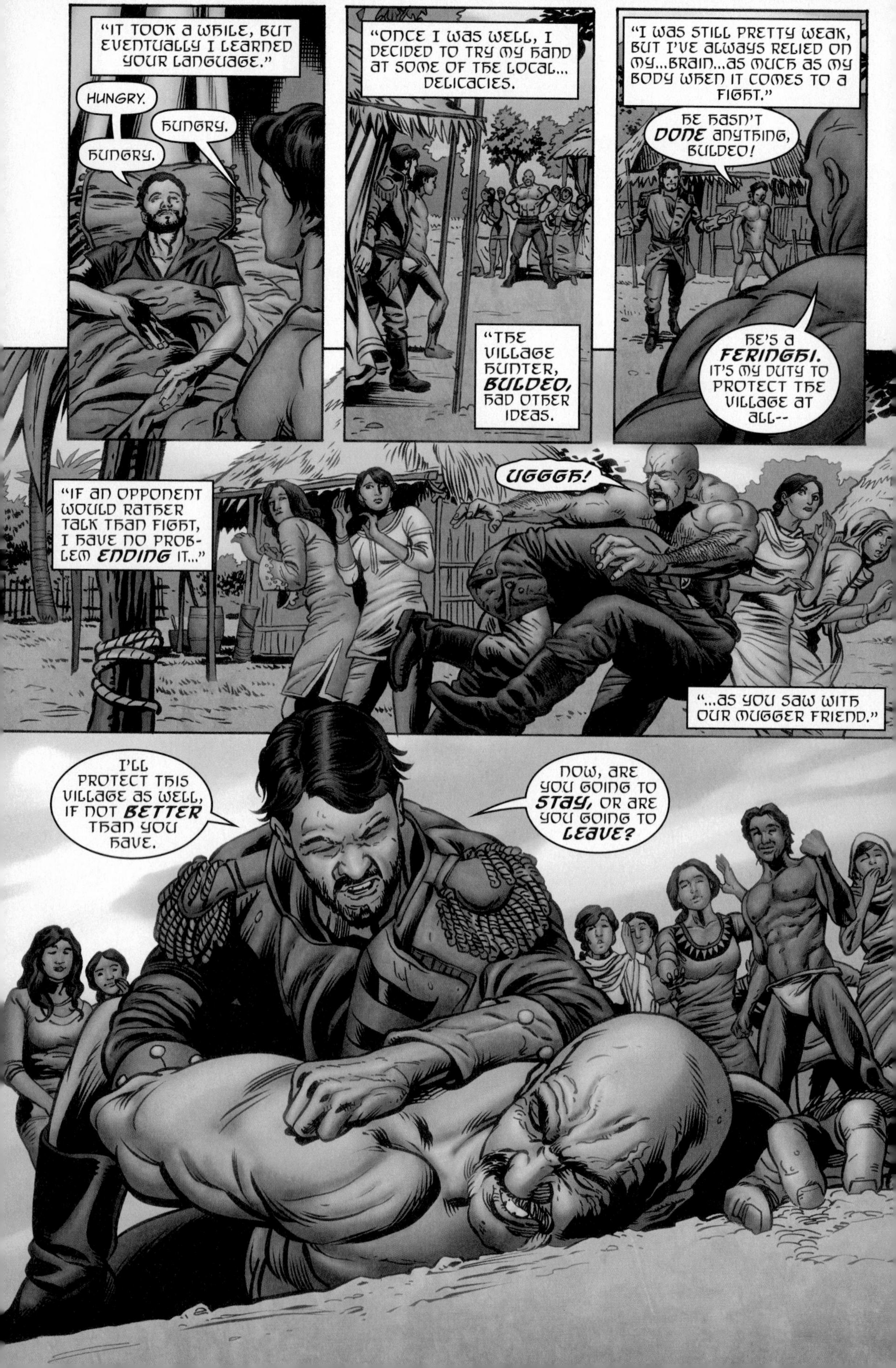
"IT TOOK A WHILE, BUT EVENTUALLY I LEARNED YOUR LANGUAGE."
HUNGRY.
HUNGRY.
HUNGRY.
"ONCE I WAS WELL, I DECIDED TO TRY MY HAND AT SOME OF THE LOCAL... DELICACIES.
"THE VILLAGE HUNTER, BULDEO, HAD OTHER IDEAS.
"I WAS STILL PRETTY WEAK, BUT I'VE ALWAYS RELIED ON MY...BRAIN...AS MUCH AS MY BODY WHEN IT COMES TO A FIGHT."
HE HASN'T DONE ANYTHING, BULDEO!
HE'S A FERINGHI. IT'S MY DUTY TO PROTECT THE VILLAGE AT ALL--
"IF AN OPPONENT WOULD RATHER TALK THAN FIGHT, I HAVE NO PROBLEM ENDING IT..."
UGGGH!
"...AS YOU SAW WITH OUR MUGGER FRIEND."
I'LL PROTECT THIS VILLAGE AS WELL, IF NOT BETTER THAN YOU HAVE.
NOW, ARE YOU GOING TO STAY, OR ARE YOU GOING TO LEAVE?

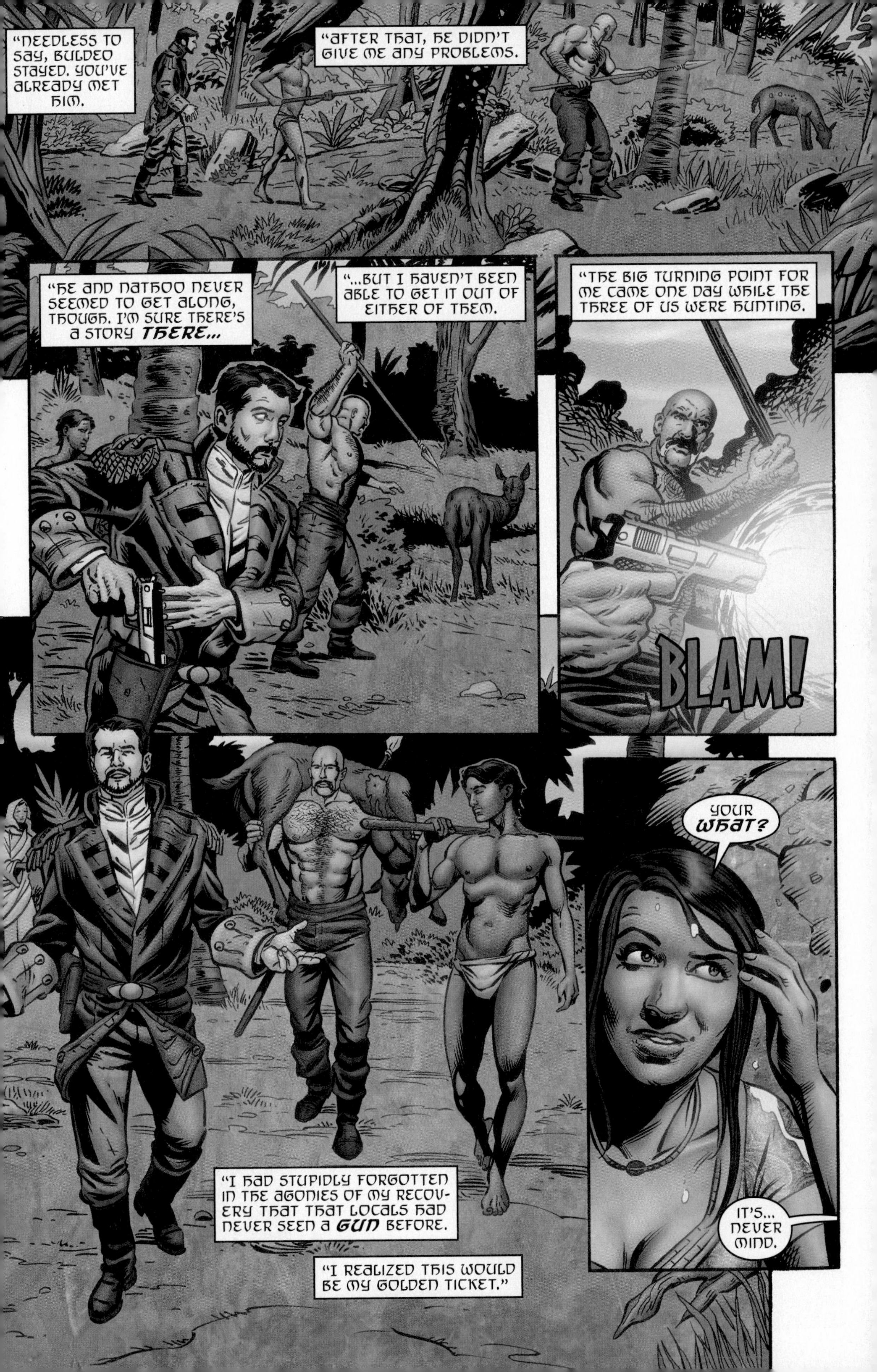
"NEEDLESS TO SAY, BULDEO STAYED. YOU'VE ALREADY MET HIM.
"AFTER THAT, HE DIDN'T GIVE ME ANY PROBLEMS.
"HE AND NATHOO NEVER SEEMED TO GET ALONG, THOUGH. I'M SURE THERE'S A STORY THERE...
"...BUT I HAVEN'T BEEN ABLE TO GET IT OUT OF EITHER OF THEM.
"THE BIG TURNING POINT FOR ME CAME ONE DAY WHILE THE THREE OF US WERE HUNTING.
BLAM!
"I HAD STUPIDLY FORGOTTEN IN THE AGONIES OF MY RECOVERY THAT THAT LOCALS HAD NEVER SEEN A GUN BEFORE.
"I REALIZED THIS WOULD BE MY GOLDEN TICKET."
YOUR WHAT?
IT'S... NEVER MIND.

"DEMONSTRATING THE POWER OF MY 'MAGICAL' *GUN*, I WAS ABLE TO BAND A FEW OF THE NEIGHBORING VILLAGES TOGETHER.

"USING WHAT ARMOR AND WEAPONS WE COULD FIND, GOBLIN OR INDU, I TRAINED THE ABLE-BODIED WOMEN OF OUR VILLAGES MYSELF...

"...AND SOON WE HAD AN *ARMY*.

"NO VILLAGE...

"...OR GOB ENCAMPMENT...

"...OR MAHARAJA COULD *DARE* OPPOSE US."

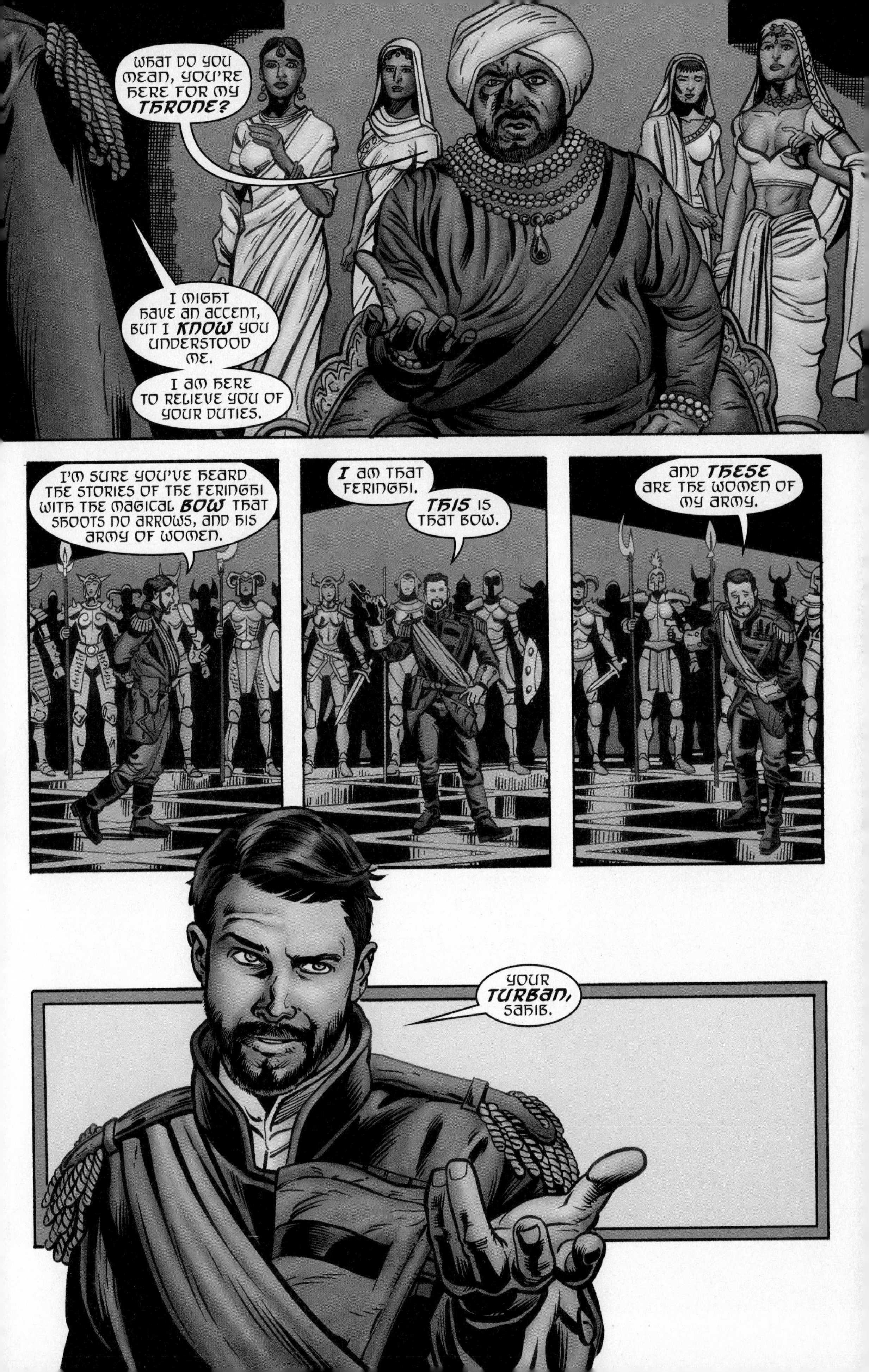
WHAT DO YOU MEAN, YOU'RE HERE FOR MY THRONE?
I MIGHT HAVE AN ACCENT, BUT I KNOW YOU UNDERSTOOD ME.
I AM HERE TO RELIEVE YOU OF YOUR DUTIES.
I'M SURE YOU'VE HEARD THE STORIES OF THE FERINGHI WITH THE MAGICAL BOW THAT SHOOTS NO ARROWS, AND HIS ARMY OF WOMEN.
I AM THAT FERINGHI.
THIS IS THAT BOW.
AND THESE ARE THE WOMEN OF MY ARMY.
YOUR TURBAN, SAHIB.

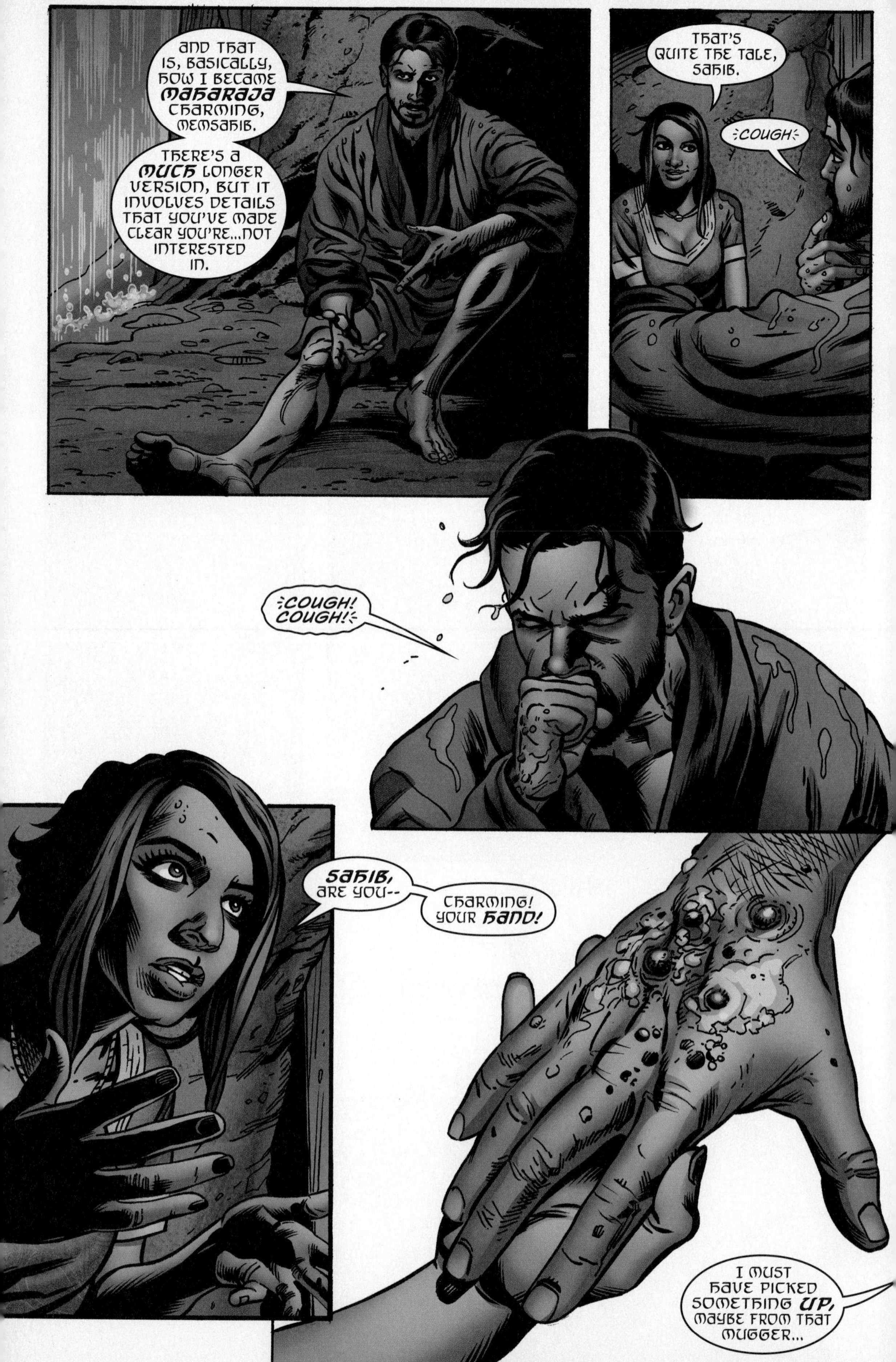
AND THAT IS, BASICALLY, HOW I BECAME MAHARAJA CHARMING, MEMSAHIB.
THERE'S A MUCH LONGER VERSION, BUT IT INVOLVES DETAILS THAT YOU'VE MADE CLEAR YOU'RE...NOT INTERESTED IN.
THAT'S QUITE THE TALE, SAHIB.
COUGH
COUGH! COUGH!
SAHIB, ARE YOU--
CHARMING! YOUR HAND!
I MUST HAVE PICKED SOMETHING UP, MAYBE FROM THAT MUGGER...

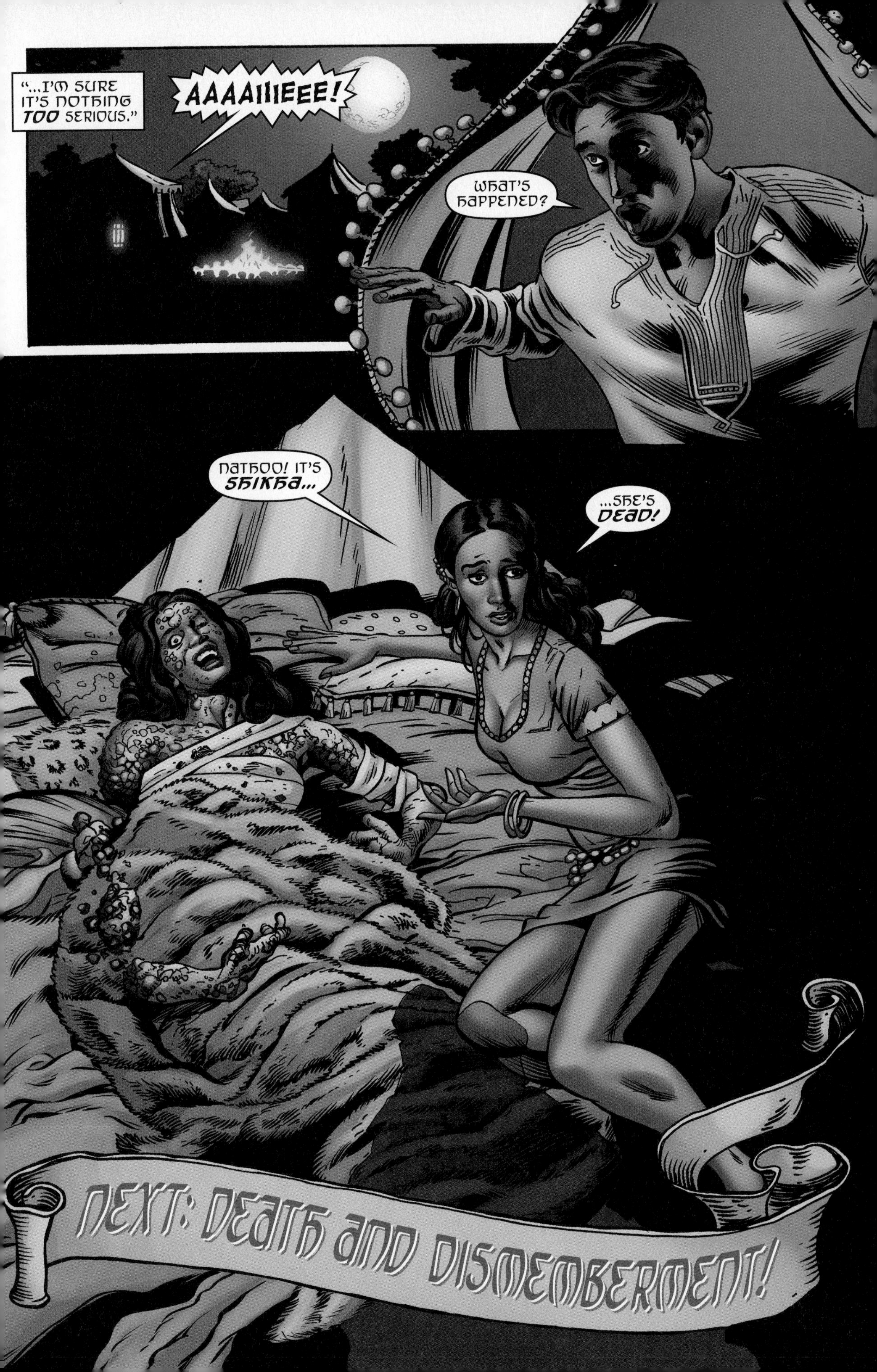
"...I'M SURE IT'S NOTHING TOO SERIOUS."
AAAAIIIIEEE!
WHAT'S HAPPENED?
NATHOO! IT'S SHIKHA...
...SHE'S DEAD!
NEXT: DEATH AND DISMEMBERMENT!

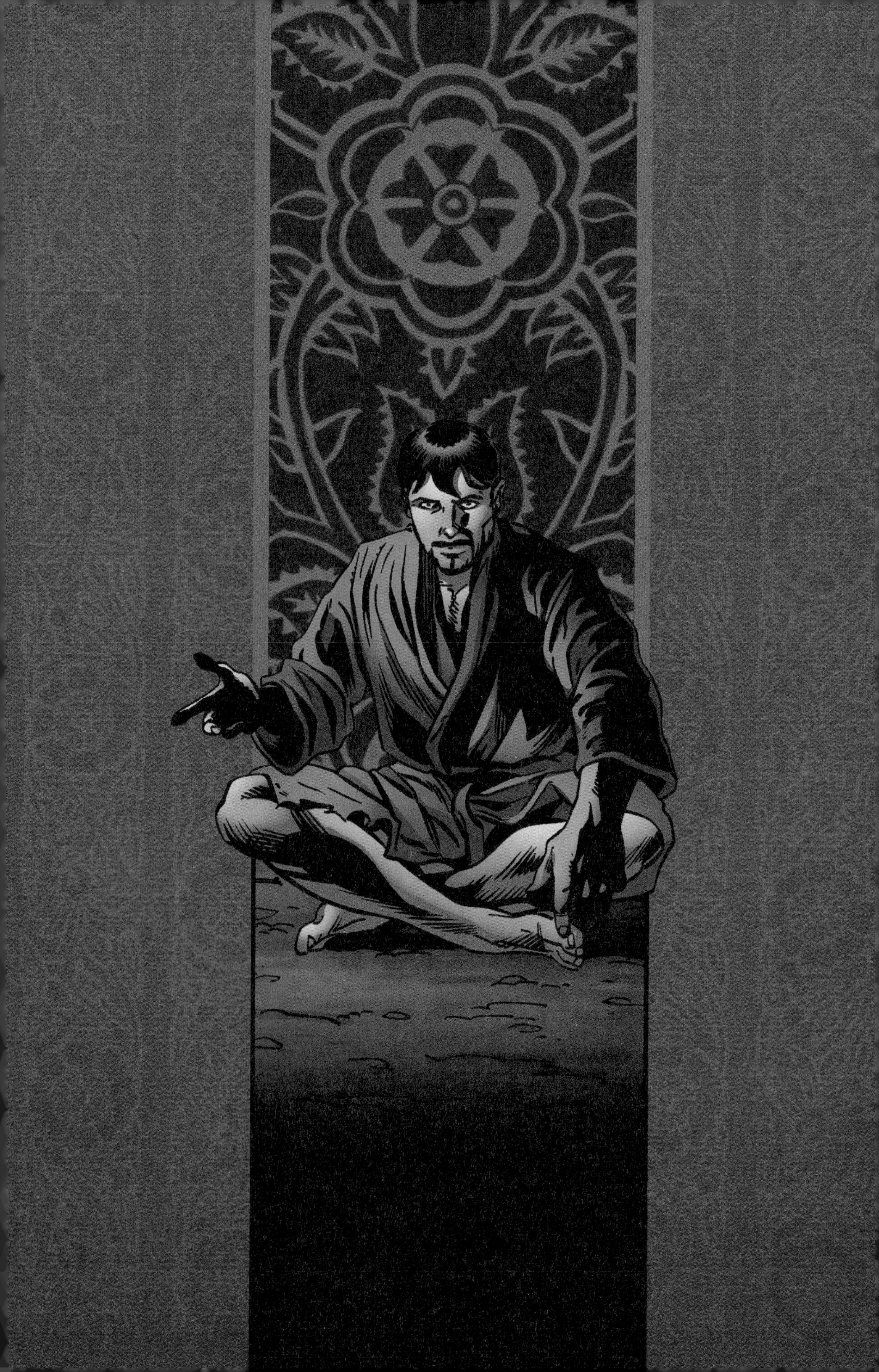

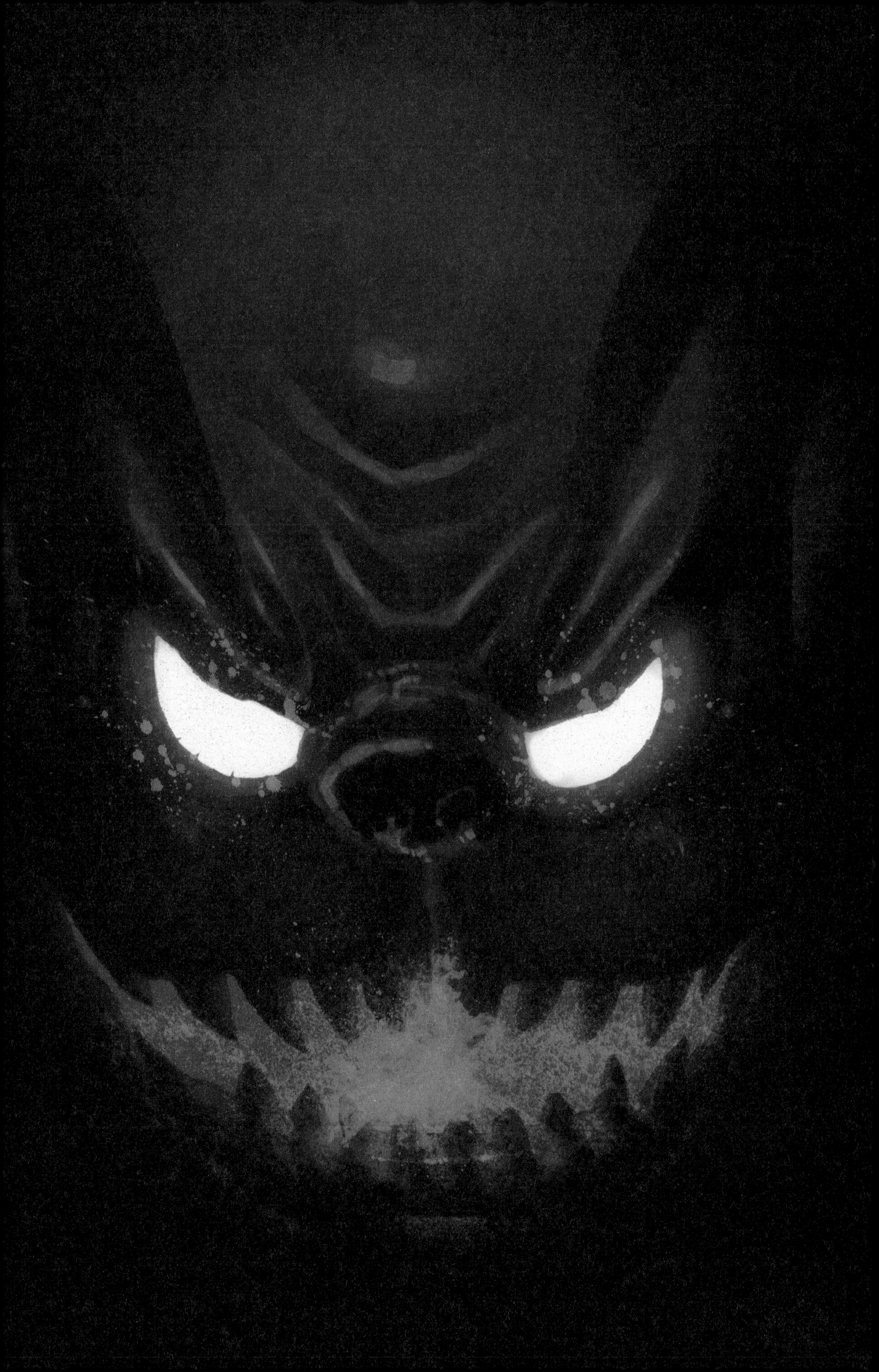

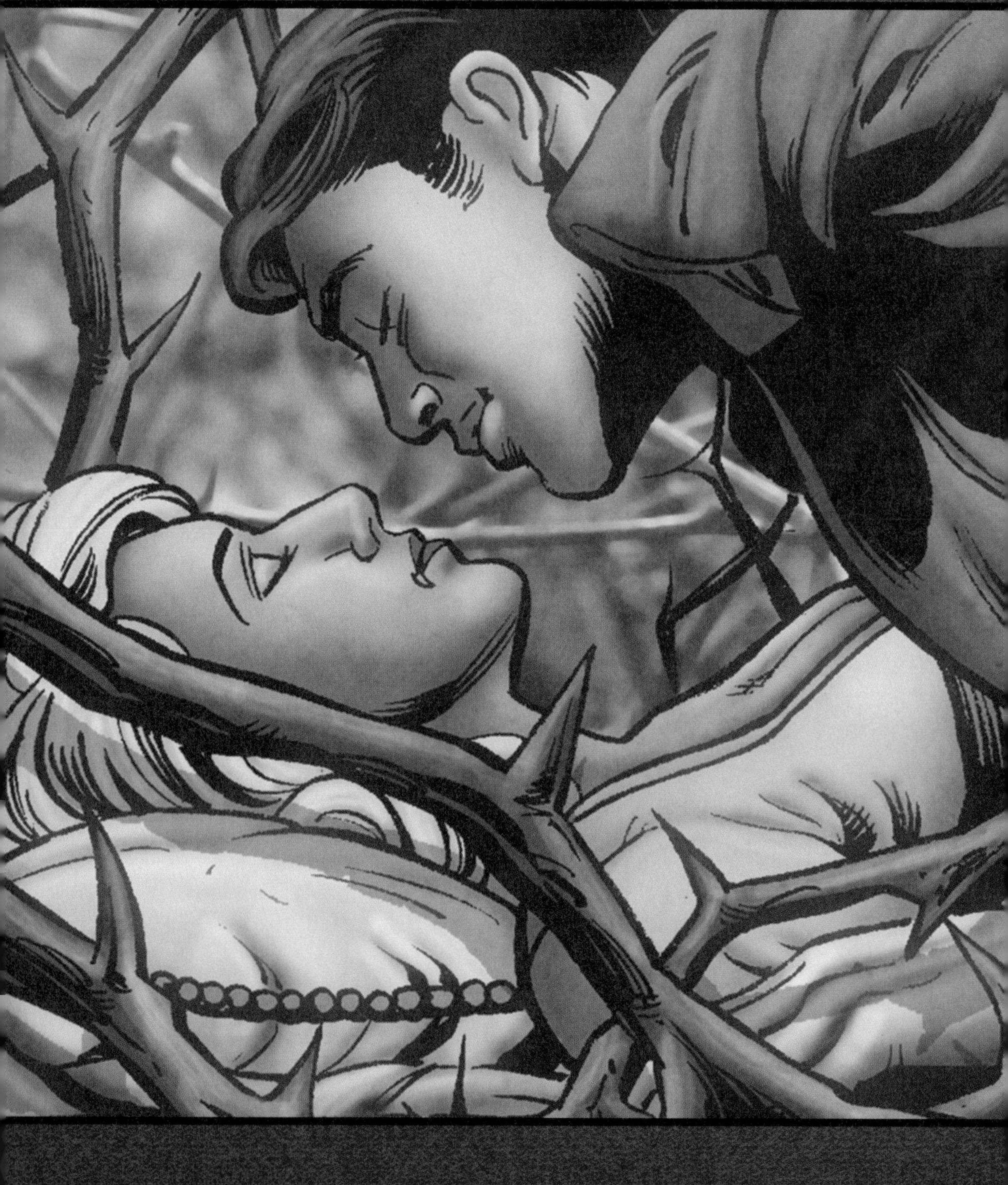

"It's funny, isn't it? How love works."

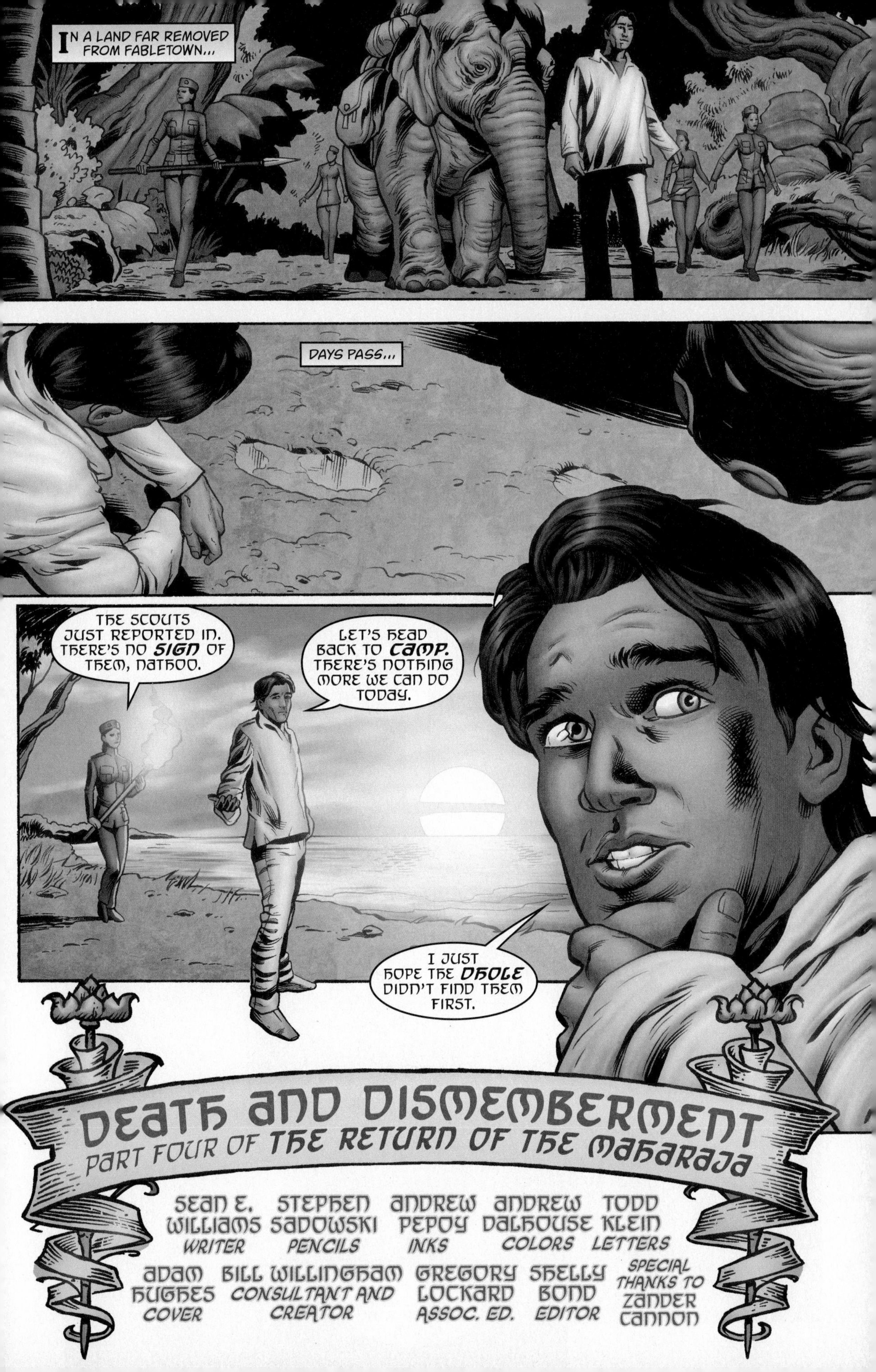
IN A LAND FAR REMOVED FROM FABLETOWN...
DAYS PASS...
THE SCOUTS JUST REPORTED IN. THERE'S NO SIGN OF THEM, NATHOO.
LET'S HEAD BACK TO CAMP. THERE'S NOTHING MORE WE CAN DO TODAY.
I JUST HOPE THE DHOLE DIDN'T FIND THEM FIRST.
DEATH AND DISMEMBERMENT
PART FOUR OF THE RETURN OF THE MAHARAJA
SEAN E. WILLIAMS WRITER
STEPHEN SADOWSKI PENCILS
ANDREW PEPOY INKS
ANDREW DALHOUSE COLORS
TODD KLEIN LETTERS
ADAM HUGHES COVER
BILL WILLINGHAM CONSULTANT AND CREATOR
GREGORY LOCKARD ASSOC. ED.
SHELLY BOND EDITOR
SPECIAL THANKS TO ZANDER CANNON

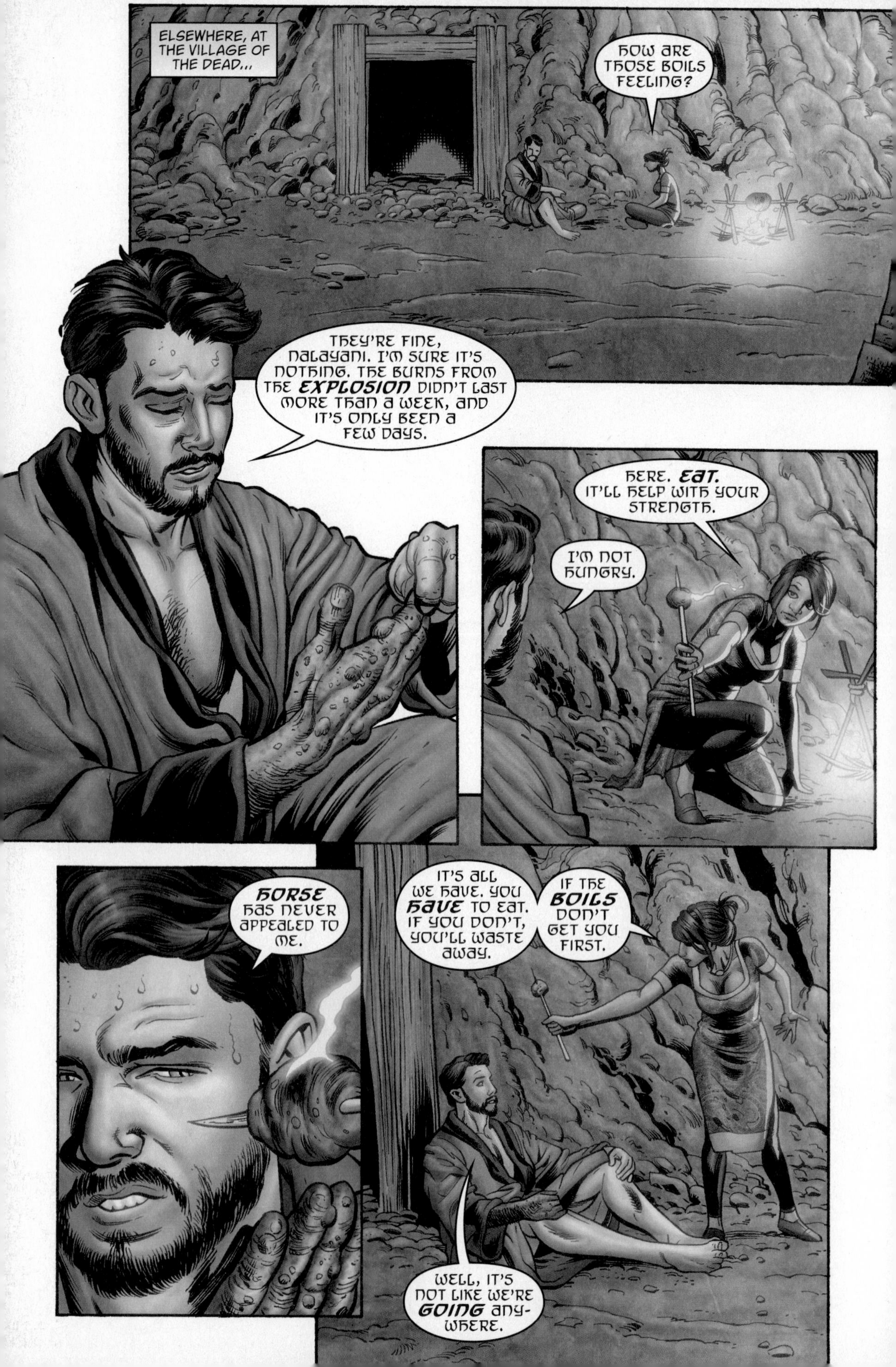
ELSEWHERE, AT THE VILLAGE OF THE DEAD...
HOW ARE THOSE BOILS FEELING?
THEY'RE FINE, NALAYANI. I'M SURE IT'S NOTHING. THE BURNS FROM THE EXPLOSION DIDN'T LAST MORE THAN A WEEK, AND IT'S ONLY BEEN A FEW DAYS.
HERE. EAT. IT'LL HELP WITH YOUR STRENGTH.
I'M NOT HUNGRY.
HORSE HAS NEVER APPEALED TO ME.
IT'S ALL WE HAVE. YOU HAVE TO EAT. IF YOU DON'T, YOU'LL WASTE AWAY.
IF THE BOILS DON'T GET YOU FIRST.
WELL, IT'S NOT LIKE WE'RE GOING ANY-WHERE.

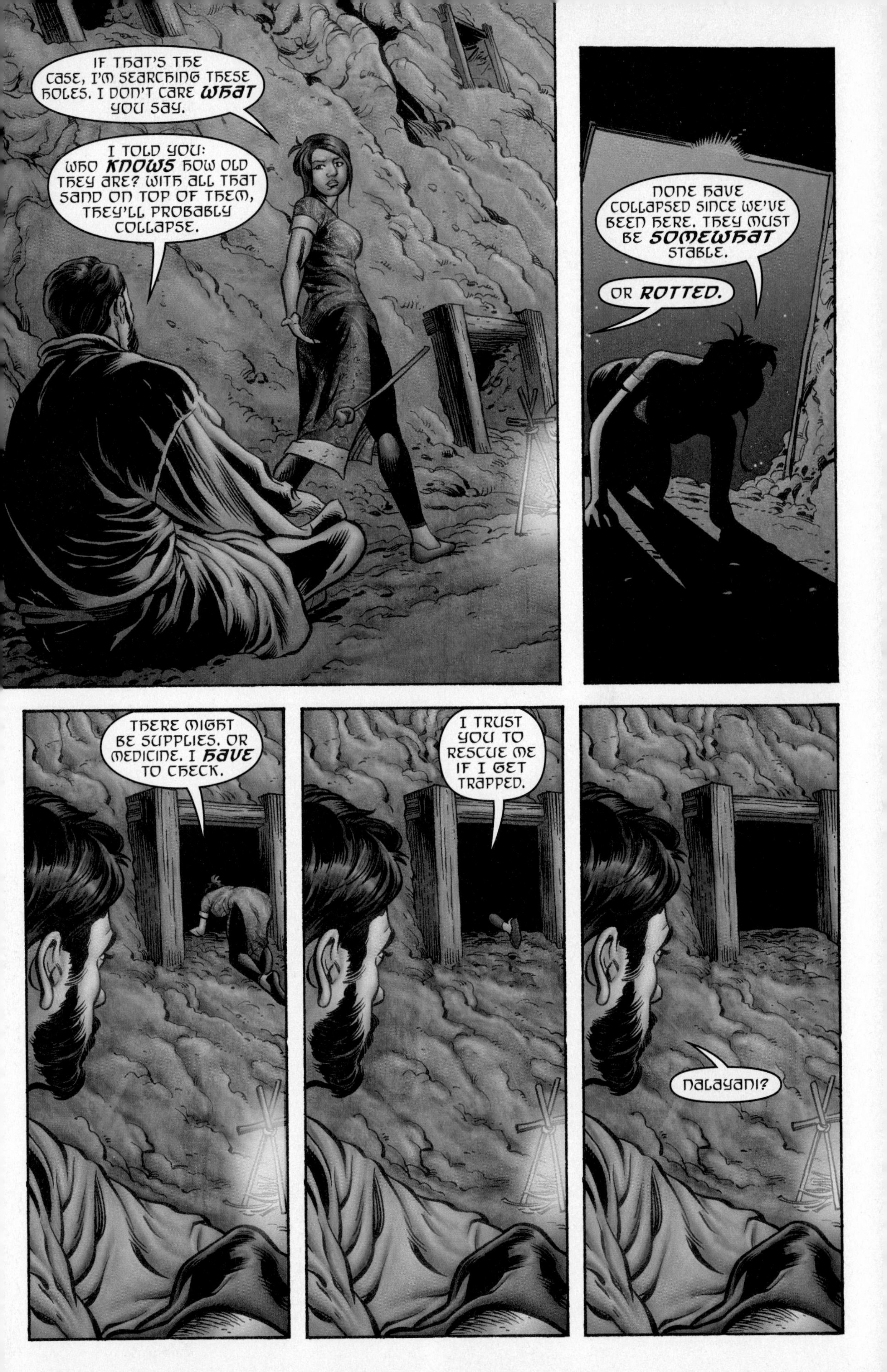
IF THAT'S THE CASE, I'M SEARCHING THESE HOLES. I DON'T CARE WHAT YOU SAY.
I TOLD YOU: WHO KNOWS HOW OLD THEY ARE? WITH ALL THAT SAND ON TOP OF THEM, THEY'LL PROBABLY COLLAPSE.
NONE HAVE COLLAPSED SINCE WE'VE BEEN HERE. THEY MUST BE SOMEWHAT STABLE.
OR ROTTED.
THERE MIGHT BE SUPPLIES. OR MEDICINE. I HAVE TO CHECK.
I TRUST YOU TO RESCUE ME IF I GET TRAPPED.
NALAYANI?

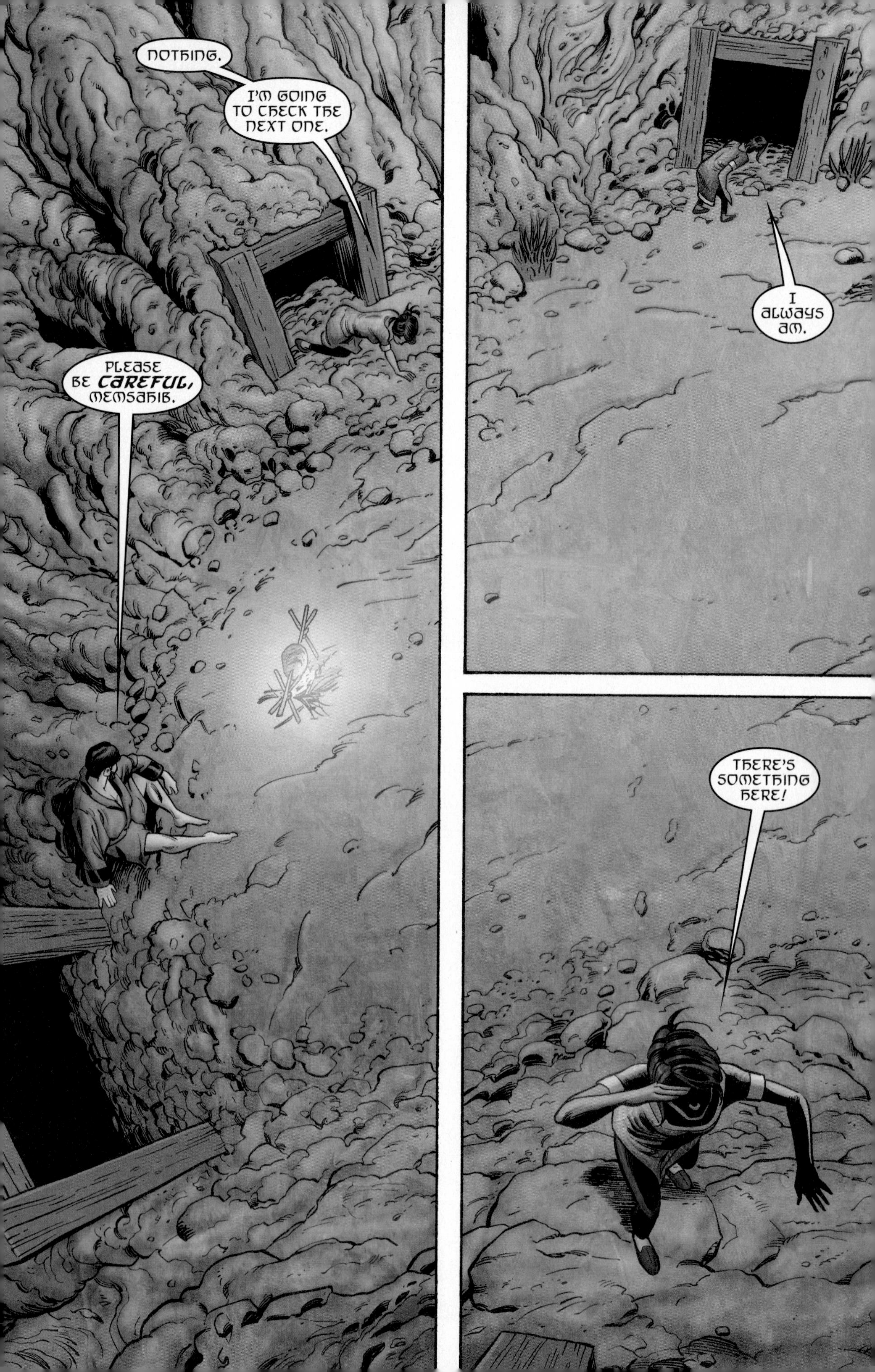
NOTHING.
I'M GOING TO CHECK THE NEXT ONE.
PLEASE BE CAREFUL, MEMSAHIB.
I ALWAYS AM.
THERE'S SOMETHING HERE!

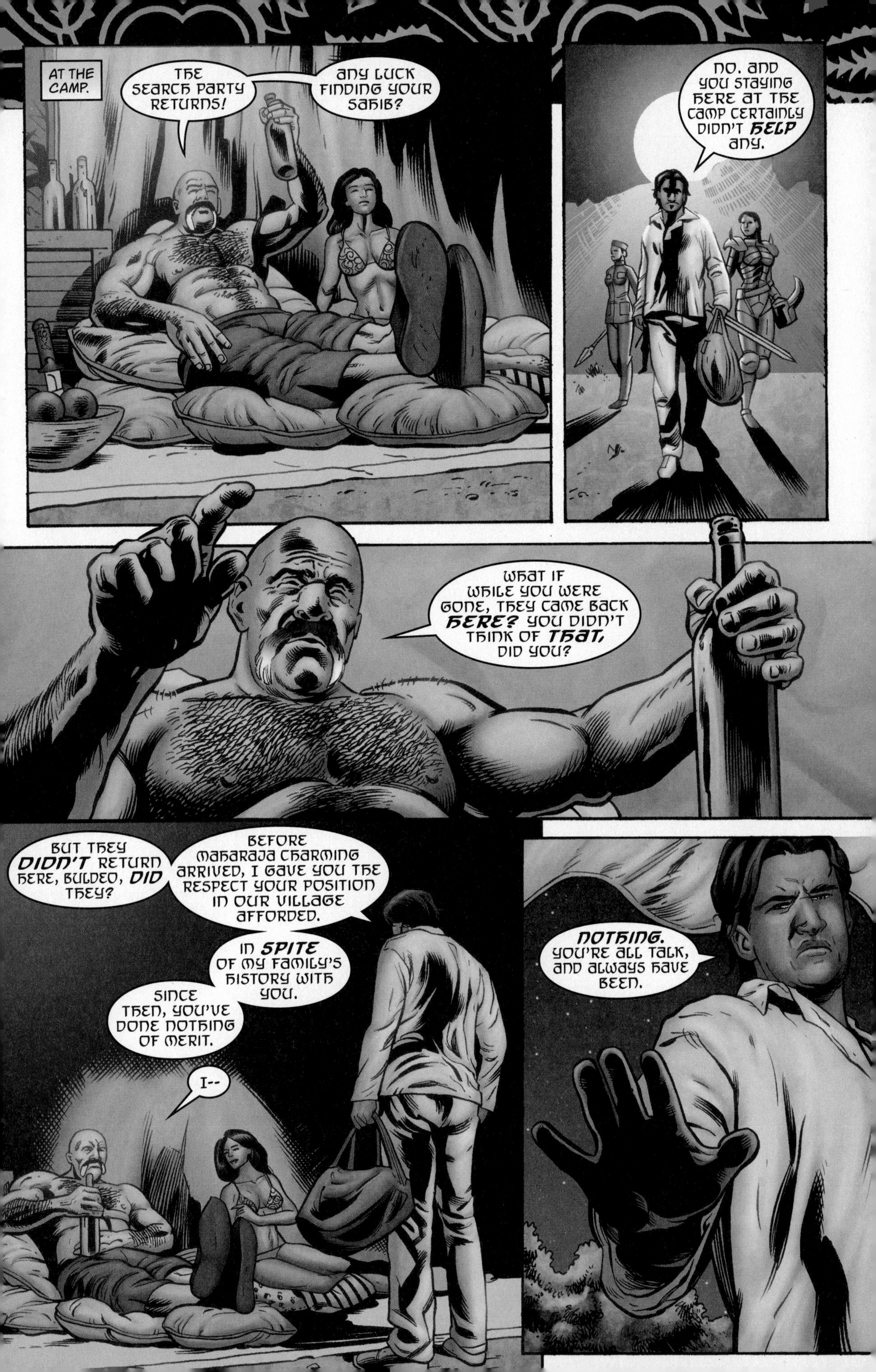
AT THE CAMP.
THE SEARCH PARTY RETURNS!
ANY LUCK FINDING YOUR SAHIB?
NO. AND YOU STAYING HERE AT THE CAMP CERTAINLY DIDN'T HELP ANY.
WHAT IF WHILE YOU WERE GONE, THEY CAME BACK HERE? YOU DIDN'T THINK OF THAT, DID YOU?
BUT THEY DIDN'T RETURN HERE, BULDEO, DID THEY?
BEFORE MAHARAJA CHARMING ARRIVED, I GAVE YOU THE RESPECT YOUR POSITION IN OUR VILLAGE AFFORDED.
IN SPITE OF MY FAMILY'S HISTORY WITH YOU.
SINCE THEN, YOU'VE DONE NOTHING OF MERIT.
I--
NOTHING. YOU'RE ALL TALK, AND ALWAYS HAVE BEEN.

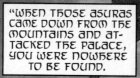

"WHEN THOSE ASURAS CAME DOWN FROM THE MOUNTAINS AND ATTACKED THE PALACE, YOU WERE NOWHERE TO BE FOUND.

"WHEN THE PISHACHA POSSESSED THAT CHILD, THEN *ATE* ALL THE PEOPLE IN HER VILLAGE, YOU SAID TO 'LEAVE IT ALONE' AND THAT IT 'MIGHT GO AWAY.'"

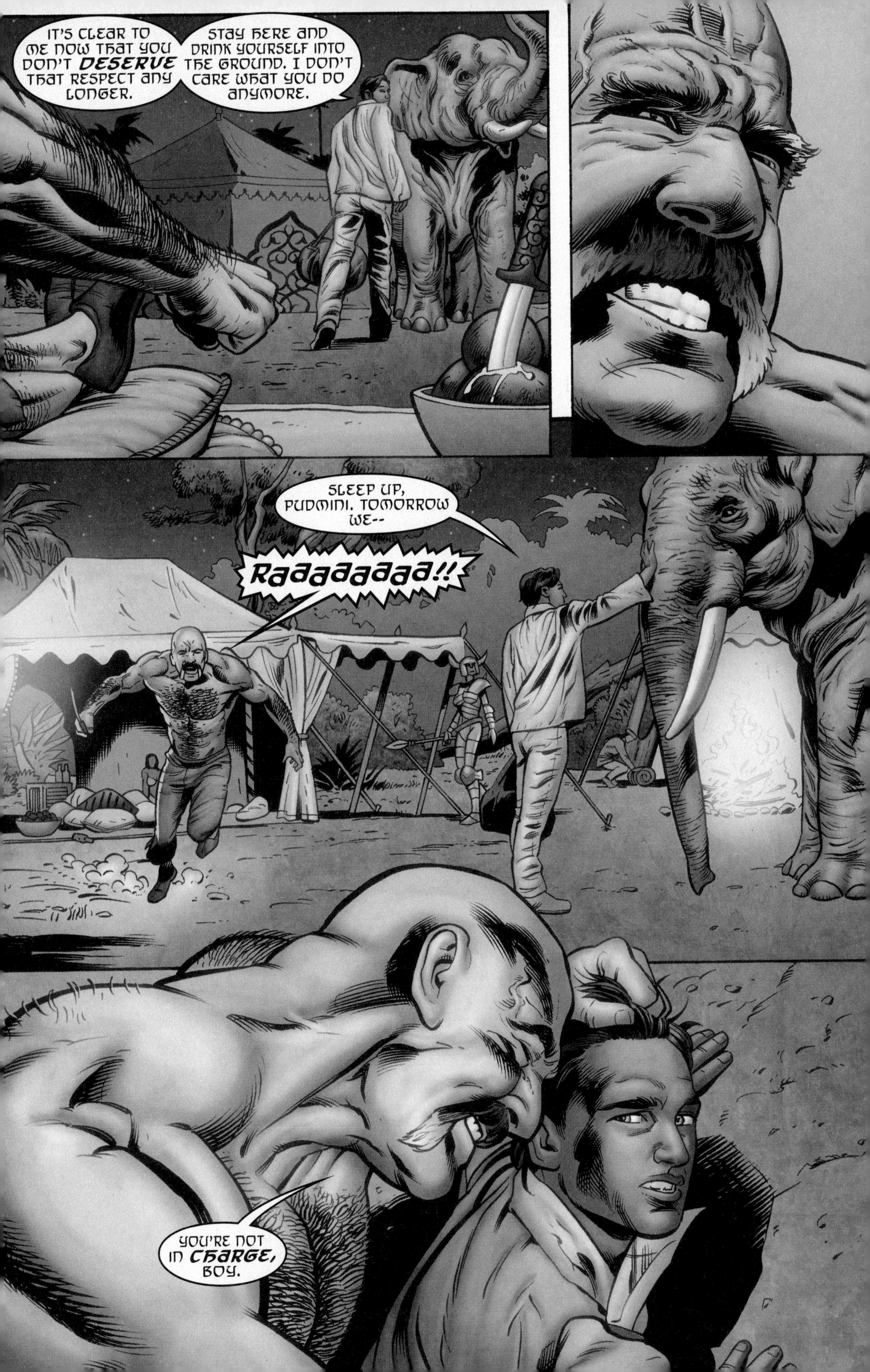
IT'S CLEAR TO ME NOW THAT YOU DON'T DESERVE THAT RESPECT ANY LONGER.
STAY HERE AND DRINK YOURSELF INTO THE GROUND. I DON'T CARE WHAT YOU DO ANYMORE.
SLEEP UP, PUDMINI. TOMORROW WE--
RAAAAAAAA!!
YOU'RE NOT IN CHARGE, BOY.

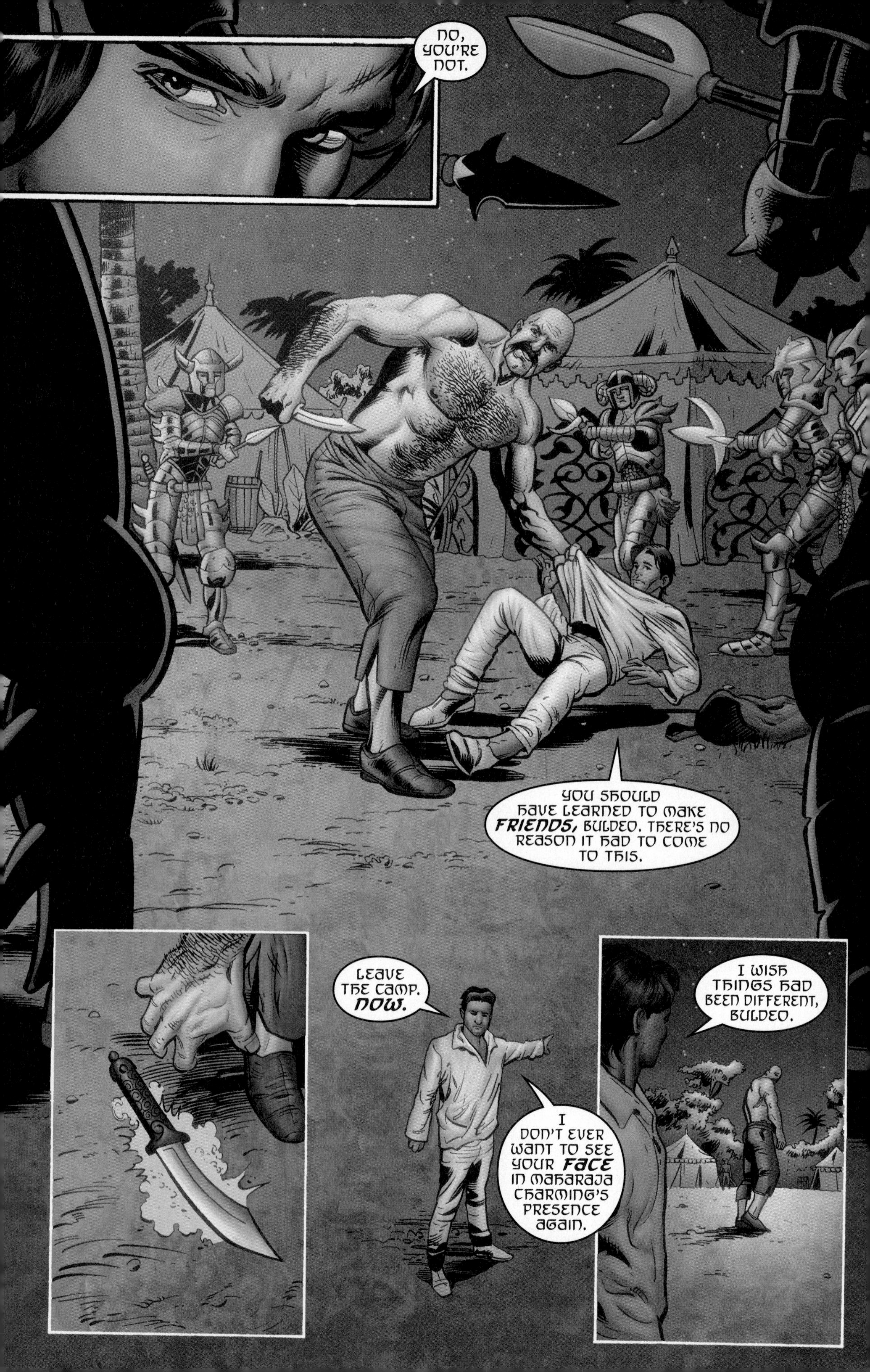
NO, YOU'RE NOT.
YOU SHOULD HAVE LEARNED TO MAKE FRIENDS, BULDEO. THERE'S NO REASON IT HAD TO COME TO THIS.
LEAVE THE CAMP. NOW.
I DON'T EVER WANT TO SEE YOUR FACE IN MAHARAJA CHARMING'S PRESENCE AGAIN.
I WISH THINGS HAD BEEN DIFFERENT, BULDEO.

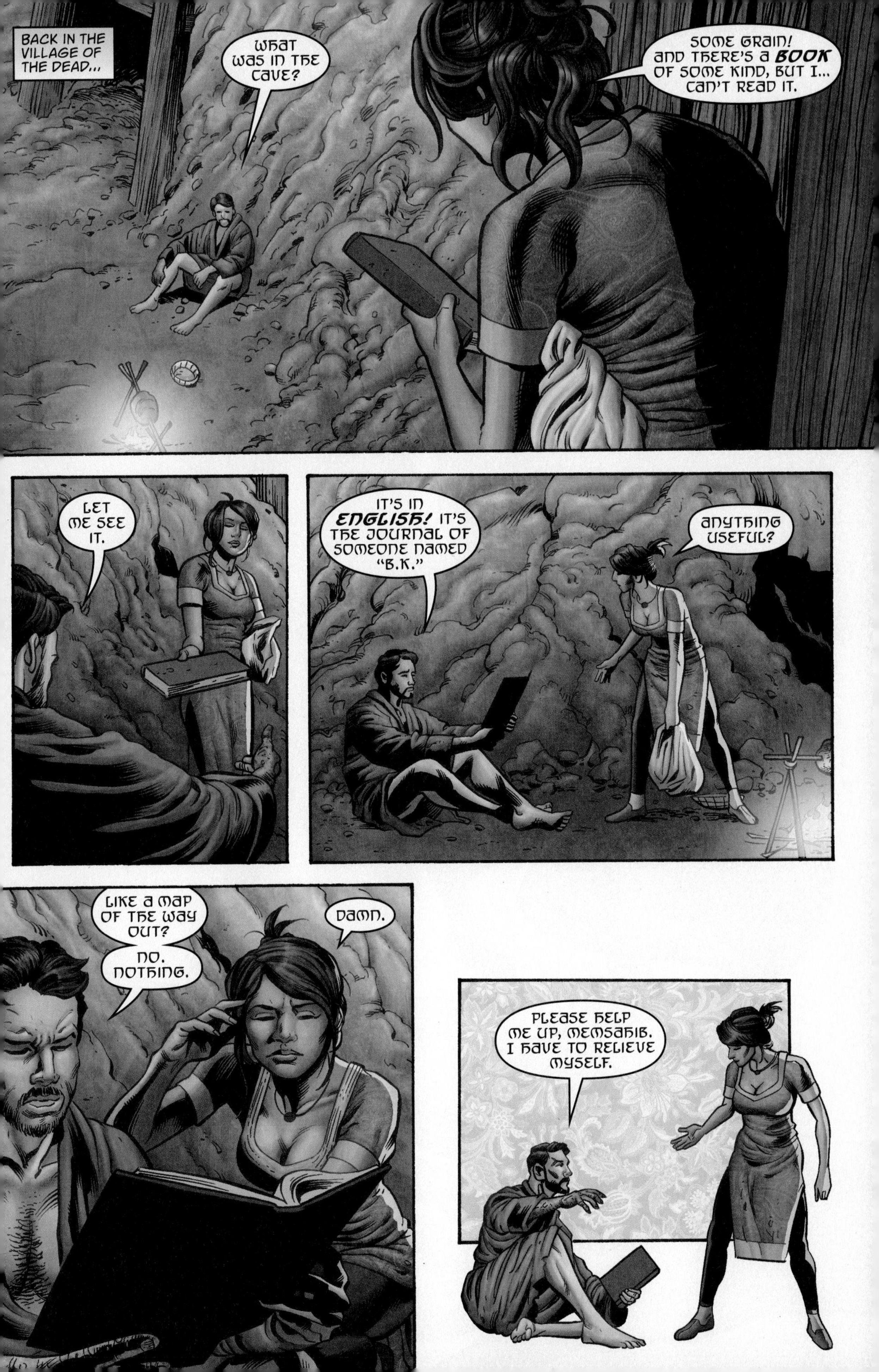
BACK IN THE VILLAGE OF THE DEAD...
WHAT WAS IN THE CAVE?
SOME GRAIN! AND THERE'S A BOOK OF SOME KIND, BUT I... CAN'T READ IT.
LET ME SEE IT.
IT'S IN ENGLISH! IT'S THE JOURNAL OF SOMEONE NAMED "B.K."
ANYTHING USEFUL?
LIKE A MAP OF THE WAY OUT?
NO. NOTHING.
DAMN.
PLEASE HELP ME UP, MEMSAHIB. I HAVE TO RELIEVE MYSELF.

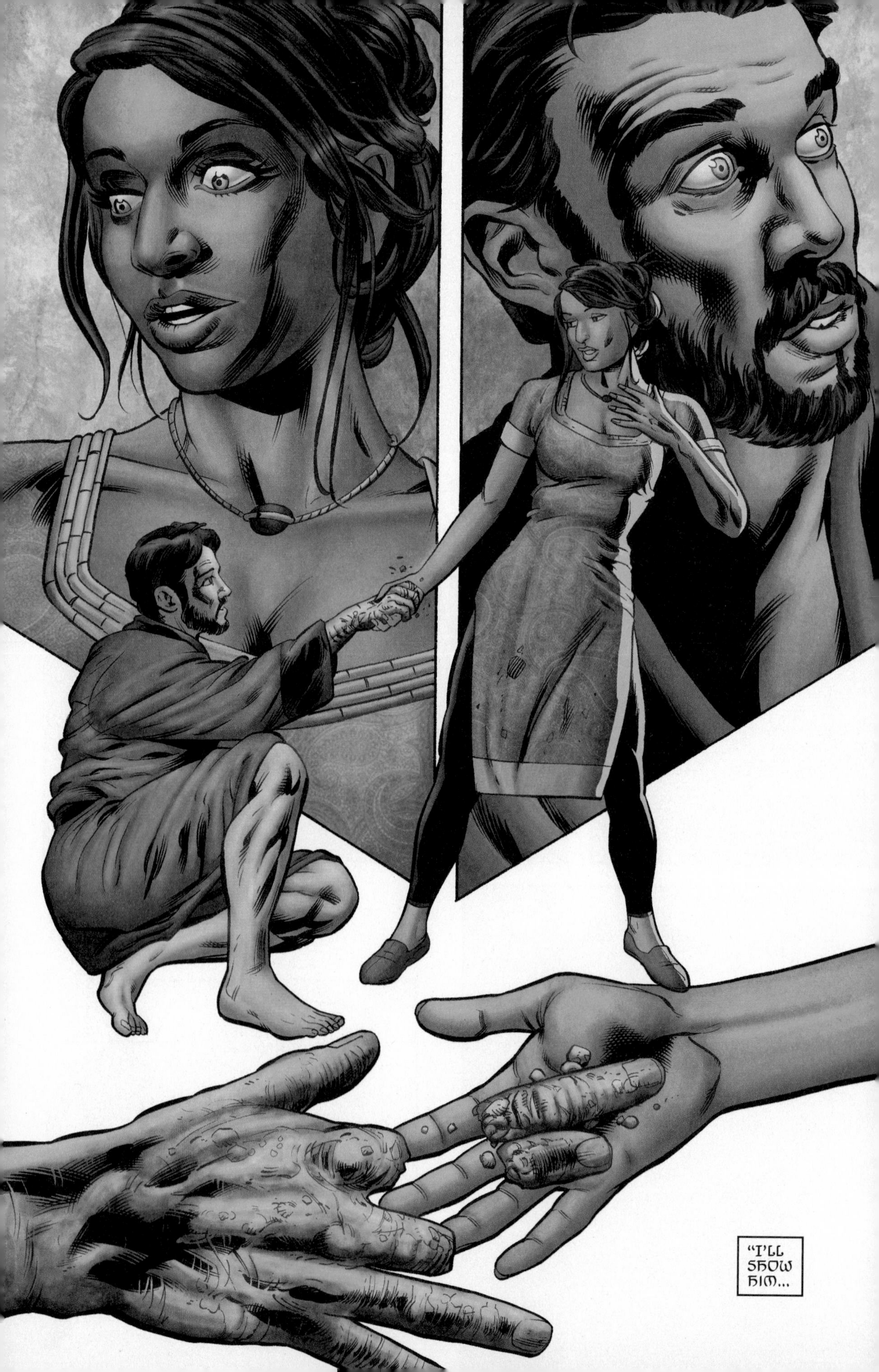
"I'LL SHOW HIM...

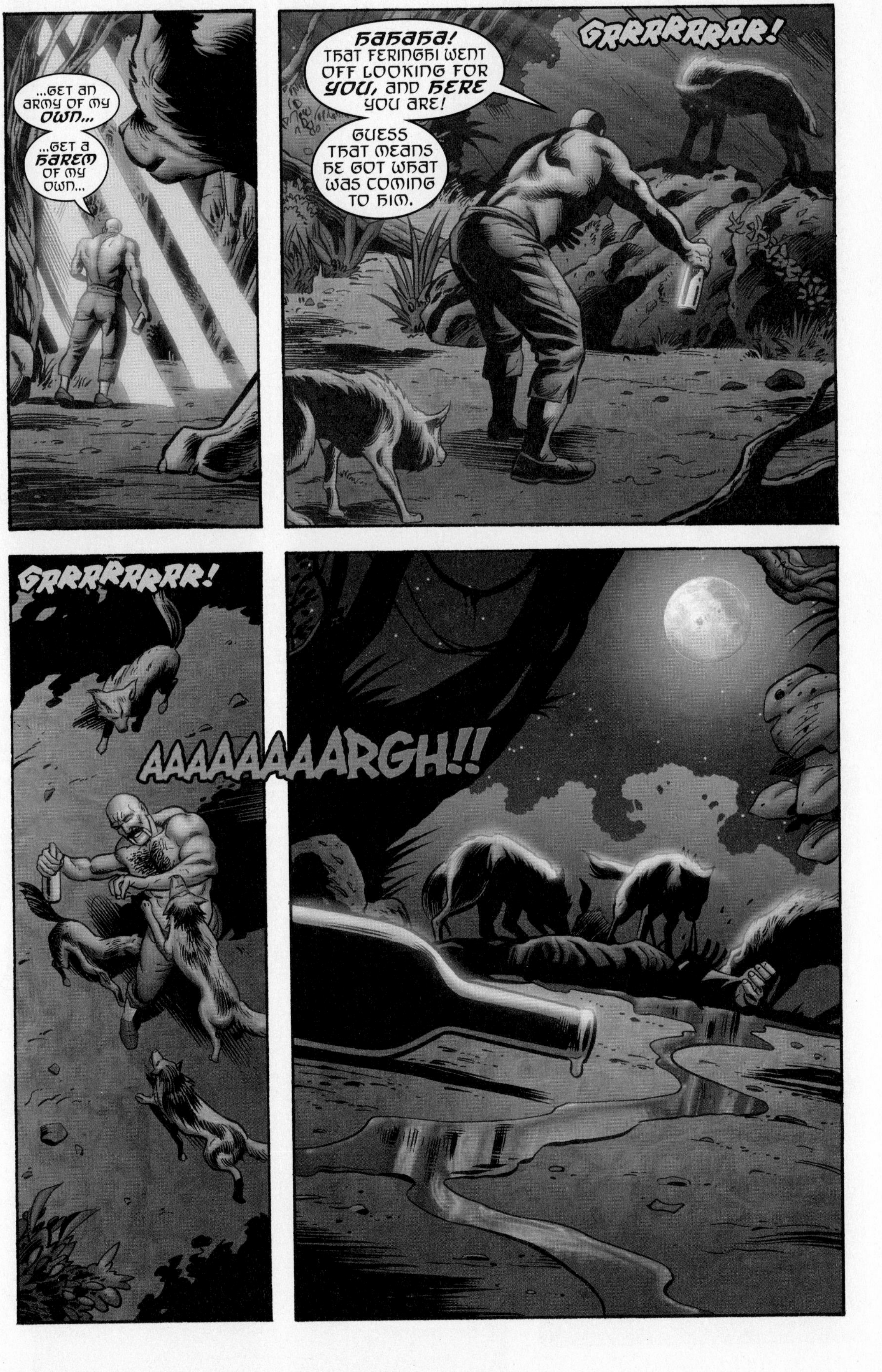
...GET AN ARMY OF MY OWN...
...GET A HAREM OF MY OWN...
GRRRRRRRR!
HAHAHA! THAT FERINGHI WENT OFF LOOKING FOR YOU, AND HERE YOU ARE!
GUESS THAT MEANS HE GOT WHAT WAS COMING TO HIM.
GRRRRRRRR!
AAAAAAAARGH!!

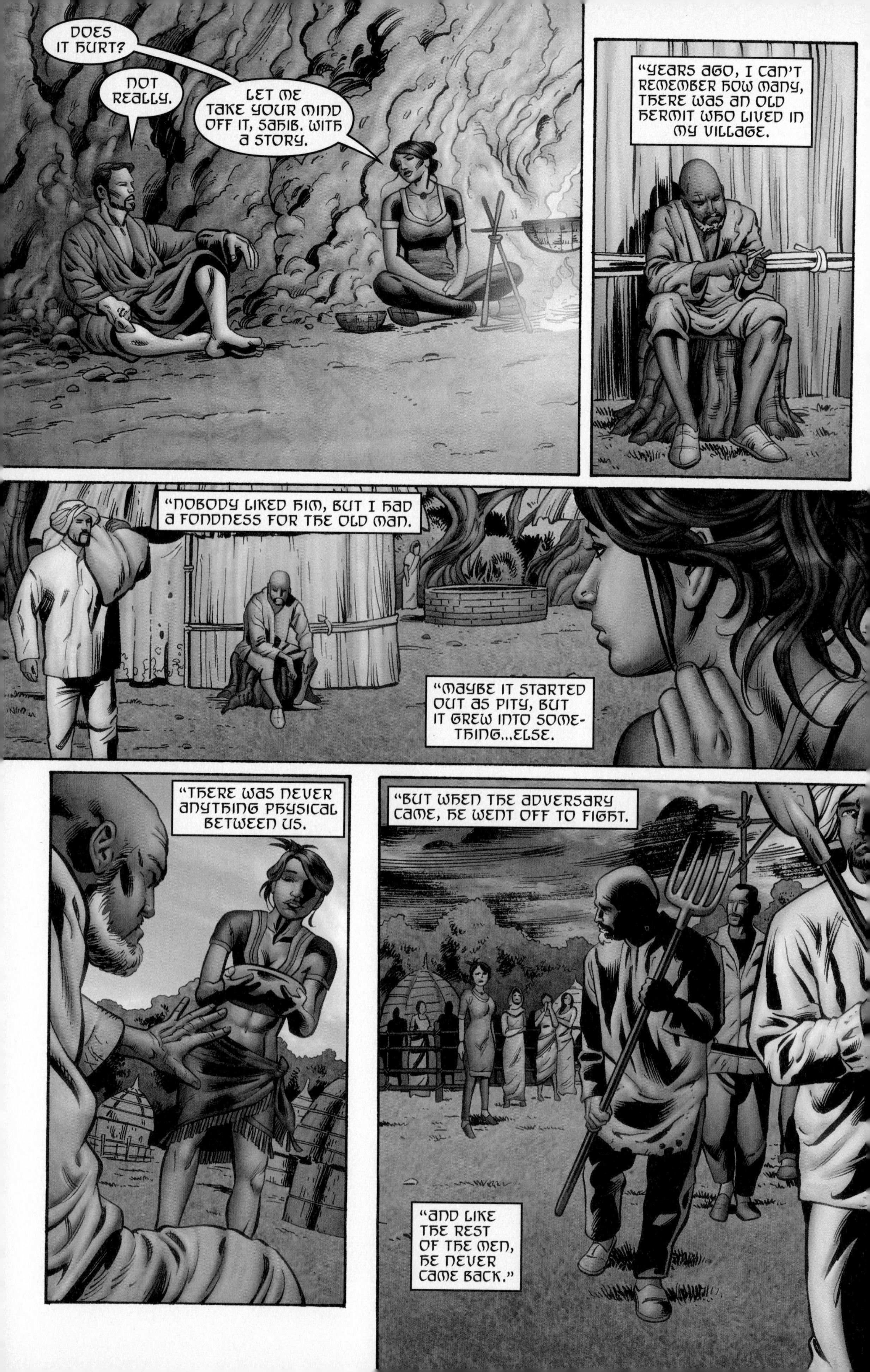
DOES IT HURT?
NOT REALLY.
LET ME TAKE YOUR MIND OFF IT, SAHIB. WITH A STORY.
"YEARS AGO, I CAN'T REMEMBER HOW MANY, THERE WAS AN OLD HERMIT WHO LIVED IN MY VILLAGE.
"NOBODY LIKED HIM, BUT I HAD A FONDNESS FOR THE OLD MAN.
"MAYBE IT STARTED OUT AS PITY, BUT IT GREW INTO SOME-THING...ELSE.
"THERE WAS NEVER ANYTHING PHYSICAL BETWEEN US.
"BUT WHEN THE ADVERSARY CAME, HE WENT OFF TO FIGHT.
"AND LIKE THE REST OF THE MEN, HE NEVER CAME BACK."

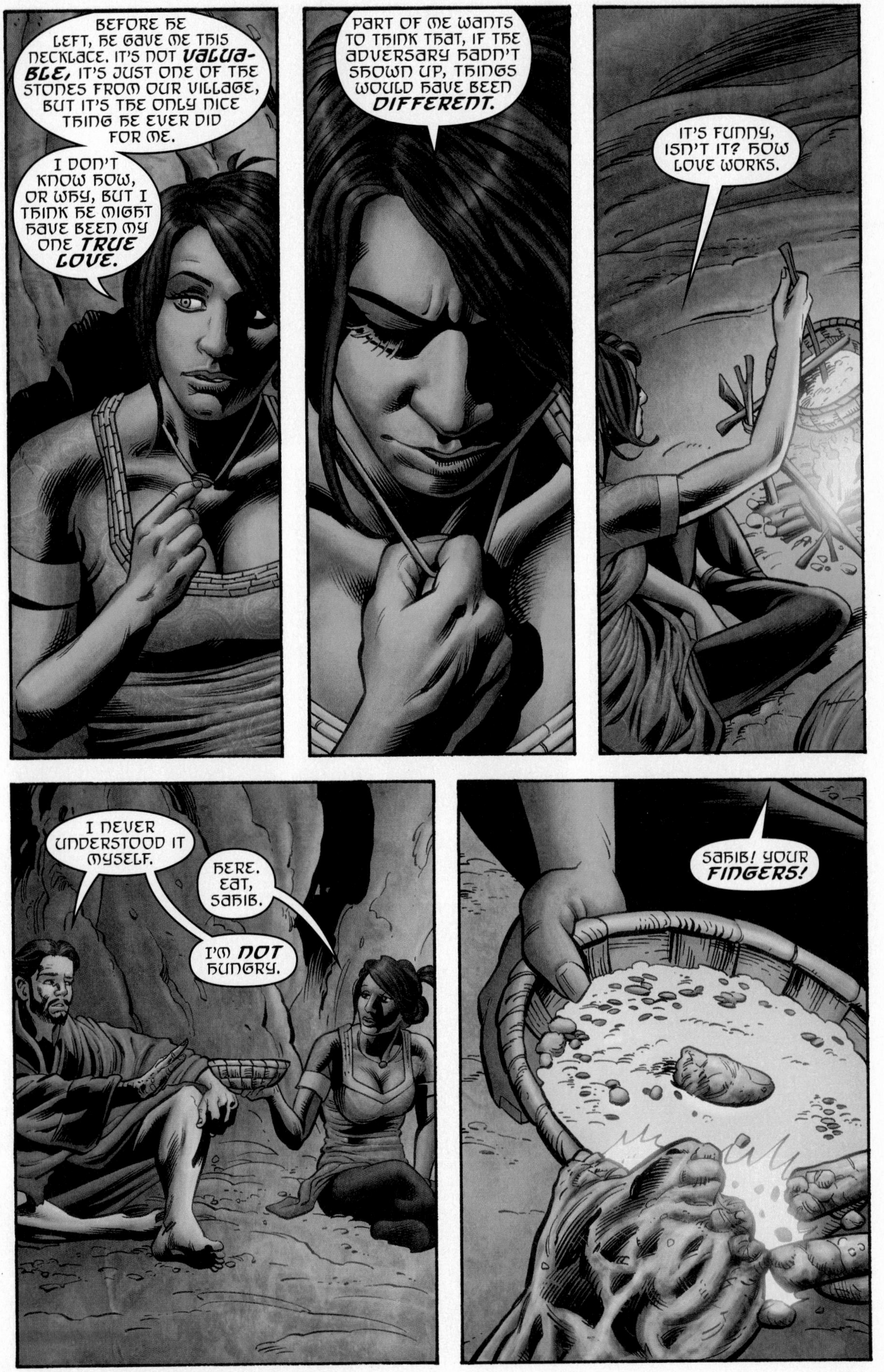
BEFORE HE LEFT, HE GAVE ME THIS NECKLACE. IT'S NOT VALUABLE, IT'S JUST ONE OF THE STONES FROM OUR VILLAGE, BUT IT'S THE ONLY NICE THING HE EVER DID FOR ME.
I DON'T KNOW HOW, OR WHY, BUT I THINK HE MIGHT HAVE BEEN MY ONE TRUE LOVE.
PART OF ME WANTS TO THINK THAT, IF THE ADVERSARY HADN'T SHOWN UP, THINGS WOULD HAVE BEEN DIFFERENT.
IT'S FUNNY, ISN'T IT? HOW LOVE WORKS.
I NEVER UNDERSTOOD IT MYSELF.
HERE. EAT, SAHIB.
I'M NOT HUNGRY.
SAHIB! YOUR FINGERS!

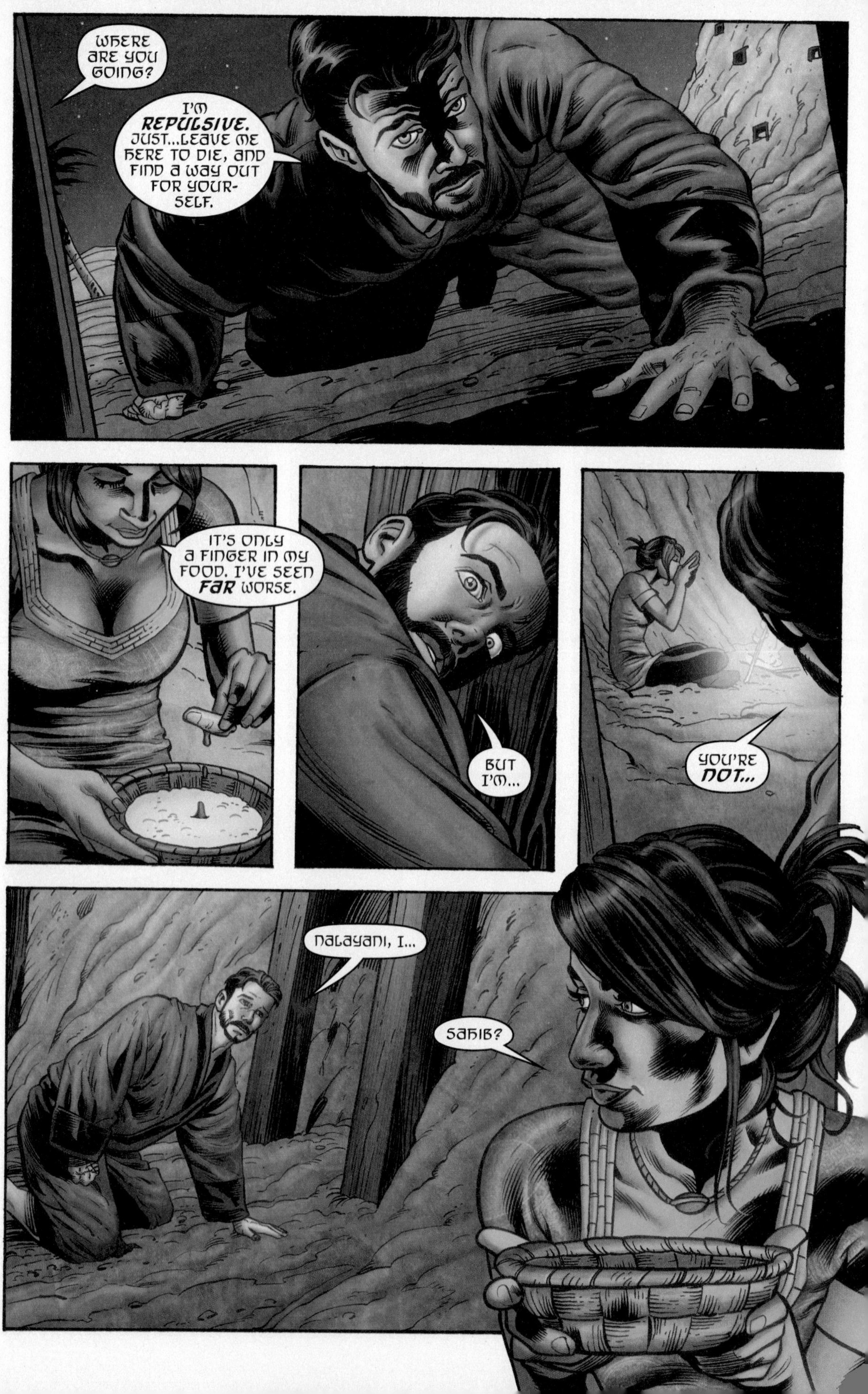
WHERE ARE YOU GOING?
I'M REPULSIVE. JUST...LEAVE ME HERE TO DIE, AND FIND A WAY OUT FOR YOUR-SELF.
IT'S ONLY A FINGER IN MY FOOD. I'VE SEEN FAR WORSE.
BUT I'M...
YOU'RE NOT...
NALAYANI, I...
SAHIB?

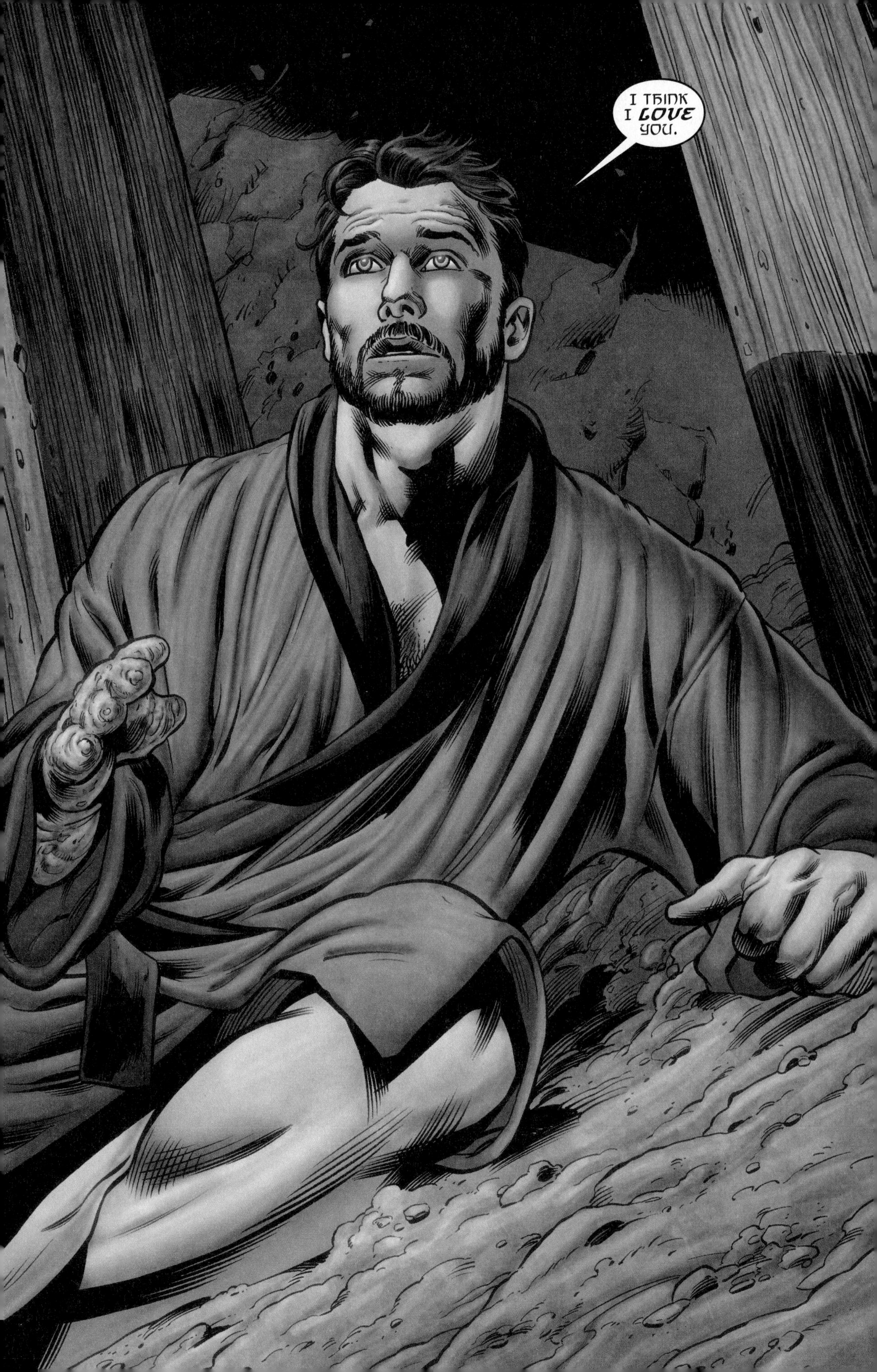
I THINK I LOVE YOU.

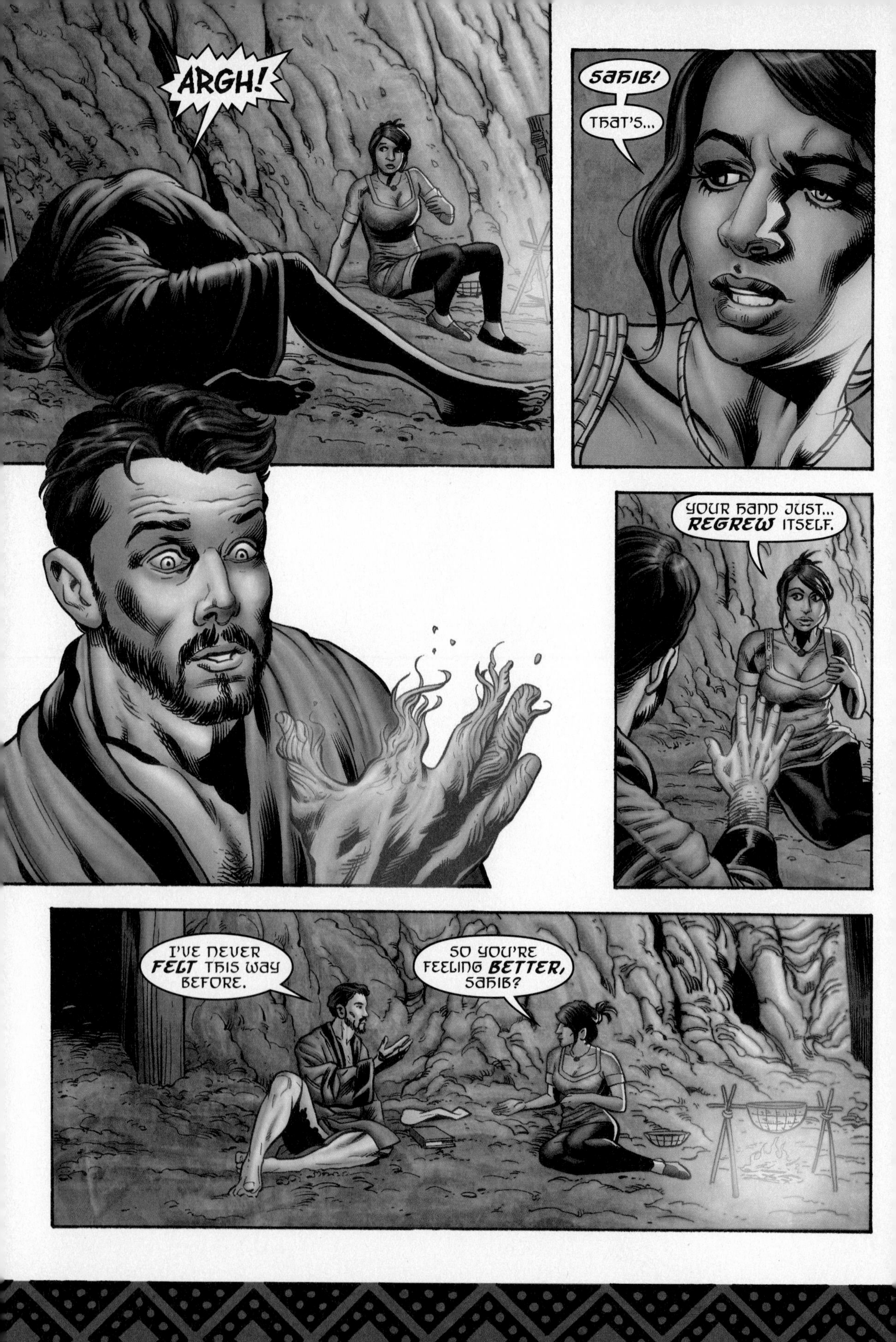
ARGH!
SAHIB!
THAT'S...
YOUR HAND JUST... REGREW ITSELF.
I'VE NEVER FELT THIS WAY BEFORE.
SO YOU'RE FEELING BETTER, SAHIB?

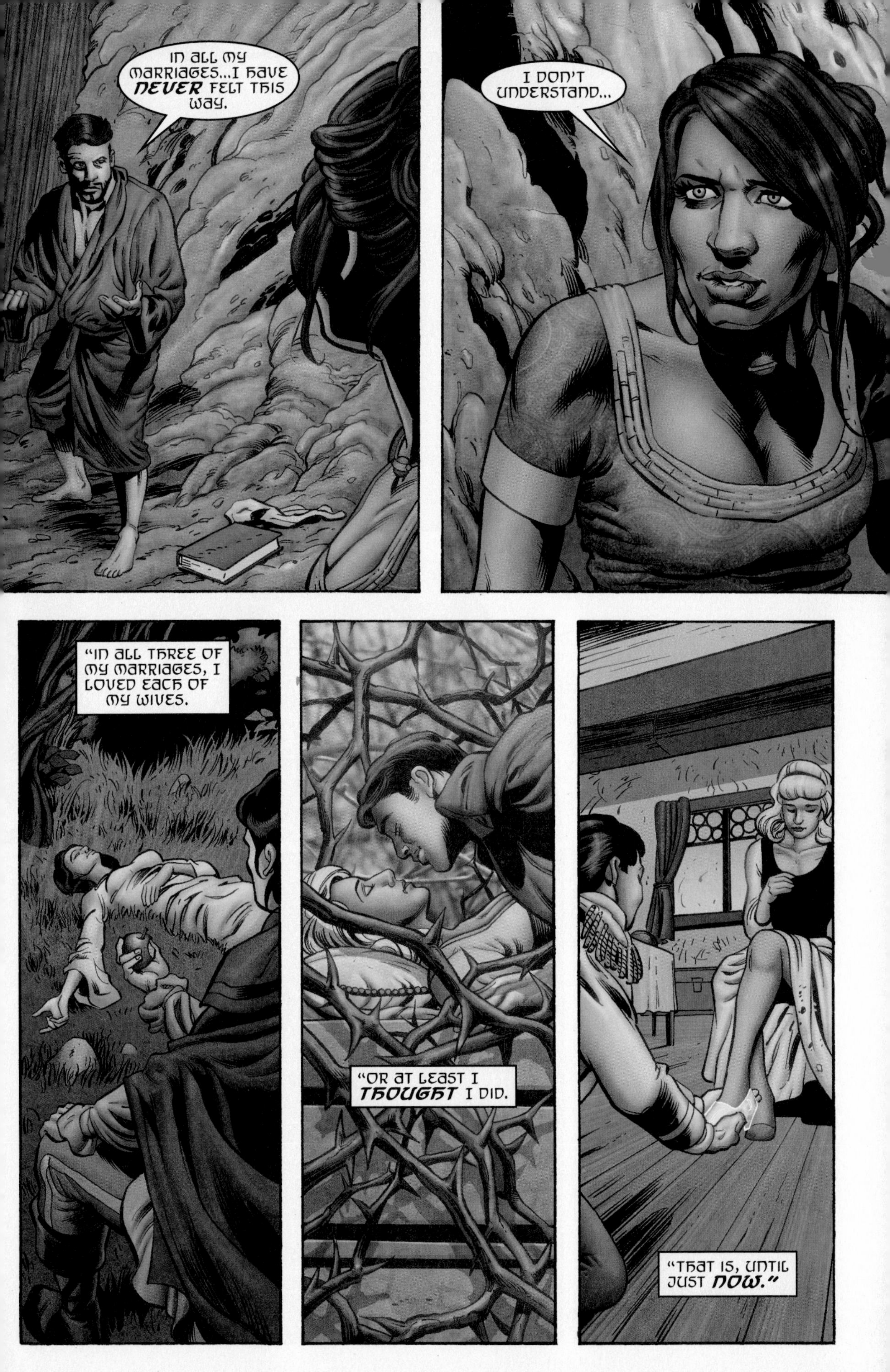
IN ALL MY MARRIAGES...I HAVE NEVER FELT THIS WAY.
I DON'T UNDERSTAND...
"IN ALL THREE OF MY MARRIAGES, I LOVED EACH OF MY WIVES.
"OR AT LEAST I THOUGHT I DID.
"THAT IS, UNTIL JUST NOW."

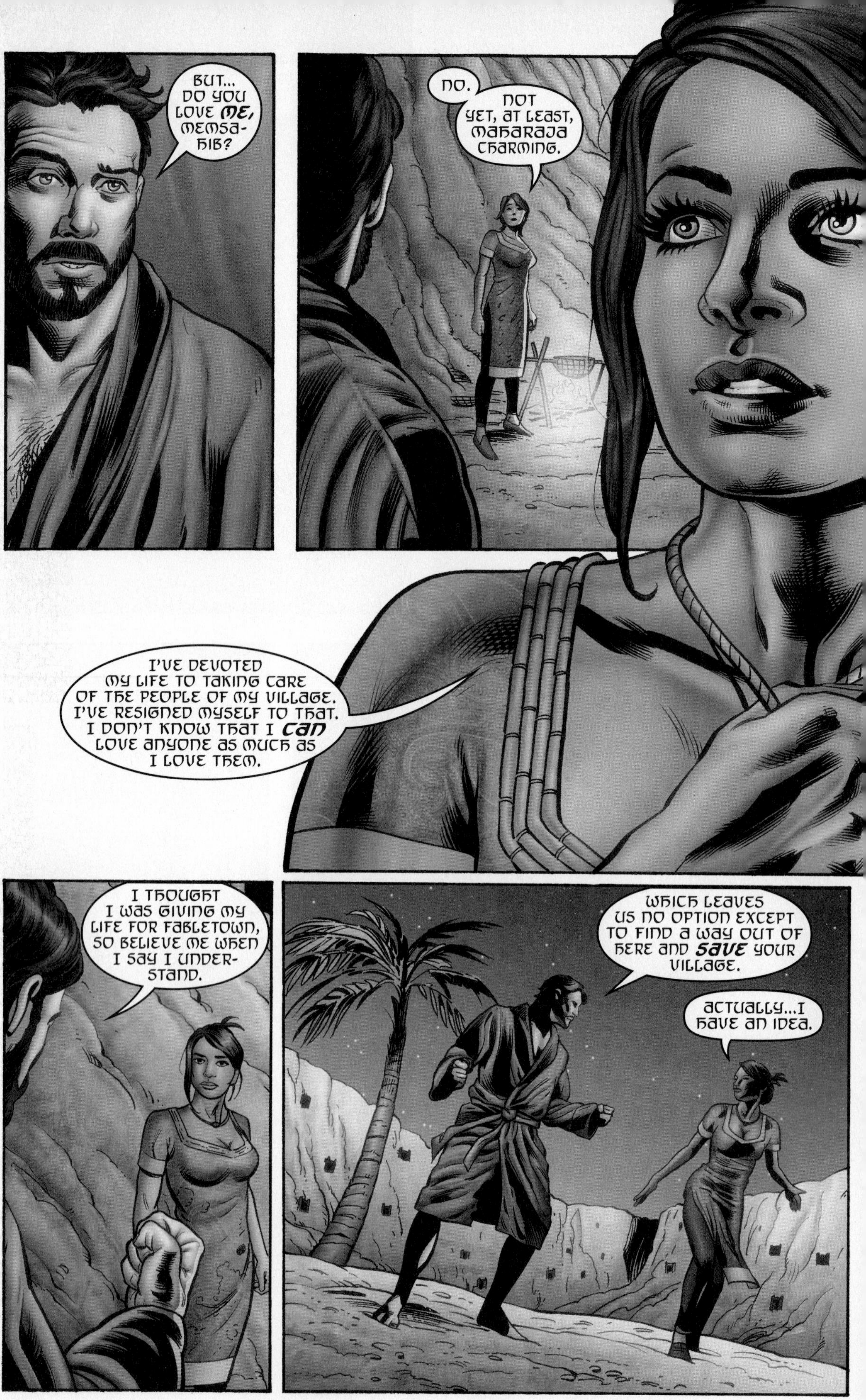
BUT... DO YOU LOVE ME, MEMSA-HIB?
NO.
NOT YET, AT LEAST, MAHARAJA CHARMING.
I'VE DEVOTED MY LIFE TO TAKING CARE OF THE PEOPLE OF MY VILLAGE. I'VE RESIGNED MYSELF TO THAT. I DON'T KNOW THAT I CAN LOVE ANYONE AS MUCH AS I LOVE THEM.
I THOUGHT I WAS GIVING MY LIFE FOR FABLETOWN, SO BELIEVE ME WHEN I SAY I UNDER-STAND.
WHICH LEAVES US NO OPTION EXCEPT TO FIND A WAY OUT OF HERE AND SAVE YOUR VILLAGE.
ACTUALLY...I HAVE AN IDEA.

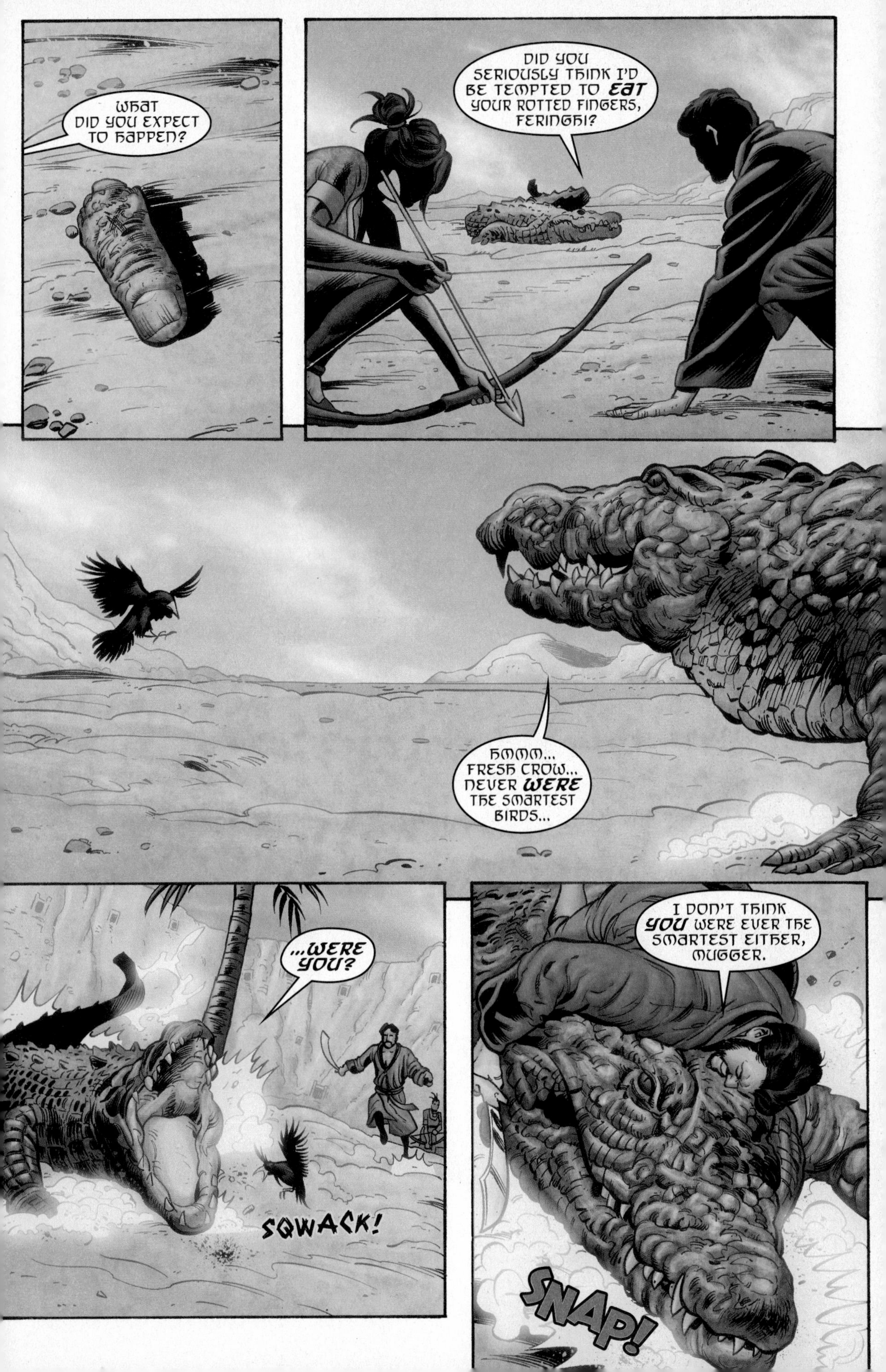
WHAT DID YOU EXPECT TO HAPPEN?
DID YOU SERIOUSLY THINK I'D BE TEMPTED TO EAT YOUR ROTTED FINGERS, FERINGHI?
HMMM... FRESH CROW... NEVER WERE THE SMARTEST BIRDS...
...WERE YOU?
SQWACK!
I DON'T THINK YOU WERE EVER THE SMARTEST EITHER, MUGGER.
SNAP!

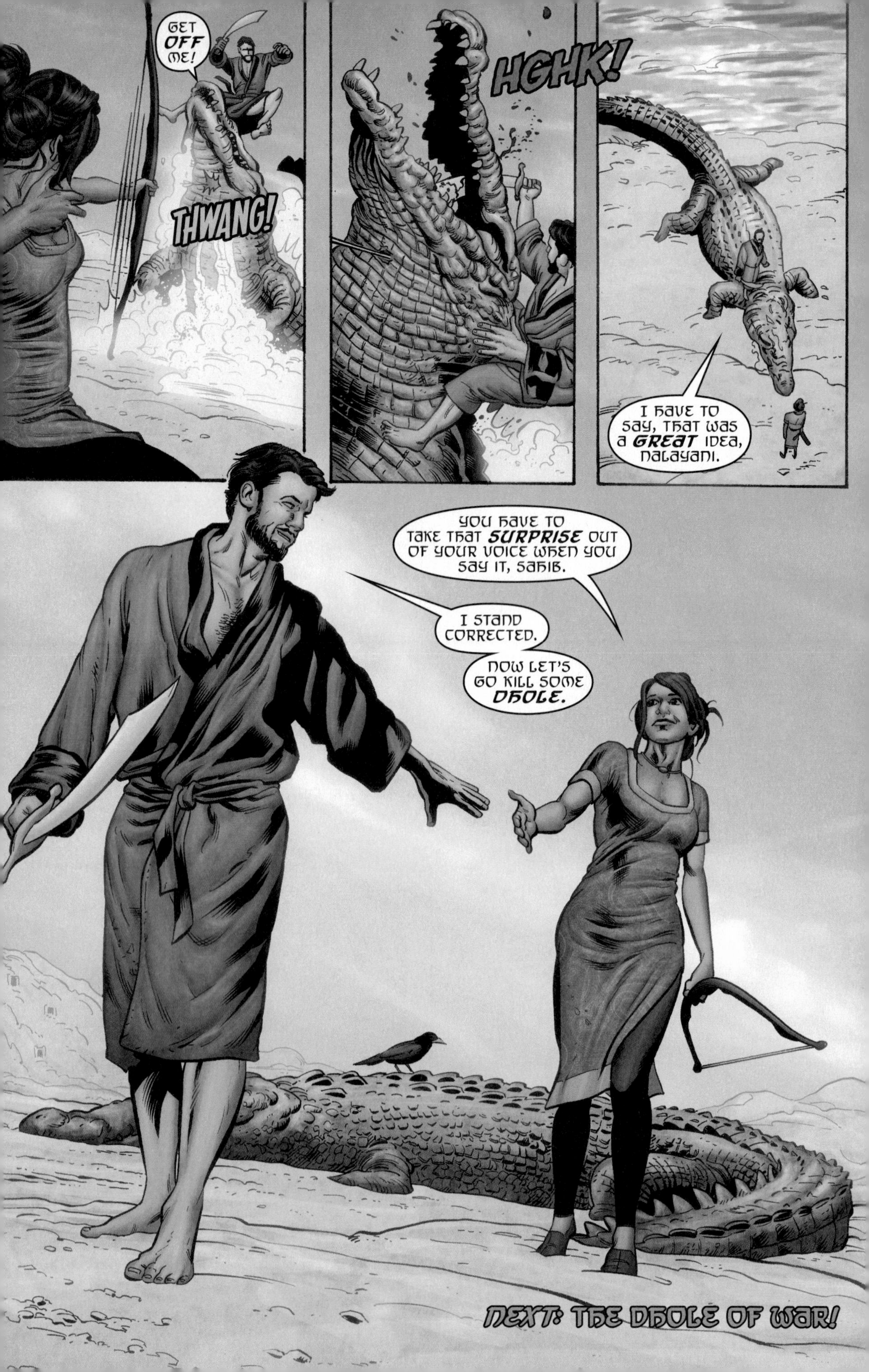
GET OFF ME!
THWANG!
HGHK!
I HAVE TO SAY, THAT WAS A GREAT IDEA, NALAYANI.
YOU HAVE TO TAKE THAT SURPRISE OUT OF YOUR VOICE WHEN YOU SAY IT, SAHIB.
I STAND CORRECTED.
NOW LET'S GO KILL SOME DHOLE.
NEXT: THE DHOLE OF WAR!

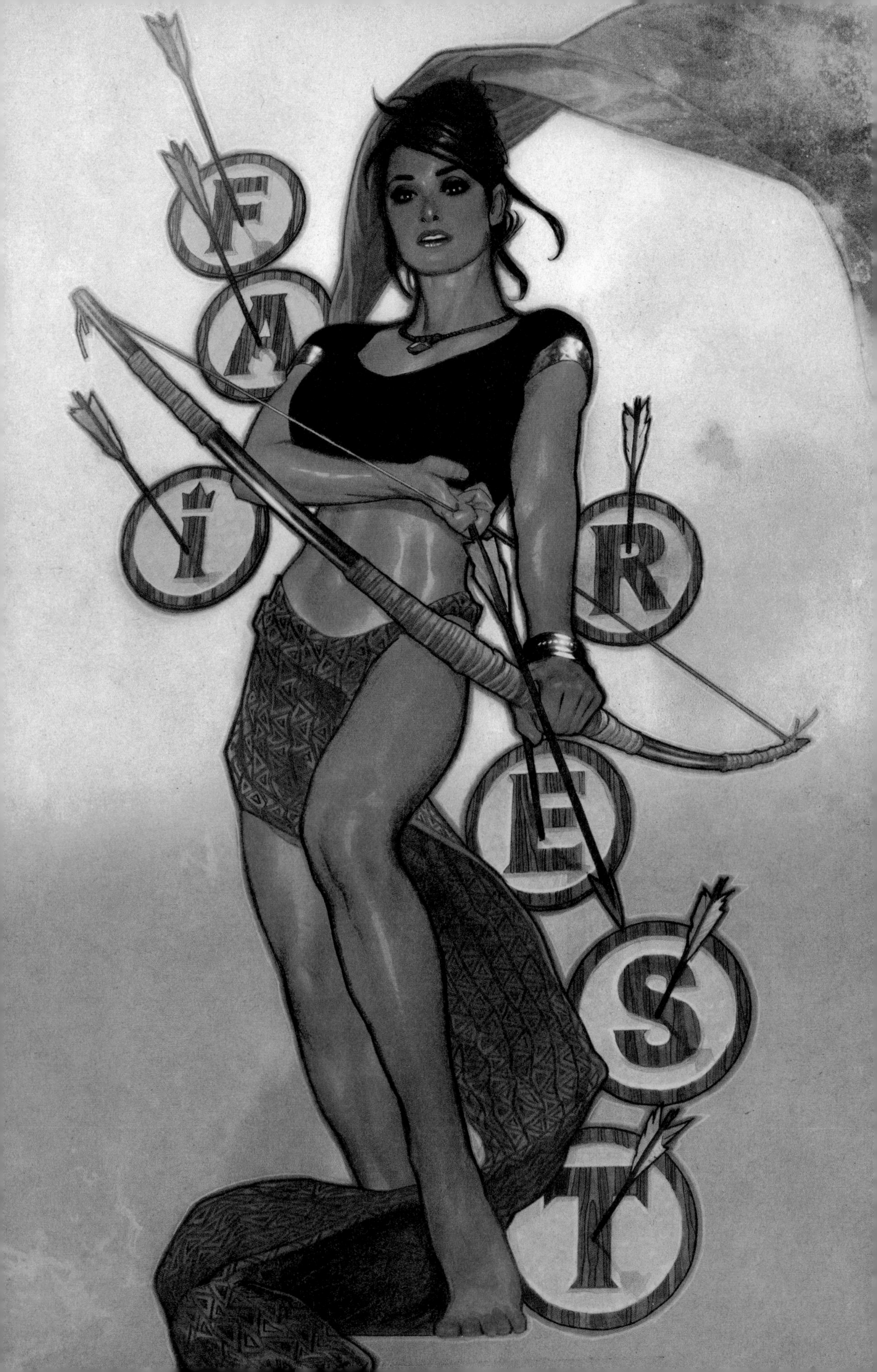
FAiREST

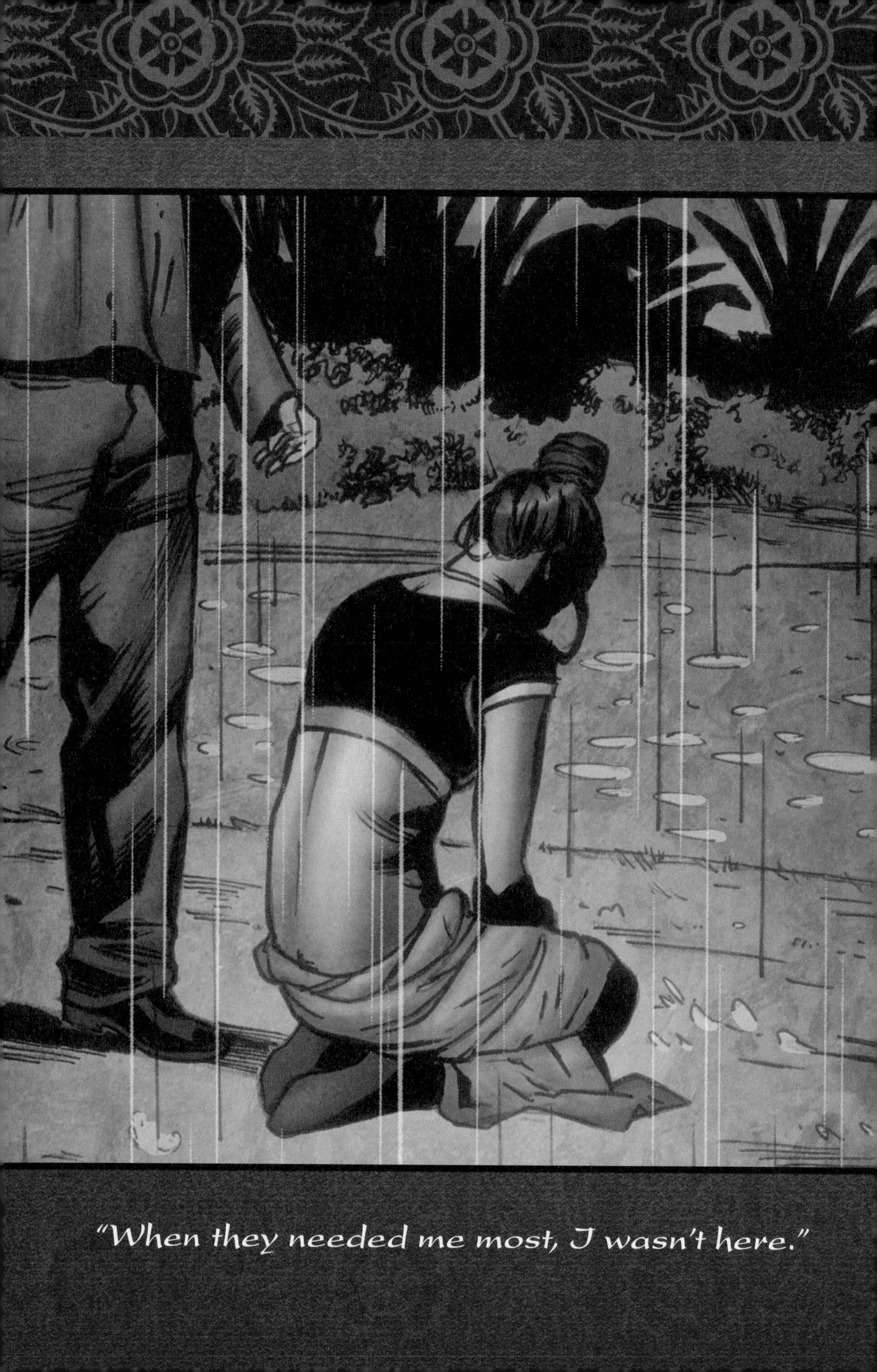

"When they needed me most, I wasn't here."

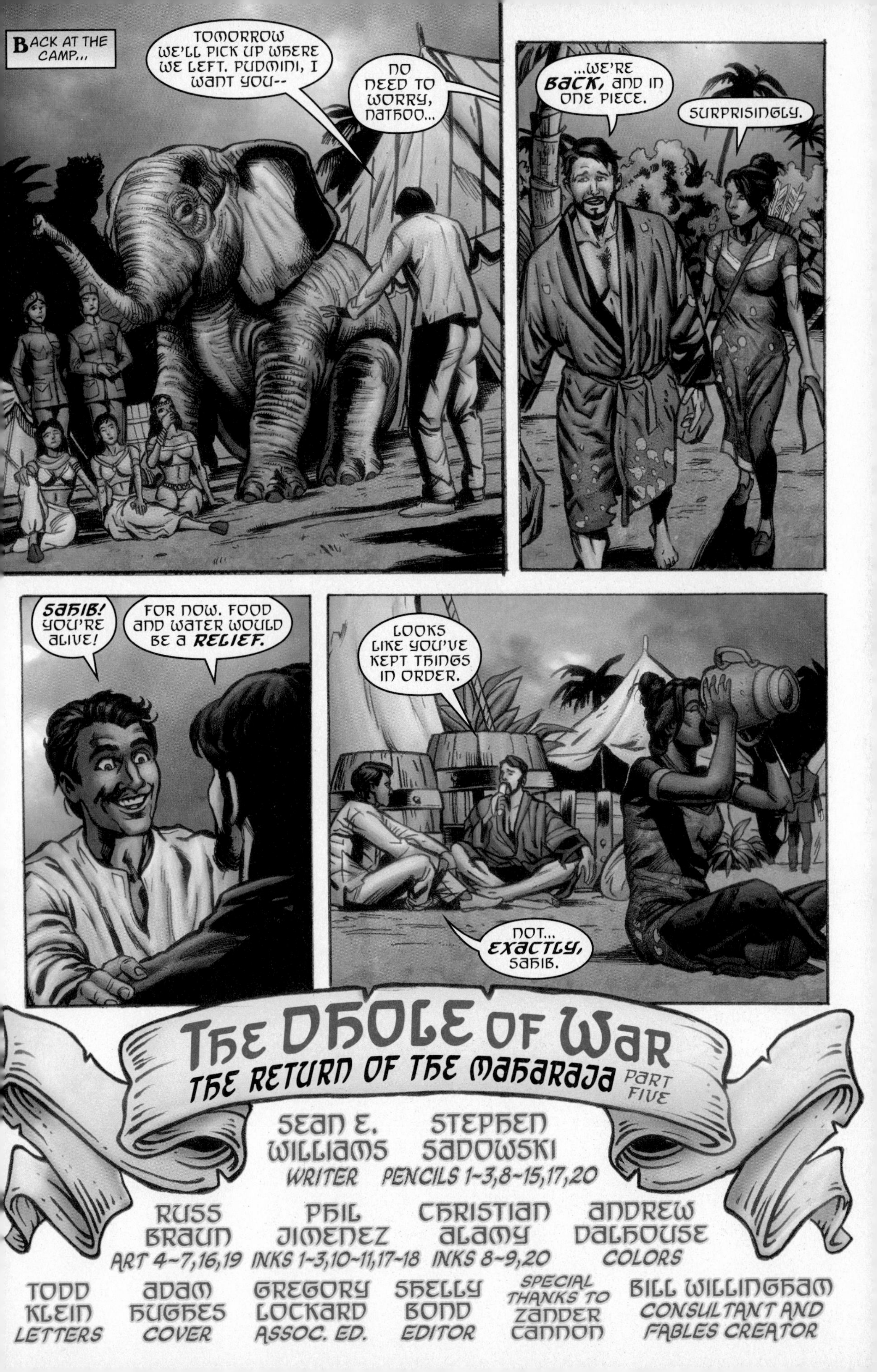
BACK AT THE CAMP...
TOMORROW WE'LL PICK UP WHERE WE LEFT. PUDMINI, I WANT YOU--
NO NEED TO WORRY, NATHOO...
...WE'RE BACK, AND IN ONE PIECE.
SURPRISINGLY.
SAHIB! YOU'RE ALIVE!
FOR NOW. FOOD AND WATER WOULD BE A RELIEF.
LOOKS LIKE YOU'VE KEPT THINGS IN ORDER.
NOT... EXACTLY, SAHIB.
THE DHOLE OF WAR
THE RETURN OF THE MAHARAJA PART FIVE
SEAN E. WILLIAMS WRITER
STEPHEN SADOWSKI PENCILS 1~3,8~15,17,20
RUSS BRAUN ART 4~7,16,19
PHIL JIMENEZ INKS 1~3,10~11,17~18
CHRISTIAN ALAMY INKS 8~9,20
ANDREW DALHOUSE COLORS
TODD KLEIN LETTERS
ADAM HUGHES COVER
GREGORY LOCKARD ASSOC. ED.
SHELLY BOND EDITOR
SPECIAL THANKS TO ZANDER CANNON
BILL WILLINGHAM CONSULTANT AND FABLES CREATOR

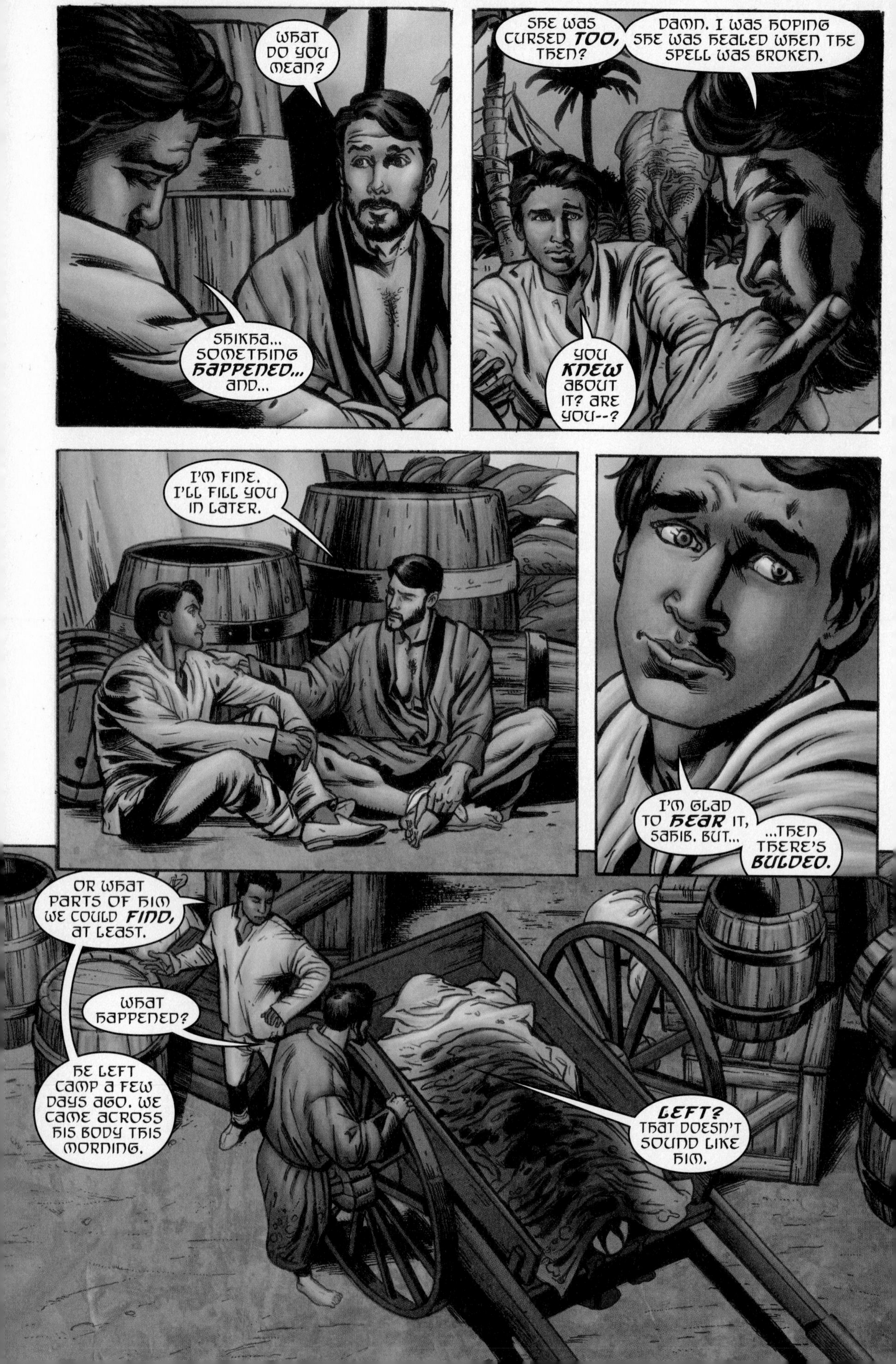
WHAT DO YOU MEAN?
SHIKHA... SOMETHING HAPPENED... AND...
SHE WAS CURSED TOO, THEN?
DAMN. I WAS HOPING SHE WAS HEALED WHEN THE SPELL WAS BROKEN.
YOU KNEW ABOUT IT? ARE YOU--?
I'M FINE. I'LL FILL YOU IN LATER.
I'M GLAD TO HEAR IT, SAHIB. BUT...
...THEN THERE'S BULDEO.
OR WHAT PARTS OF HIM WE COULD FIND, AT LEAST.
WHAT HAPPENED?
HE LEFT CAMP A FEW DAYS AGO. WE CAME ACROSS HIS BODY THIS MORNING.
LEFT? THAT DOESN'T SOUND LIKE HIM.

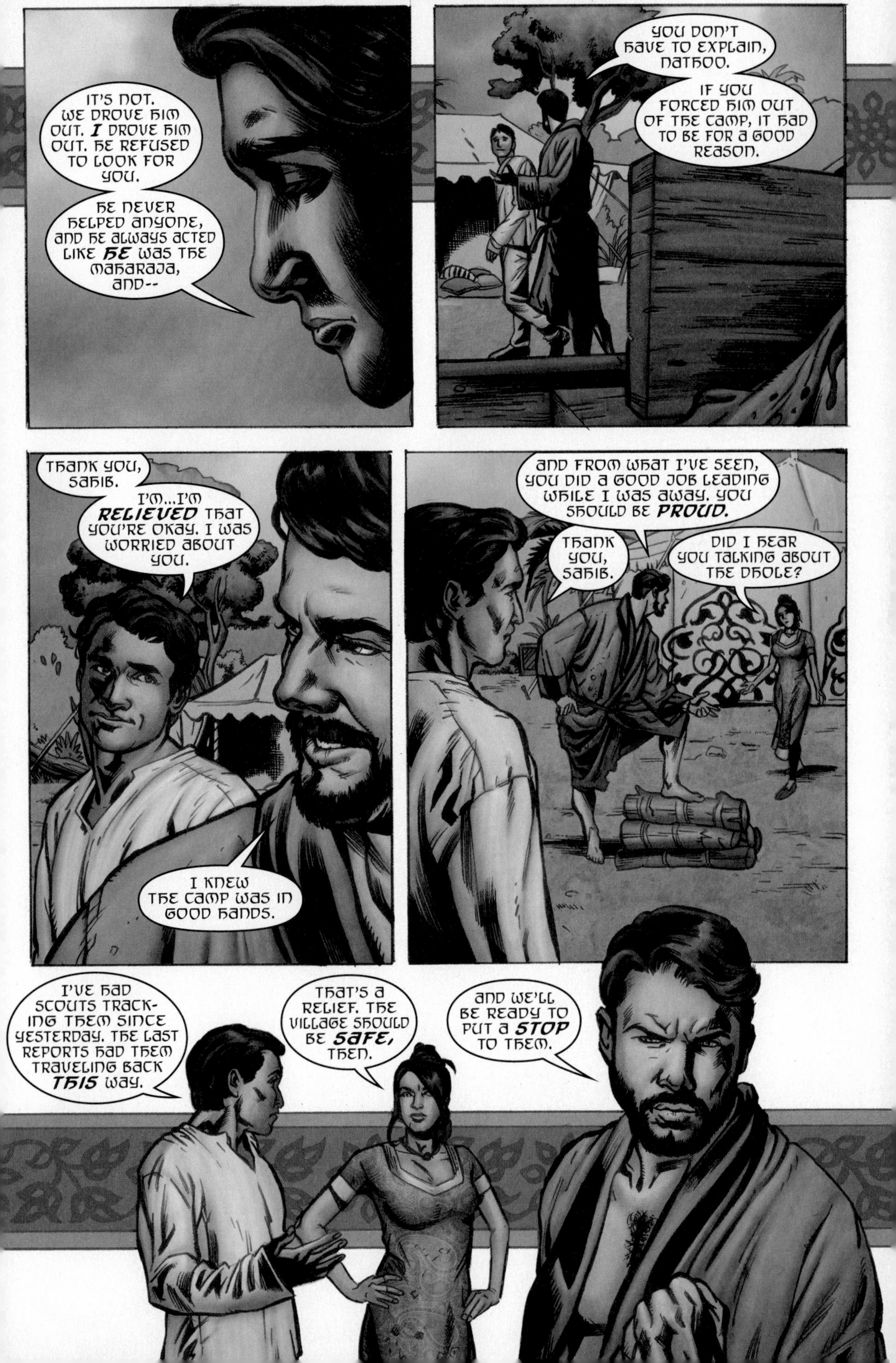
IT'S NOT. WE DROVE HIM OUT. I DROVE HIM OUT. HE REFUSED TO LOOK FOR YOU.
HE NEVER HELPED ANYONE, AND HE ALWAYS ACTED LIKE HE WAS THE MAHARAJA, AND--
YOU DON'T HAVE TO EXPLAIN, NATHOO.
IF YOU FORCED HIM OUT OF THE CAMP, IT HAD TO BE FOR A GOOD REASON.
THANK YOU, SAHIB.
I'M...I'M RELIEVED THAT YOU'RE OKAY. I WAS WORRIED ABOUT YOU.
I KNEW THE CAMP WAS IN GOOD HANDS.
AND FROM WHAT I'VE SEEN, YOU DID A GOOD JOB LEADING WHILE I WAS AWAY. YOU SHOULD BE PROUD.
THANK YOU, SAHIB.
DID I HEAR YOU TALKING ABOUT THE DHOLE?
I'VE HAD SCOUTS TRACKING THEM SINCE YESTERDAY. THE LAST REPORTS HAD THEM TRAVELING BACK THIS WAY.
THAT'S A RELIEF. THE VILLAGE SHOULD BE SAFE, THEN.
AND WE'LL BE READY TO PUT A STOP TO THEM.

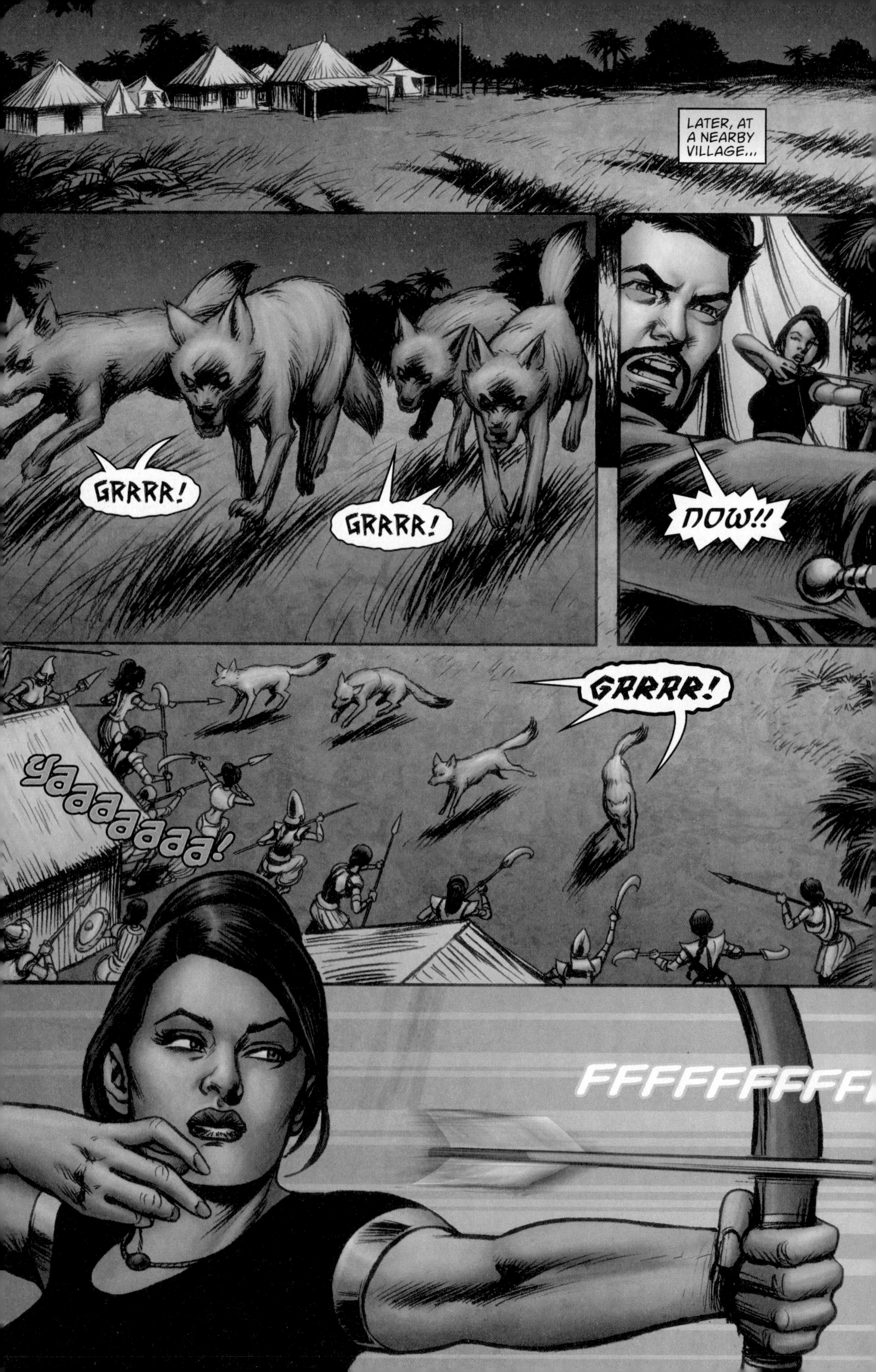
LATER, AT A NEARBY VILLAGE...
GRRRR!
GRRRR!
NOW!!
GRRRR!
yaaaaaaaa!
FFFFFFFFFF

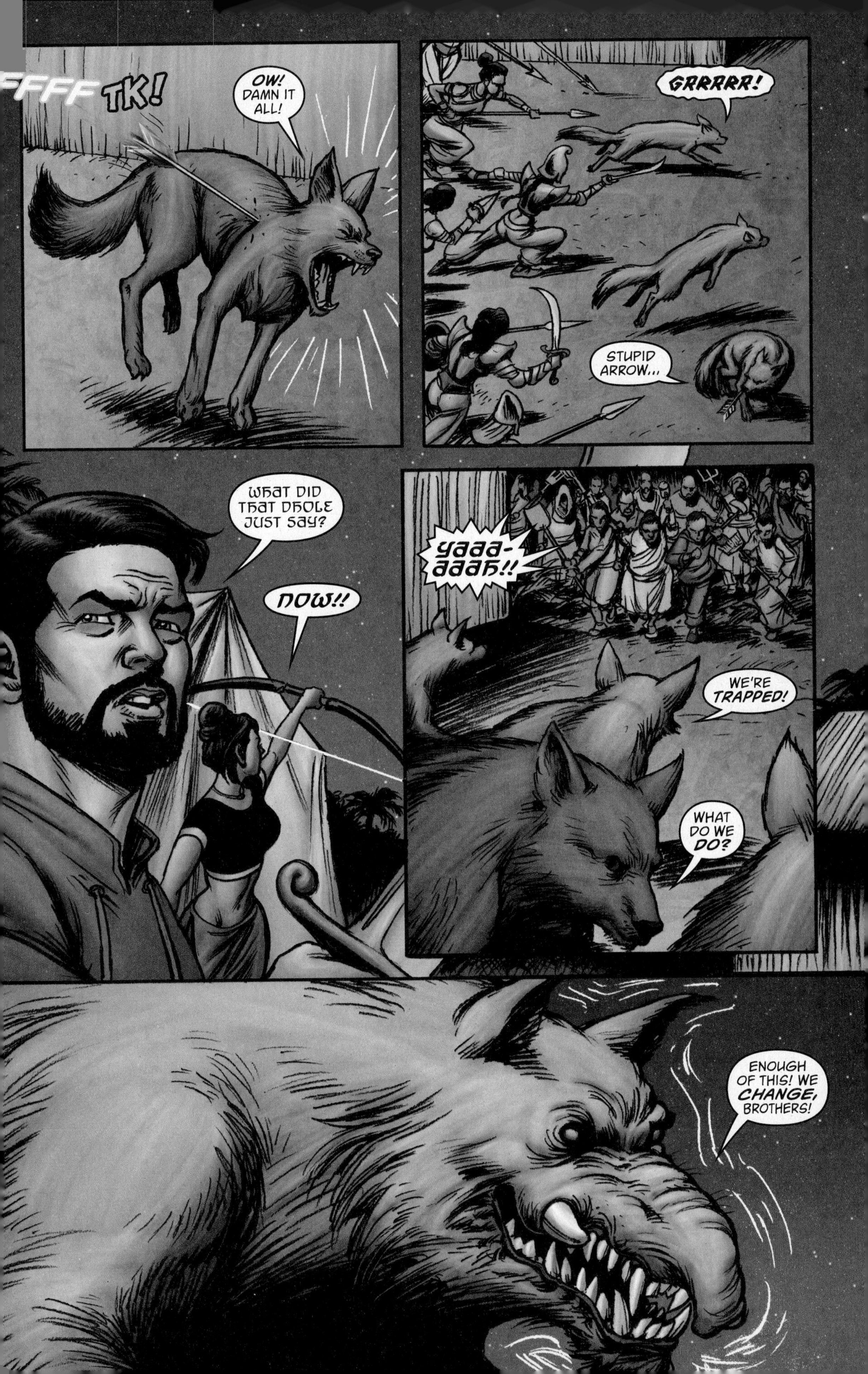
FFFFF TK!
OW! DAMN IT ALL!
GRRRRR!
STUPID ARROW...
WHAT DID THAT DHOLE JUST SAY?
NOW!!
YAAA-AAAH!!
WE'RE TRAPPED!
WHAT DO WE DO?
ENOUGH OF THIS! WE CHANGE, BROTHERS!

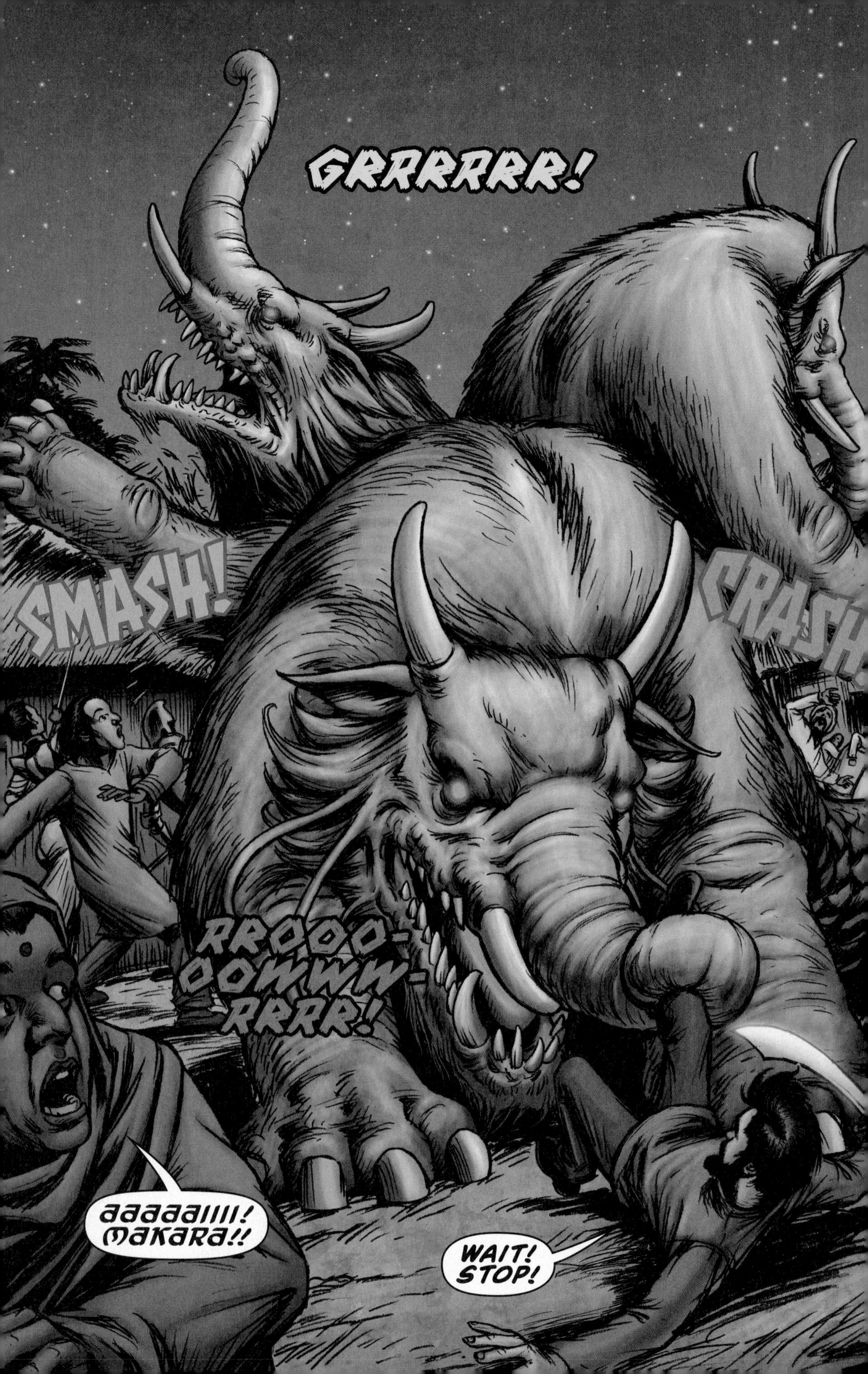
GRRRRRR!
SMASH!
CRASH!
RROOO-OOWWW-RRRR!
AAAAAIIIII! MAKARA!!
WAIT! STOP!

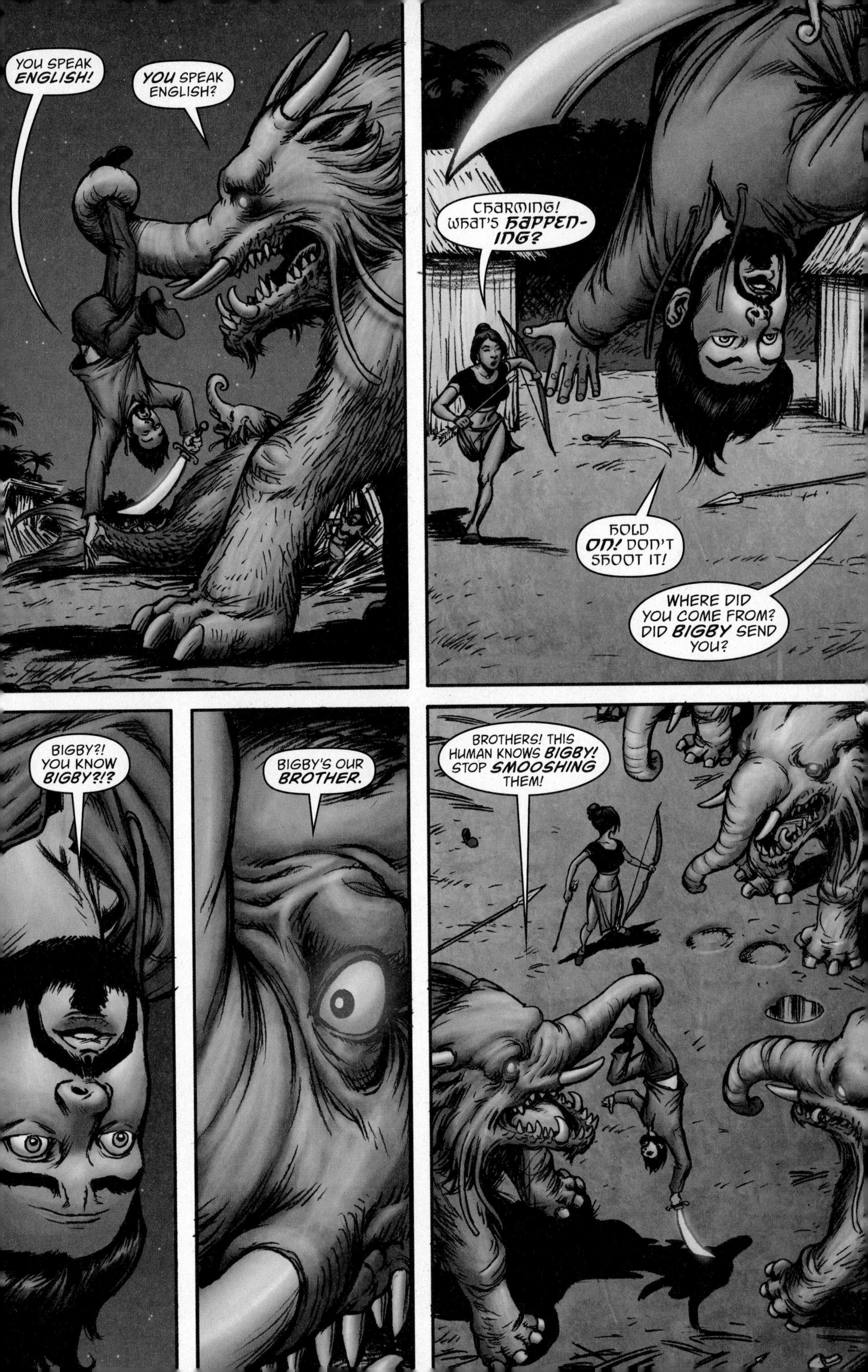
YOU SPEAK ENGLISH!
YOU SPEAK ENGLISH?
CHARMING! WHAT'S HAPPEN-ING?
HOLD ON! DON'T SHOOT IT!
WHERE DID YOU COME FROM? DID BIGBY SEND YOU?
BIGBY?! YOU KNOW BIGBY?!?
BIGBY'S OUR BROTHER.
BROTHERS! THIS HUMAN KNOWS BIGBY! STOP SMOOSHING THEM!

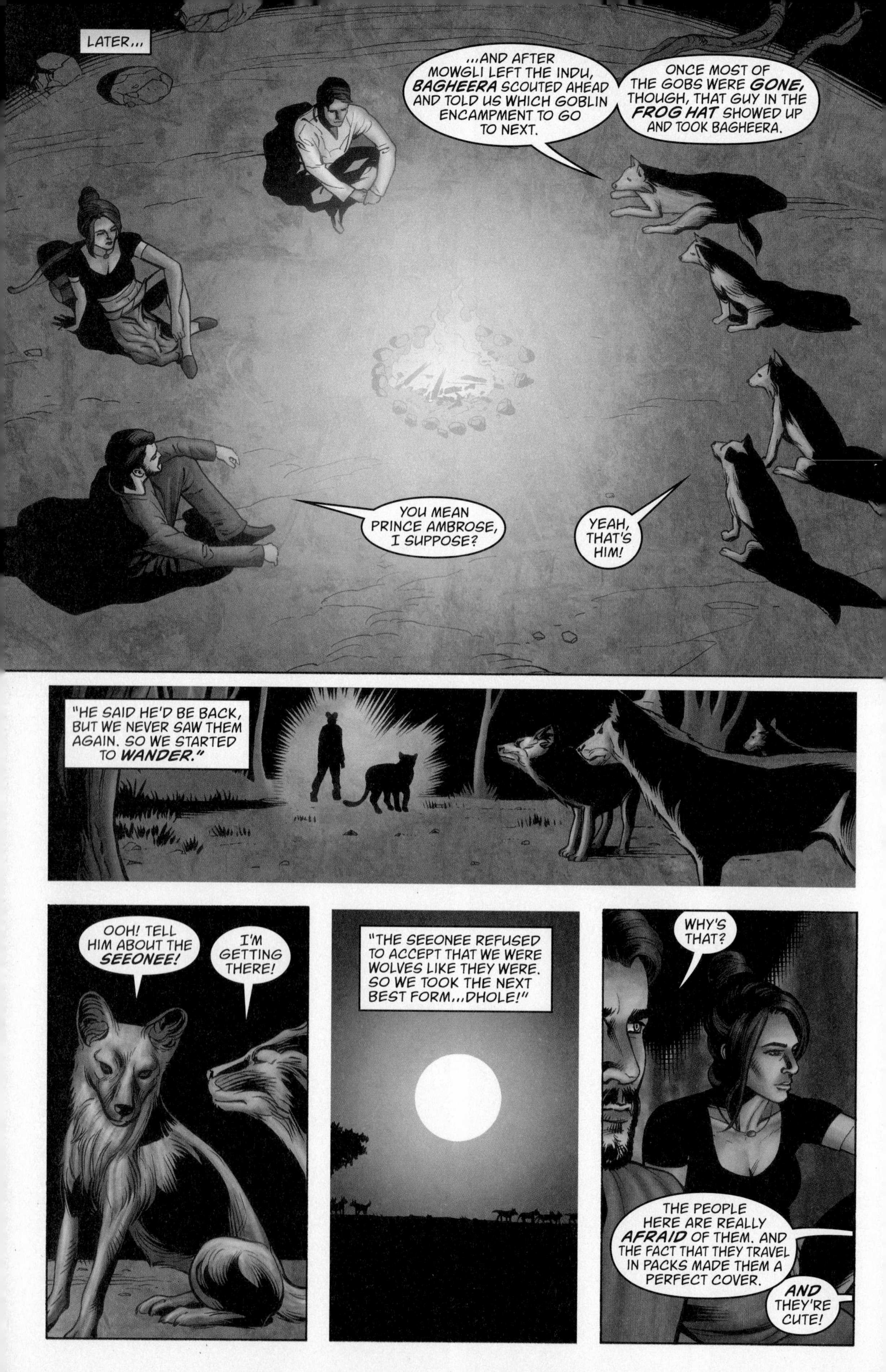
LATER...
...AND AFTER MOWGLI LEFT THE INDU, BAGHEERA SCOUTED AHEAD AND TOLD US WHICH GOBLIN ENCAMPMENT TO GO TO NEXT.
ONCE MOST OF THE GOBS WERE GONE, THOUGH, THAT GUY IN THE FROG HAT SHOWED UP AND TOOK BAGHEERA.
YOU MEAN PRINCE AMBROSE, I SUPPOSE?
YEAH, THAT'S HIM!
"HE SAID HE'D BE BACK, BUT WE NEVER SAW THEM AGAIN. SO WE STARTED TO WANDER."
OOH! TELL HIM ABOUT THE SEEONEE!
I'M GETTING THERE!
"THE SEEONEE REFUSED TO ACCEPT THAT WE WERE WOLVES LIKE THEY WERE. SO WE TOOK THE NEXT BEST FORM...DHOLE!"
WHY'S THAT?
THE PEOPLE HERE ARE REALLY AFRAID OF THEM. AND THE FACT THAT THEY TRAVEL IN PACKS MADE THEM A PERFECT COVER.
AND THEY'RE CUTE!

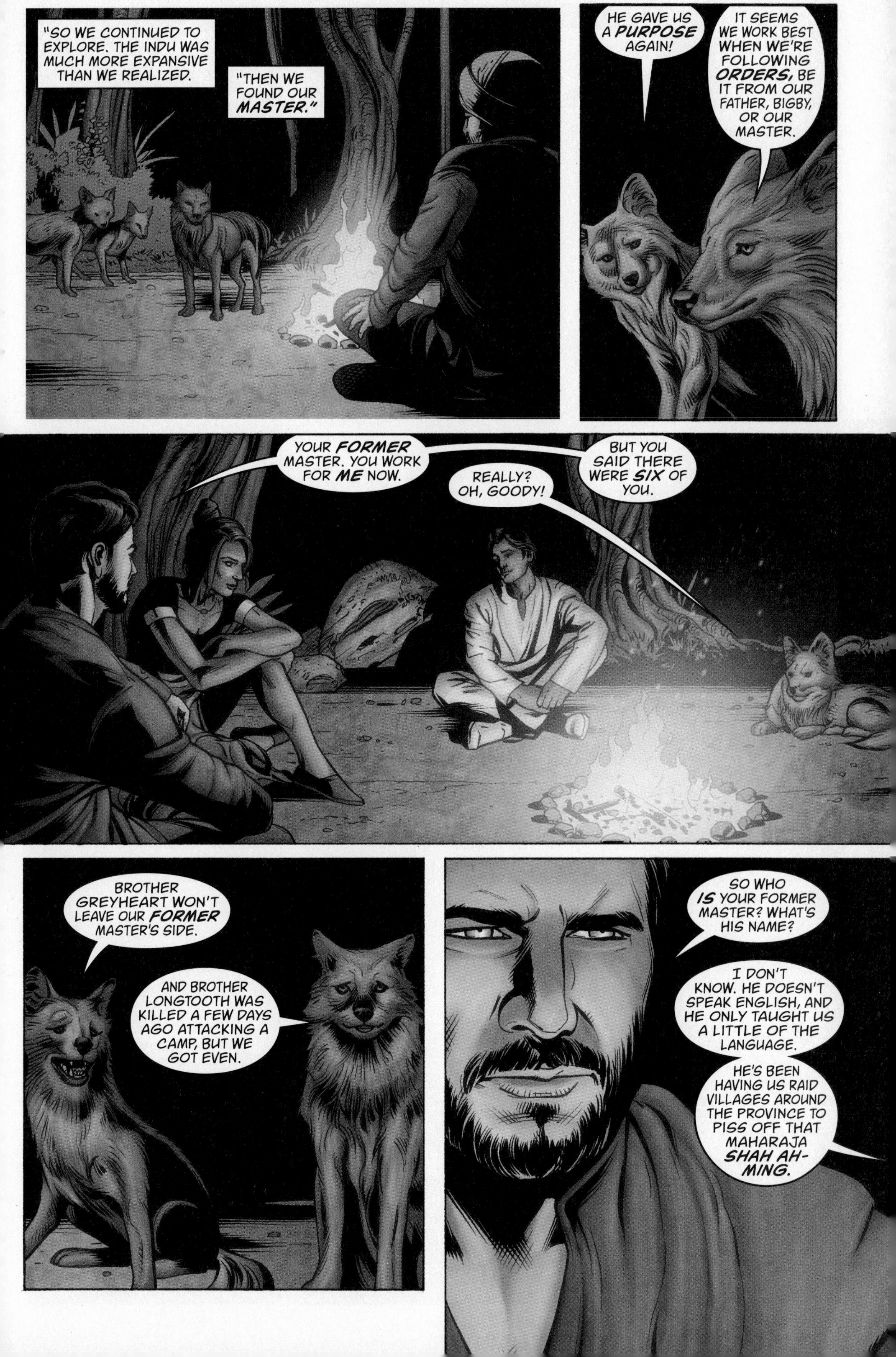
"SO WE CONTINUED TO EXPLORE. THE INDU WAS MUCH MORE EXPANSIVE THAN WE REALIZED.
"THEN WE FOUND OUR MASTER."
HE GAVE US A PURPOSE AGAIN!
IT SEEMS WE WORK BEST WHEN WE'RE FOLLOWING ORDERS, BE IT FROM OUR FATHER, BIGBY, OR OUR MASTER.
YOUR FORMER MASTER. YOU WORK FOR ME NOW.
REALLY? OH, GOODY!
BUT YOU SAID THERE WERE SIX OF YOU.
BROTHER GREYHEART WON'T LEAVE OUR FORMER MASTER'S SIDE.
AND BROTHER LONGTOOTH WAS KILLED A FEW DAYS AGO ATTACKING A CAMP, BUT WE GOT EVEN.
SO WHO IS YOUR FORMER MASTER? WHAT'S HIS NAME?
I DON'T KNOW. HE DOESN'T SPEAK ENGLISH, AND HE ONLY TAUGHT US A LITTLE OF THE LANGUAGE.
HE'S BEEN HAVING US RAID VILLAGES AROUND THE PROVINCE TO PISS OFF THAT MAHARAJA SHAH AH-MING.

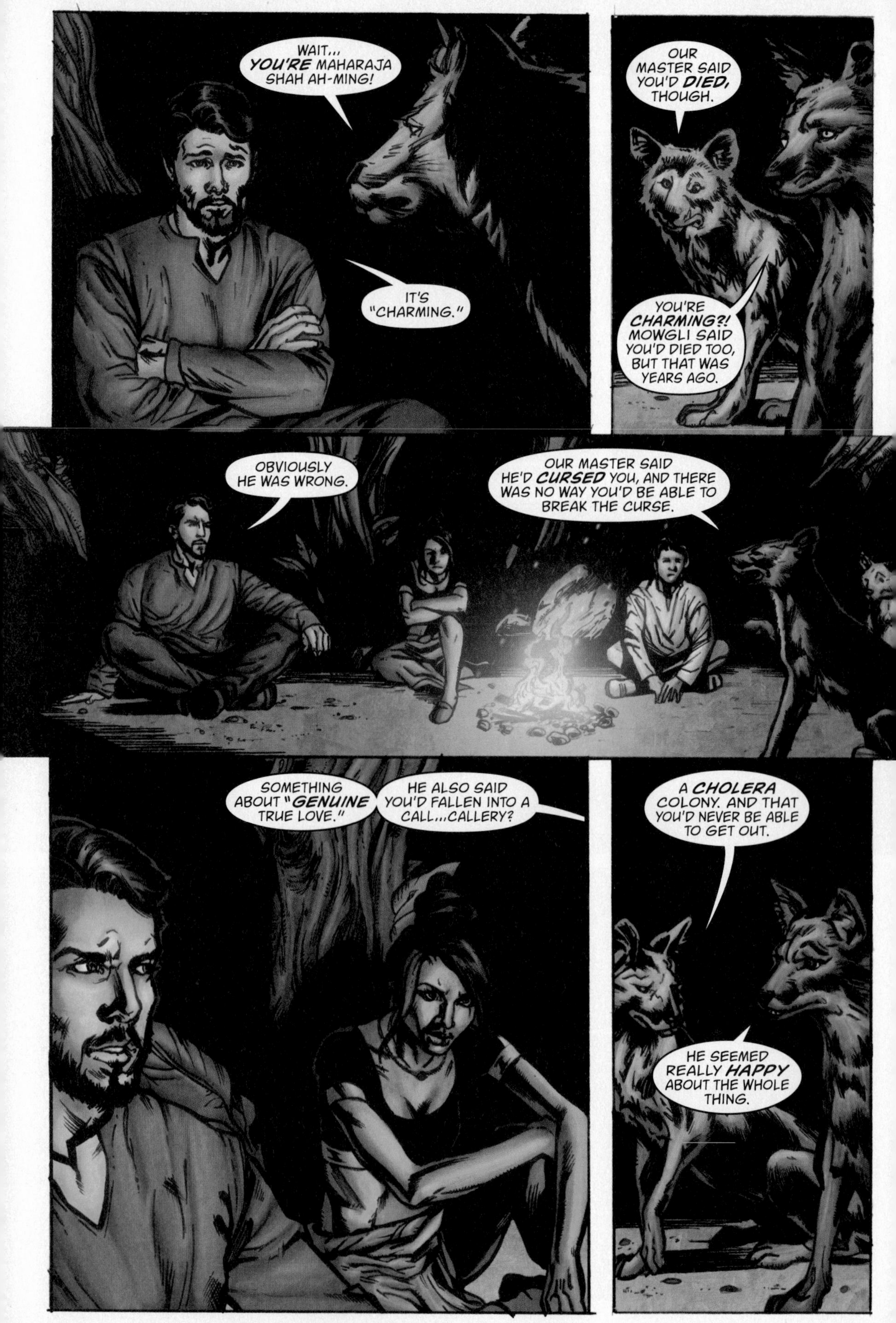
WAIT... **YOU'RE** MAHARAJA SHAH AH-MING!
IT'S "CHARMING."
OUR MASTER SAID YOU'D **DIED,** THOUGH.
YOU'RE **CHARMING?!** MOWGLI SAID YOU'D DIED TOO, BUT THAT WAS YEARS AGO.
OBVIOUSLY HE WAS WRONG.
OUR MASTER SAID HE'D **CURSED** YOU, AND THERE WAS NO WAY YOU'D BE ABLE TO BREAK THE CURSE.
SOMETHING ABOUT "**GENUINE** TRUE LOVE."
HE ALSO SAID YOU'D FALLEN INTO A CALL...CALLERY?
A **CHOLERA** COLONY. AND THAT YOU'D NEVER BE ABLE TO GET OUT.
HE SEEMED REALLY **HAPPY** ABOUT THE WHOLE THING.

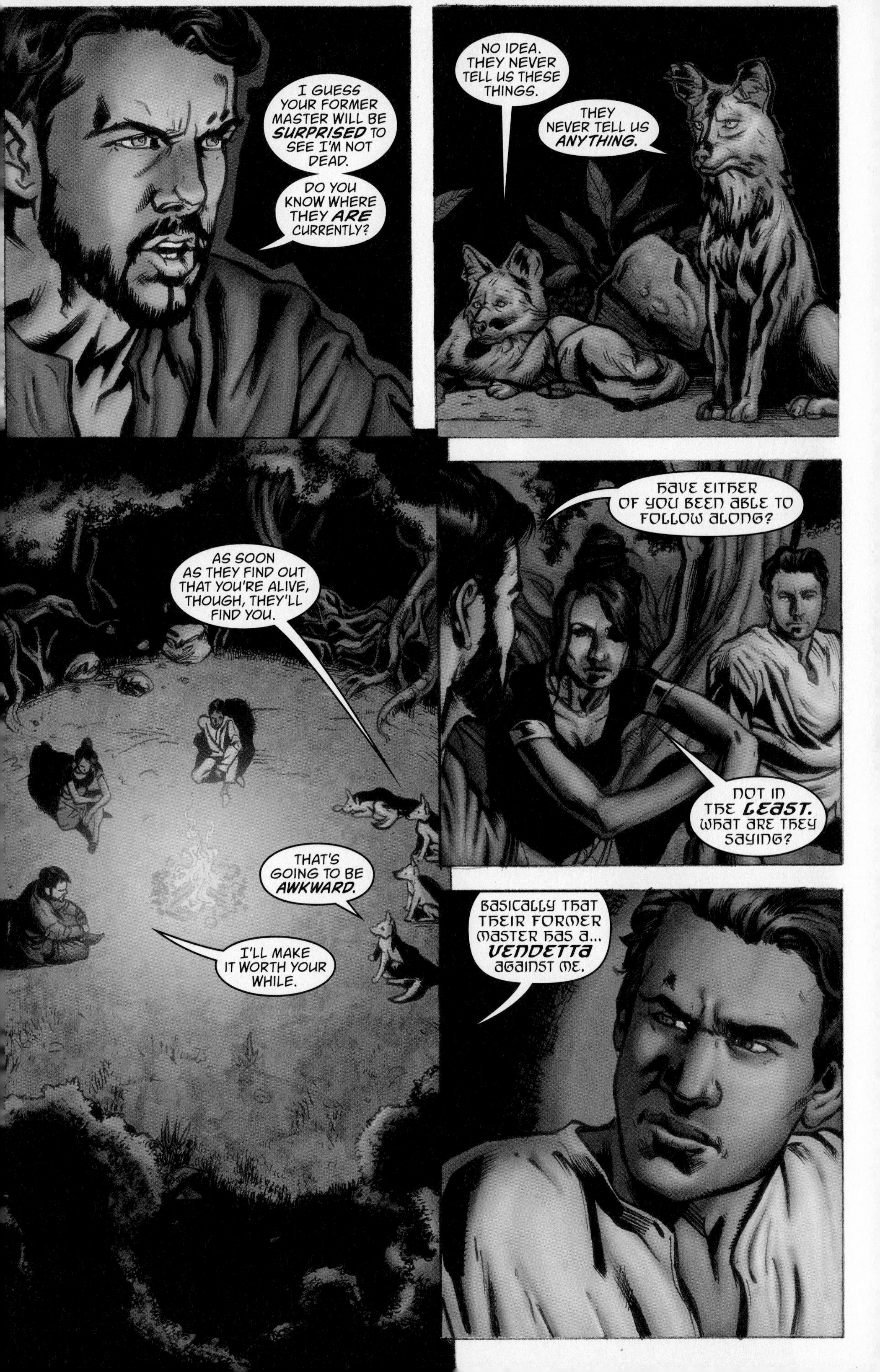
I GUESS YOUR FORMER MASTER WILL BE SURPRISED TO SEE I'M NOT DEAD.
DO YOU KNOW WHERE THEY ARE CURRENTLY?
NO IDEA. THEY NEVER TELL US THESE THINGS.
THEY NEVER TELL US ANYTHING.
AS SOON AS THEY FIND OUT THAT YOU'RE ALIVE, THOUGH, THEY'LL FIND YOU.
THAT'S GOING TO BE AWKWARD.
I'LL MAKE IT WORTH YOUR WHILE.
HAVE EITHER OF YOU BEEN ABLE TO FOLLOW ALONG?
NOT IN THE LEAST. WHAT ARE THEY SAYING?
BASICALLY THAT THEIR FORMER MASTER HAS A... VENDETTA AGAINST ME.

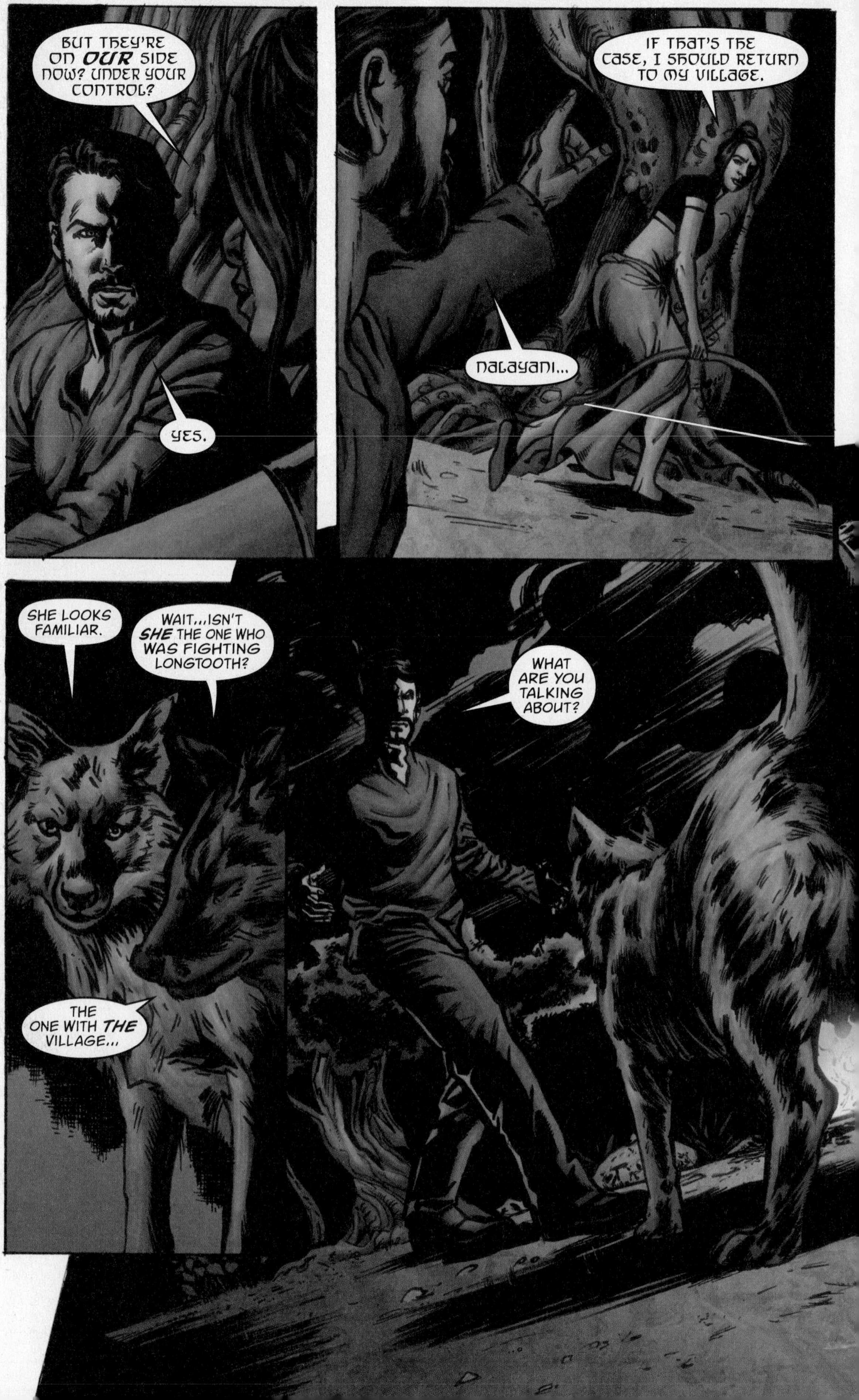
BUT THEY'RE ON OUR SIDE NOW? UNDER YOUR CONTROL?
YES.
IF THAT'S THE CASE, I SHOULD RETURN TO MY VILLAGE.
NALAYANI...
SHE LOOKS FAMILIAR.
WAIT...ISN'T SHE THE ONE WHO WAS FIGHTING LONGTOOTH?
THE ONE WITH THE VILLAGE...
WHAT ARE YOU TALKING ABOUT?

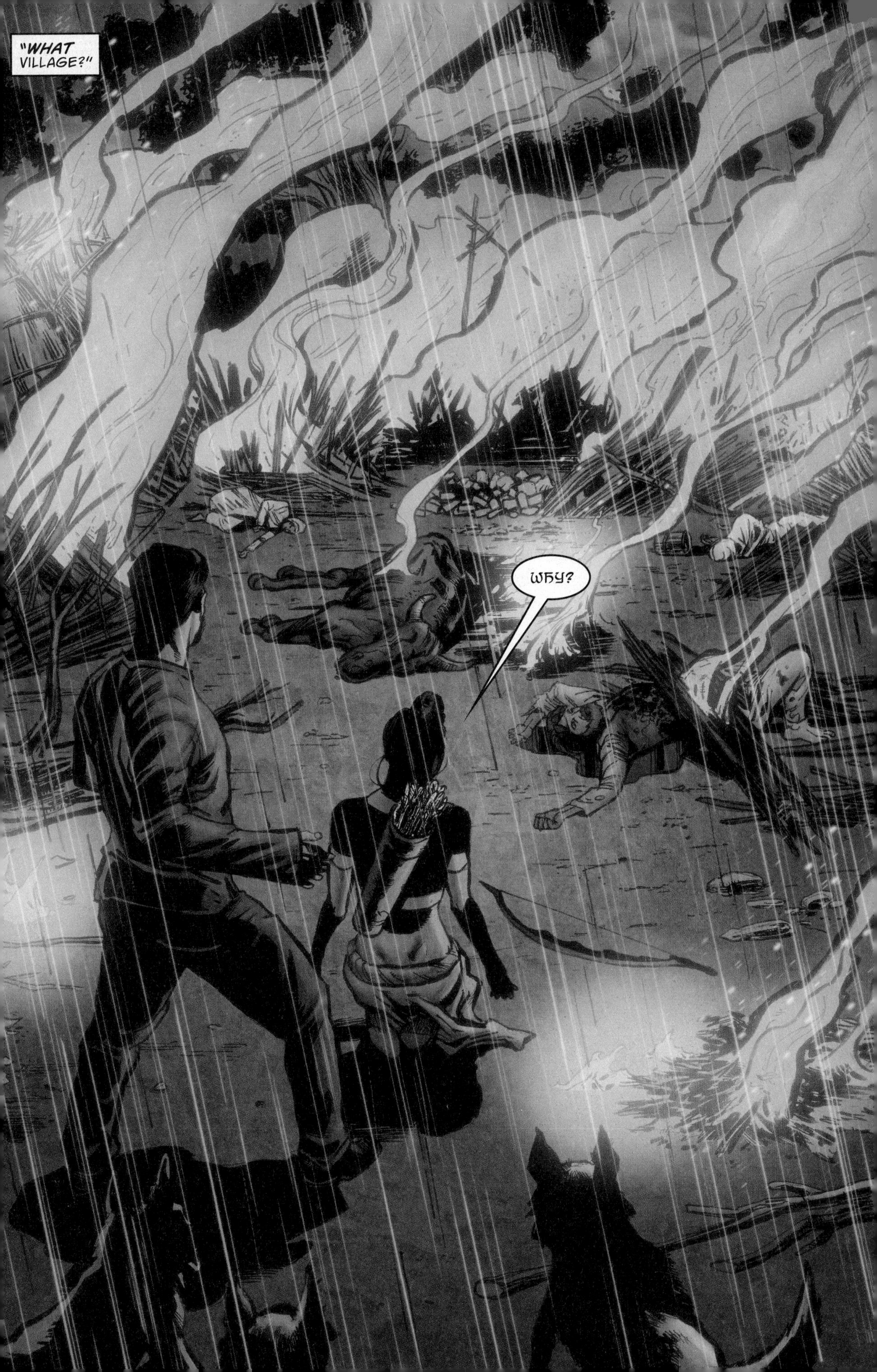
"WHAT VILLAGE?"
WHY?

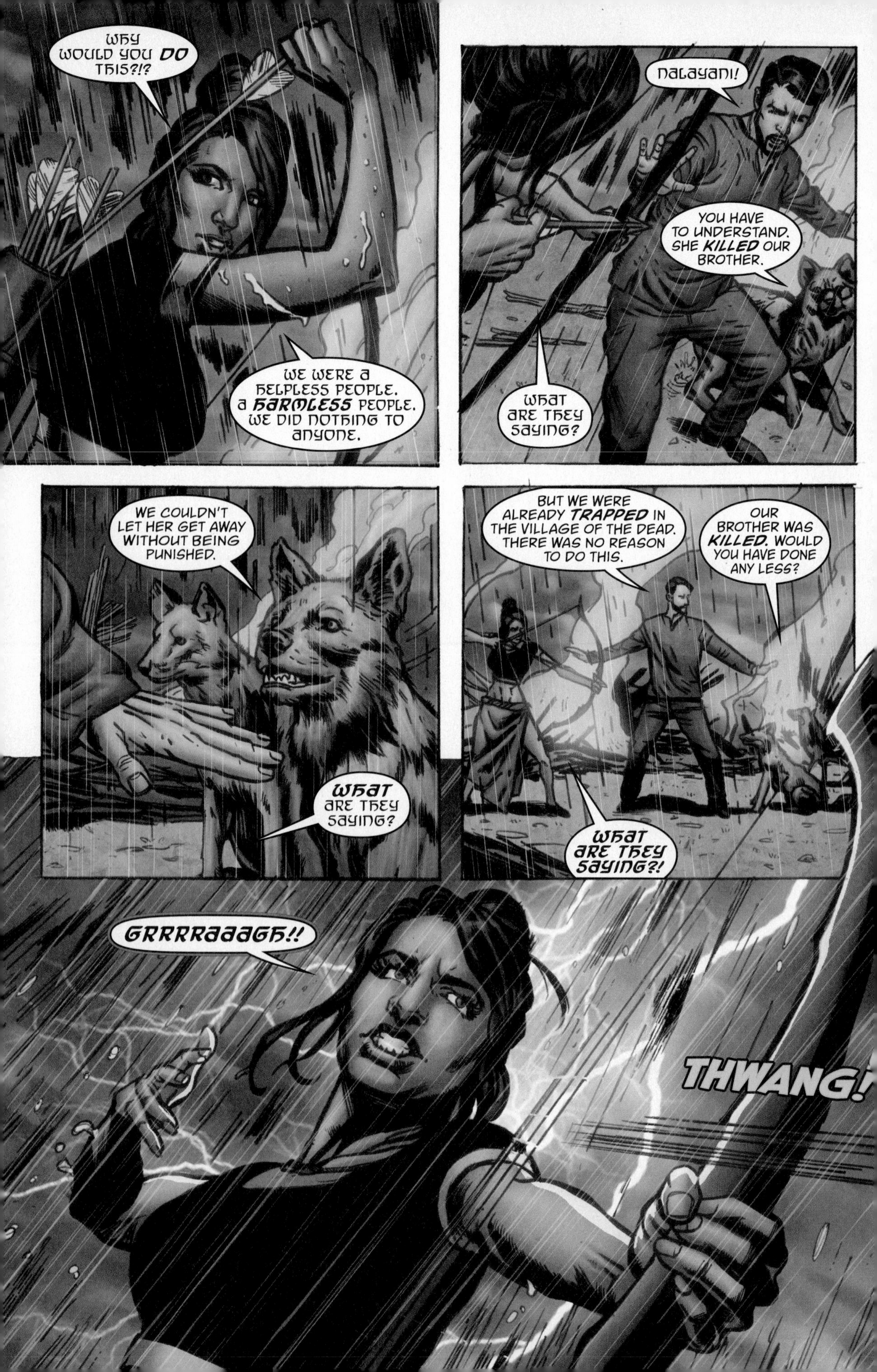
WHY WOULD YOU DO THIS?!?
WE WERE A HELPLESS PEOPLE. A HARMLESS PEOPLE. WE DID NOTHING TO ANYONE.
NALAYANI!
YOU HAVE TO UNDERSTAND. SHE KILLED OUR BROTHER.
WHAT ARE THEY SAYING?
WE COULDN'T LET HER GET AWAY WITHOUT BEING PUNISHED.
WHAT ARE THEY SAYING?
BUT WE WERE ALREADY TRAPPED IN THE VILLAGE OF THE DEAD. THERE WAS NO REASON TO DO THIS.
OUR BROTHER WAS KILLED. WOULD YOU HAVE DONE ANY LESS?
WHAT ARE THEY SAYING?!
GRRRRAAAGH!!
THWANG!

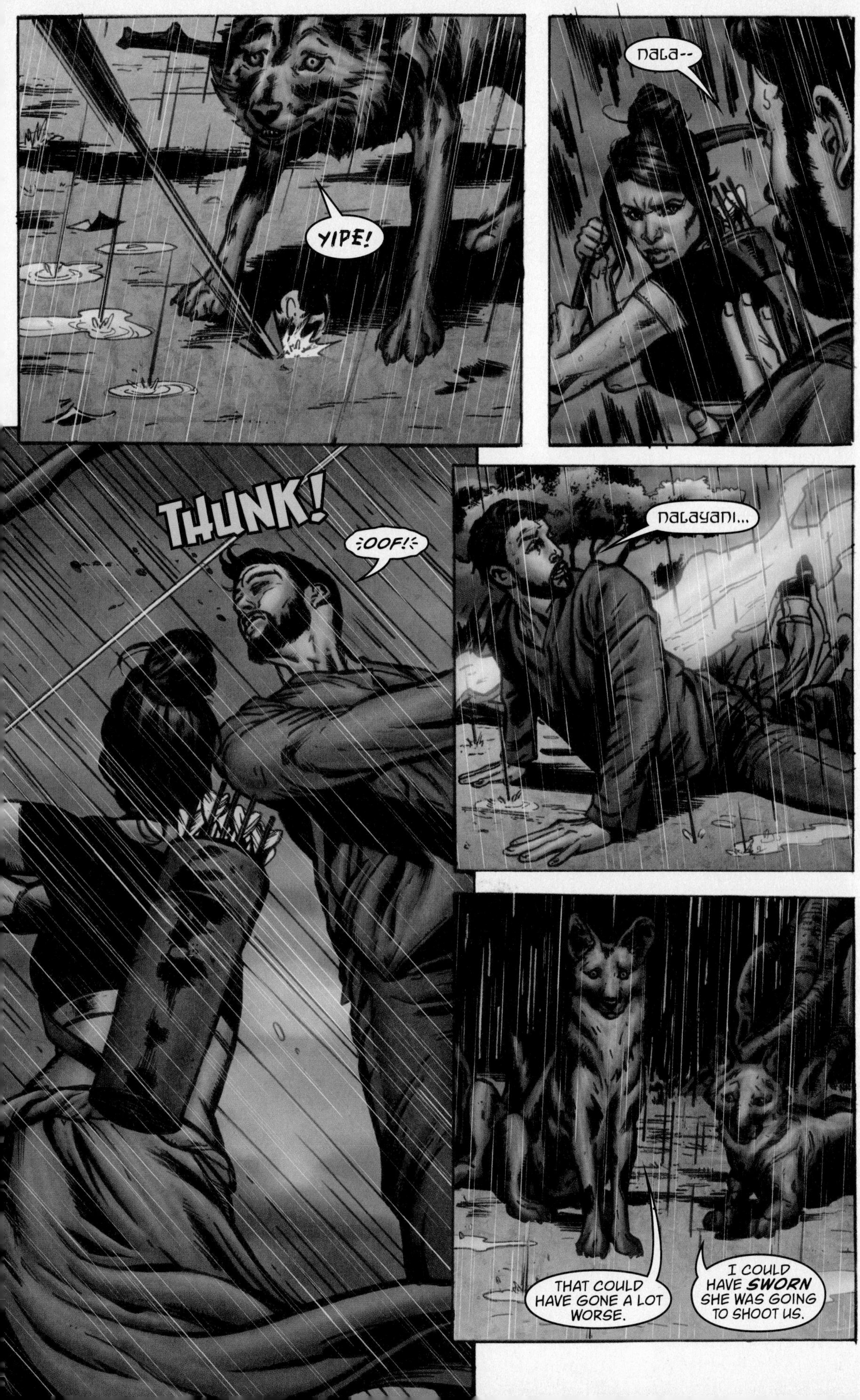
YIPE!
NALA--
THUNK!
OOF!
NALAYANI...
THAT COULD HAVE GONE A LOT WORSE.
I COULD HAVE SWORN SHE WAS GOING TO SHOOT US.

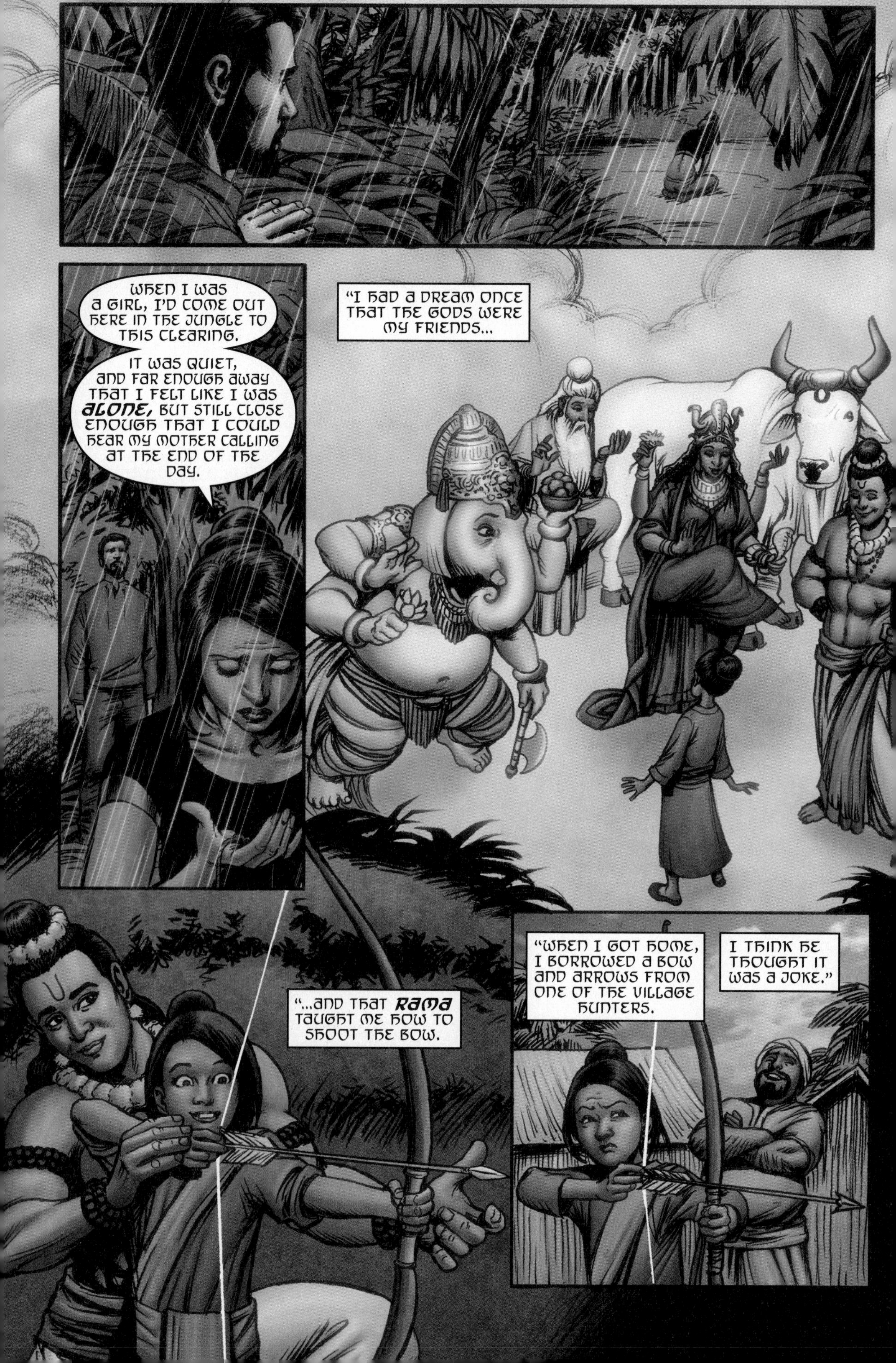

WHEN I WAS A GIRL, I'D COME OUT HERE IN THE JUNGLE TO THIS CLEARING.
IT WAS QUIET, AND FAR ENOUGH AWAY THAT I FELT LIKE I WAS ALONE, BUT STILL CLOSE ENOUGH THAT I COULD HEAR MY MOTHER CALLING AT THE END OF THE DAY.
"I HAD A DREAM ONCE THAT THE GODS WERE MY FRIENDS...
"...AND THAT RAMA TAUGHT ME HOW TO SHOOT THE BOW.
"WHEN I GOT HOME, I BORROWED A BOW AND ARROWS FROM ONE OF THE VILLAGE HUNTERS.
I THINK HE THOUGHT IT WAS A JOKE."

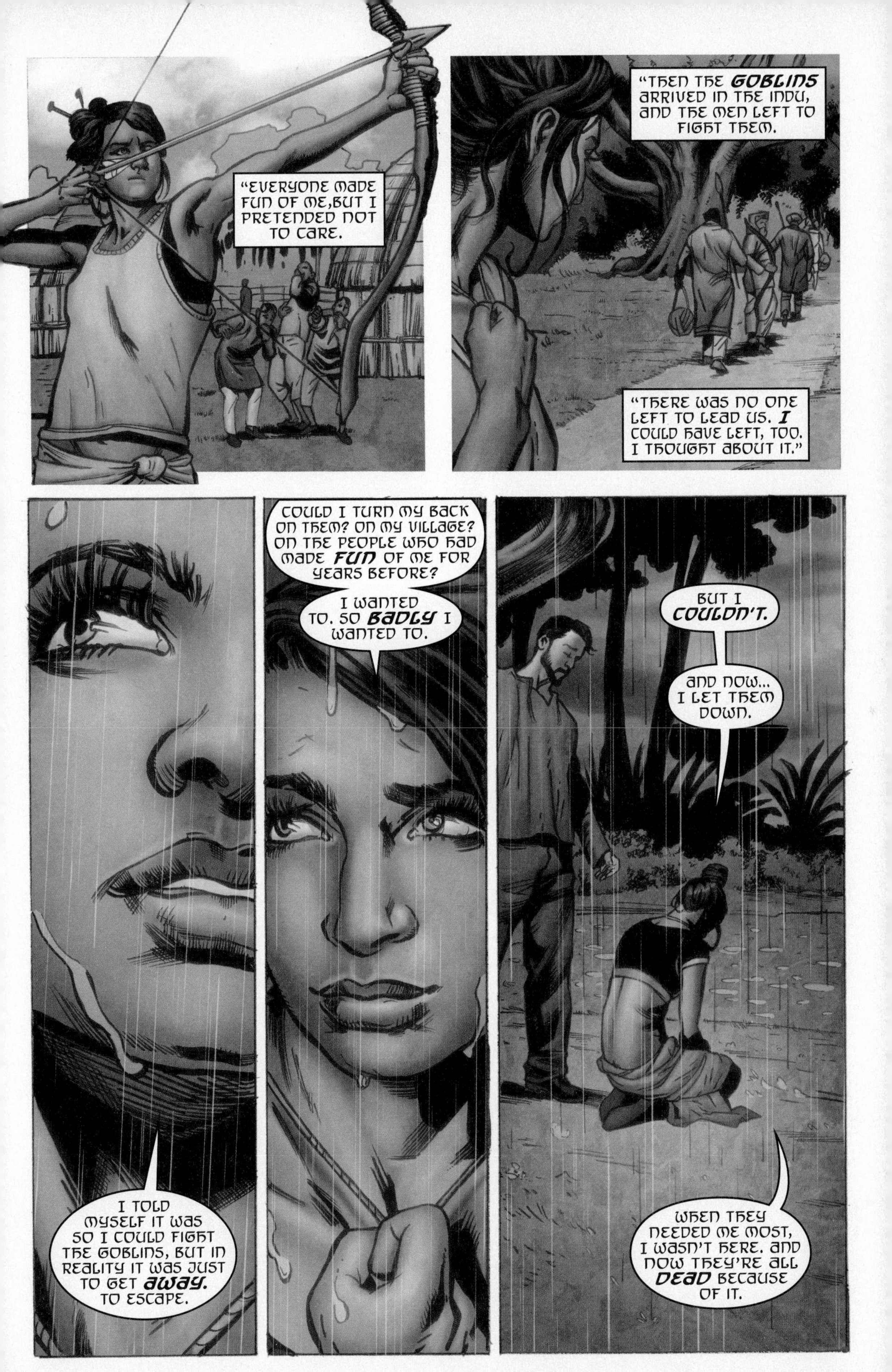
"EVERYONE MADE FUN OF ME, BUT I PRETENDED NOT TO CARE.
"THEN THE GOBLINS ARRIVED IN THE INDU, AND THE MEN LEFT TO FIGHT THEM.
"THERE WAS NO ONE LEFT TO LEAD US. I COULD HAVE LEFT, TOO. I THOUGHT ABOUT IT."
I TOLD MYSELF IT WAS SO I COULD FIGHT THE GOBLINS, BUT IN REALITY IT WAS JUST TO GET AWAY. TO ESCAPE.
COULD I TURN MY BACK ON THEM? ON MY VILLAGE? ON THE PEOPLE WHO HAD MADE FUN OF ME FOR YEARS BEFORE?
I WANTED TO. SO BADLY I WANTED TO.
BUT I COULDN'T.
AND NOW... I LET THEM DOWN.
WHEN THEY NEEDED ME MOST, I WASN'T HERE. AND NOW THEY'RE ALL DEAD BECAUSE OF IT.

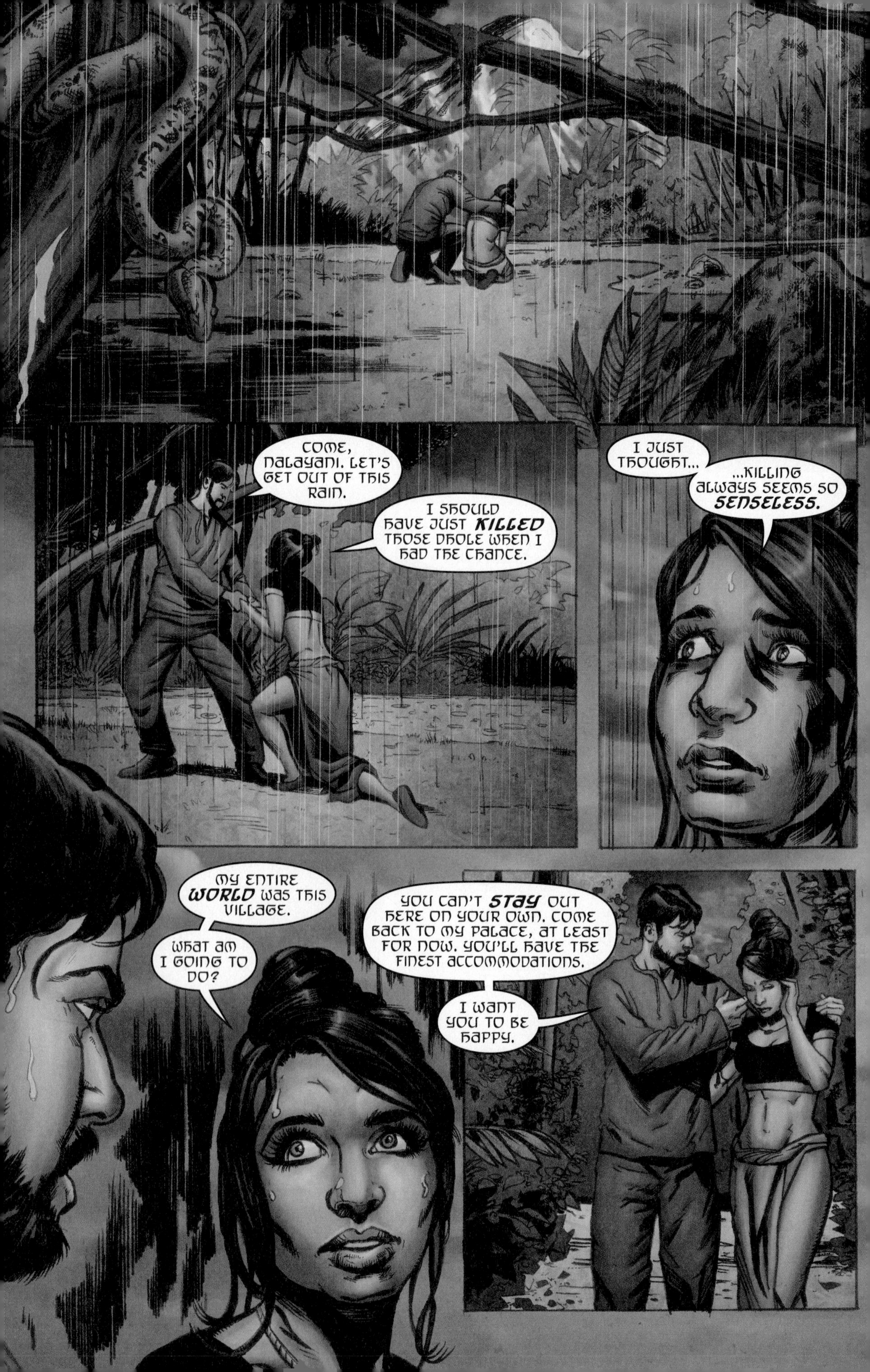
COME, NALAYANI. LET'S GET OUT OF THIS RAIN.
I SHOULD HAVE JUST KILLED THOSE DHOLE WHEN I HAD THE CHANCE.
I JUST THOUGHT...
...KILLING ALWAYS SEEMS SO SENSELESS.
MY ENTIRE WORLD WAS THIS VILLAGE.
WHAT AM I GOING TO DO?
YOU CAN'T STAY OUT HERE ON YOUR OWN. COME BACK TO MY PALACE, AT LEAST FOR NOW. YOU'LL HAVE THE FINEST ACCOMMODATIONS.
I WANT YOU TO BE HAPPY.

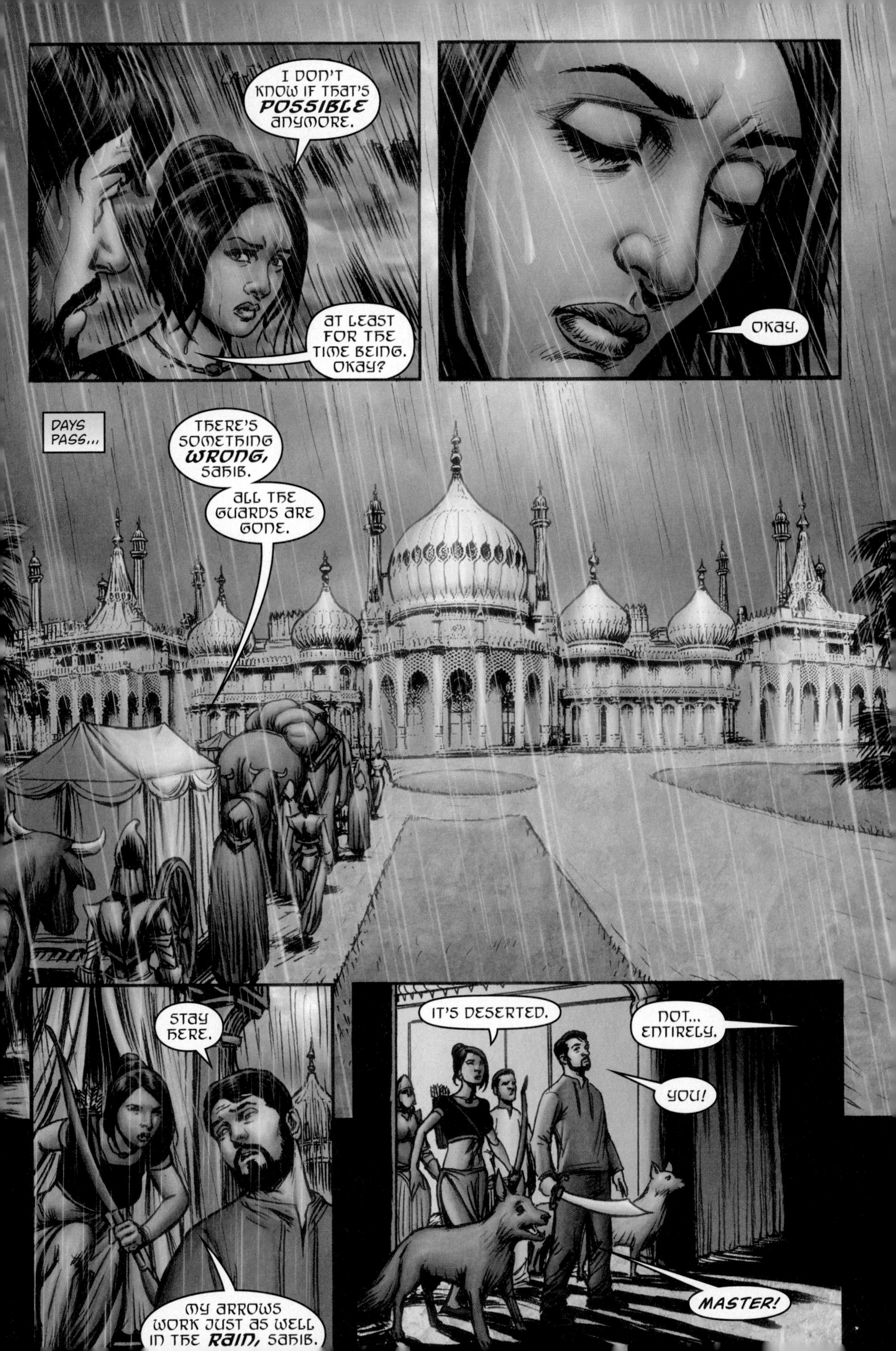
I DON'T KNOW IF THAT'S POSSIBLE ANYMORE.
AT LEAST FOR THE TIME BEING. OKAY?
OKAY.
DAYS PASS...
THERE'S SOMETHING WRONG, SAHIB.
ALL THE GUARDS ARE GONE.
STAY HERE.
MY ARROWS WORK JUST AS WELL IN THE RAIN, SAHIB.
IT'S DESERTED.
NOT... ENTIRELY.
YOU!
MASTER!

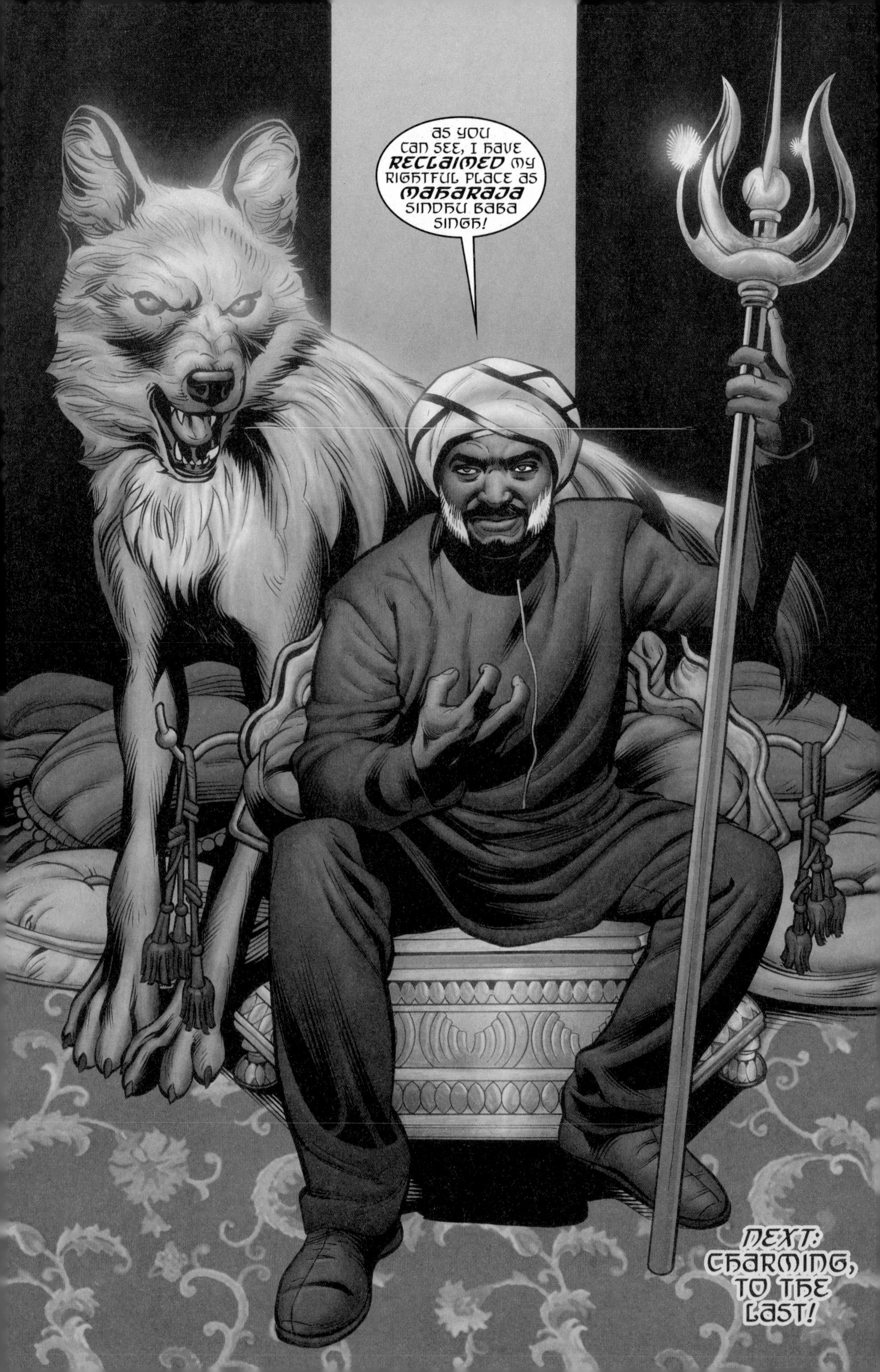
AS YOU CAN SEE, I HAVE RECLAIMED MY RIGHTFUL PLACE AS MAHARAJA SINDHU BABA SINGH!
NEXT: CHARMING, TO THE LAST!

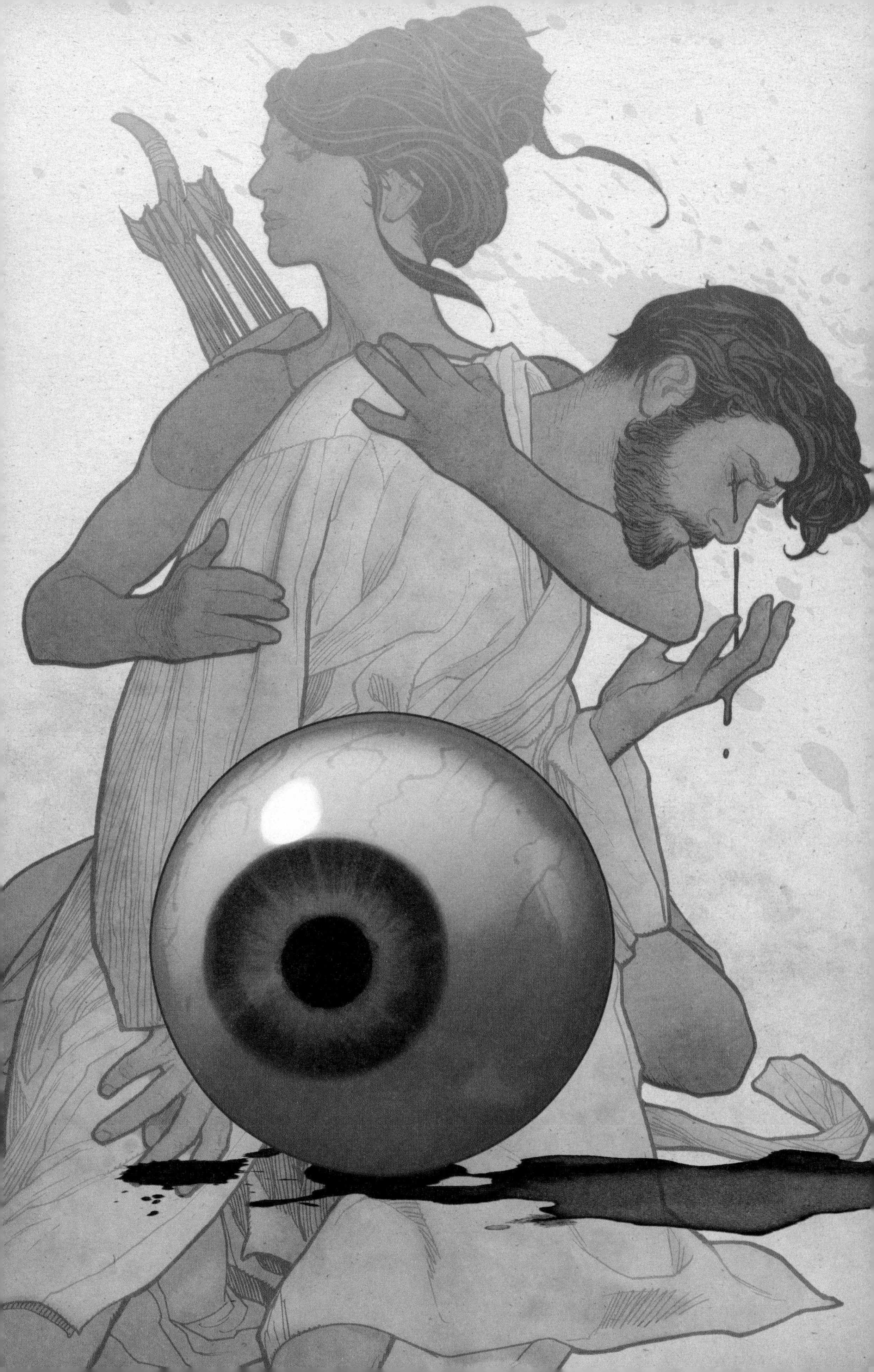

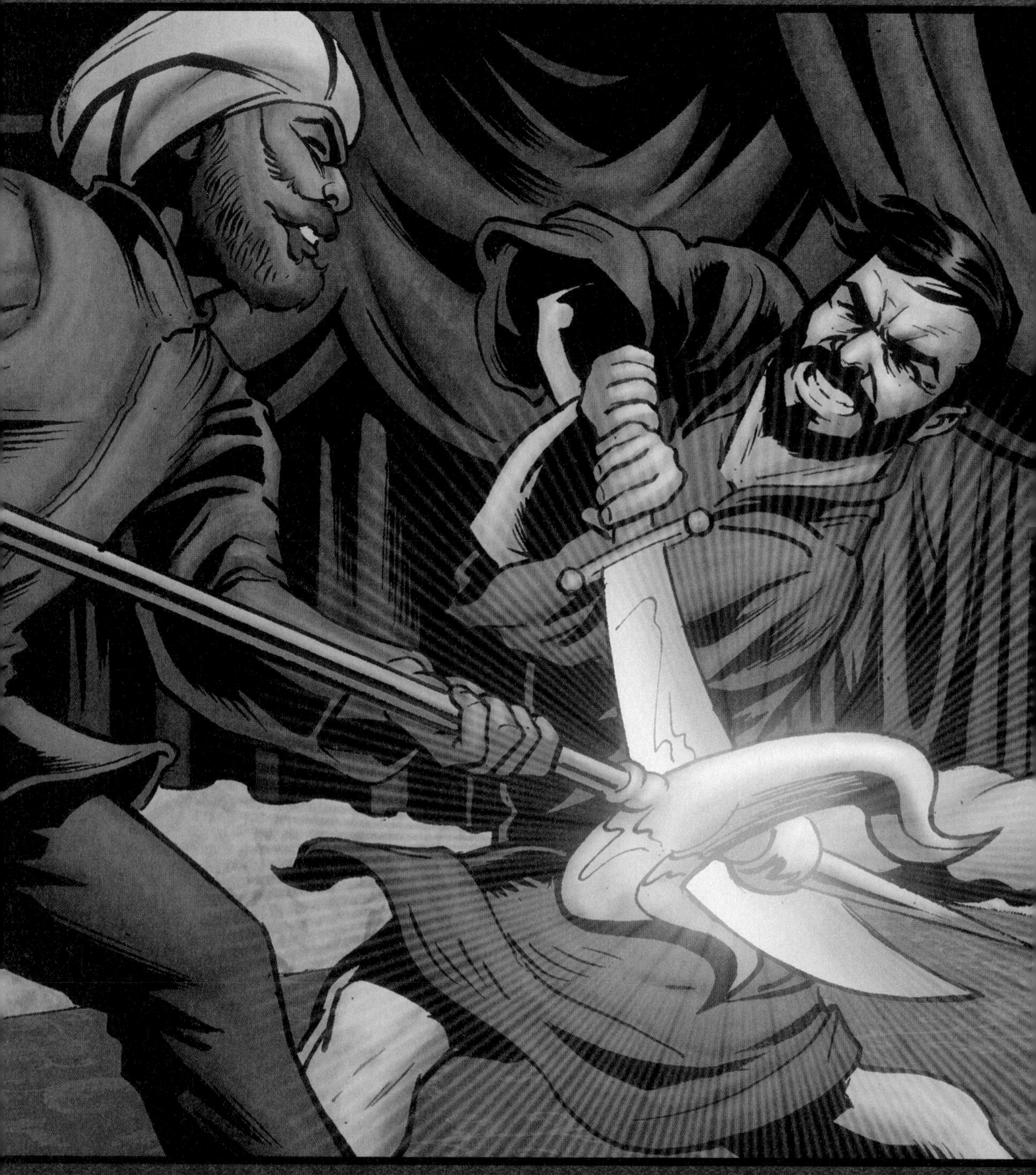

"That's a nice story.
I'll be sure to write it down once you're dead."

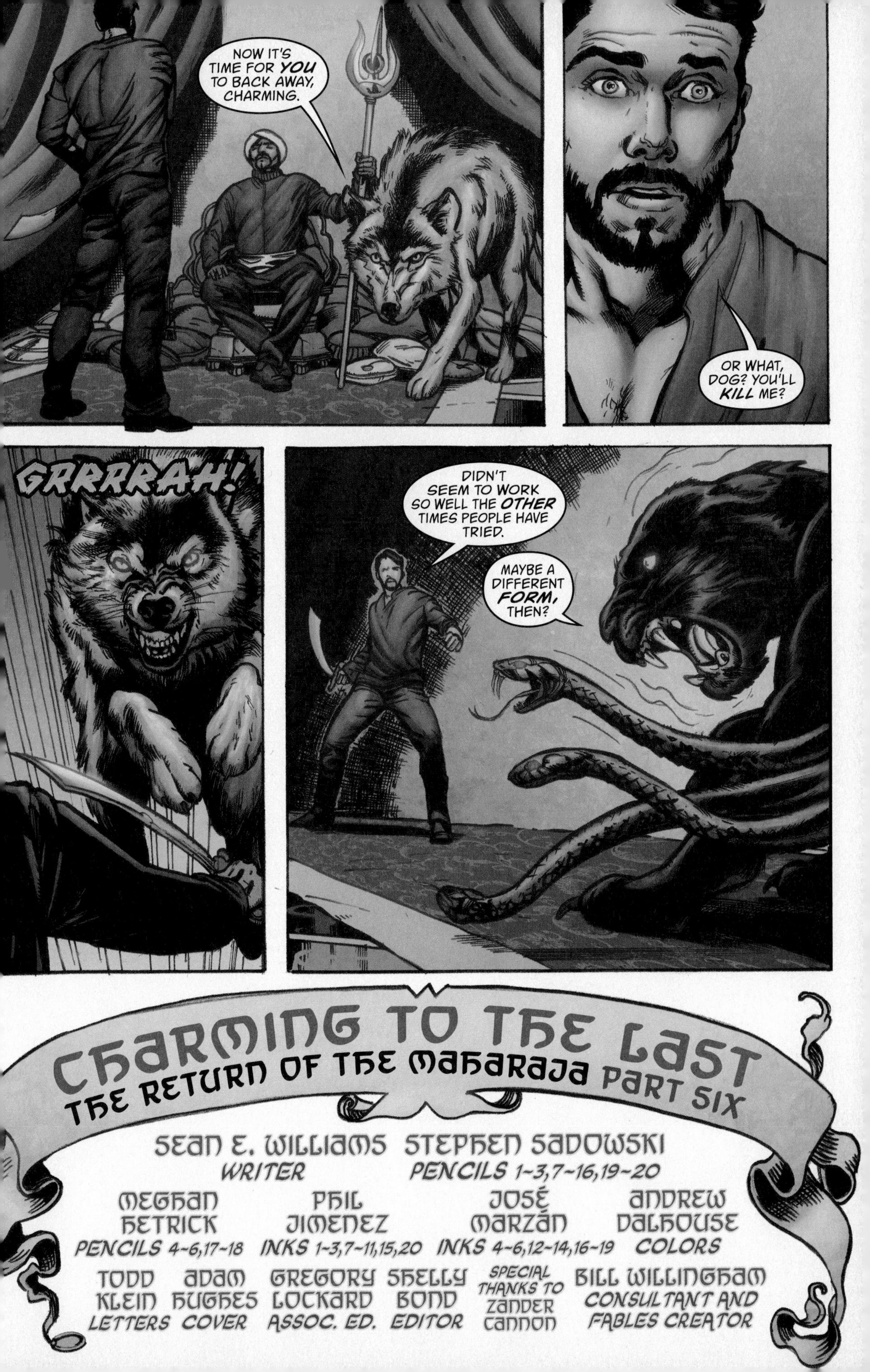
NOW IT'S TIME FOR YOU TO BACK AWAY, CHARMING.
OR WHAT, DOG? YOU'LL KILL ME?
GRRRRAH!
DIDN'T SEEM TO WORK SO WELL THE OTHER TIMES PEOPLE HAVE TRIED.
MAYBE A DIFFERENT FORM, THEN?

CHARMING TO THE LAST

THE RETURN OF THE MAHARAJA PART SIX

SEAN E. WILLIAMS *WRITER*

STEPHEN SADOWSKI *PENCILS 1~3,7~16,19~20*

MEGHAN HETRICK *PENCILS 4~6,17~18*

PHIL JIMENEZ *INKS 1~3,7~11,15,20*

JOSÉ MARZÁN *INKS 4~6,12~14,16~19*

ANDREW DALHOUSE *COLORS*

TODD KLEIN *LETTERS*

ADAM HUGHES *COVER*

GREGORY LOCKARD *ASSOC. ED.*

SHELLY BOND *EDITOR*

SPECIAL THANKS TO ZANDER CANNON

BILL WILLINGHAM *CONSULTANT AND FABLES CREATOR*

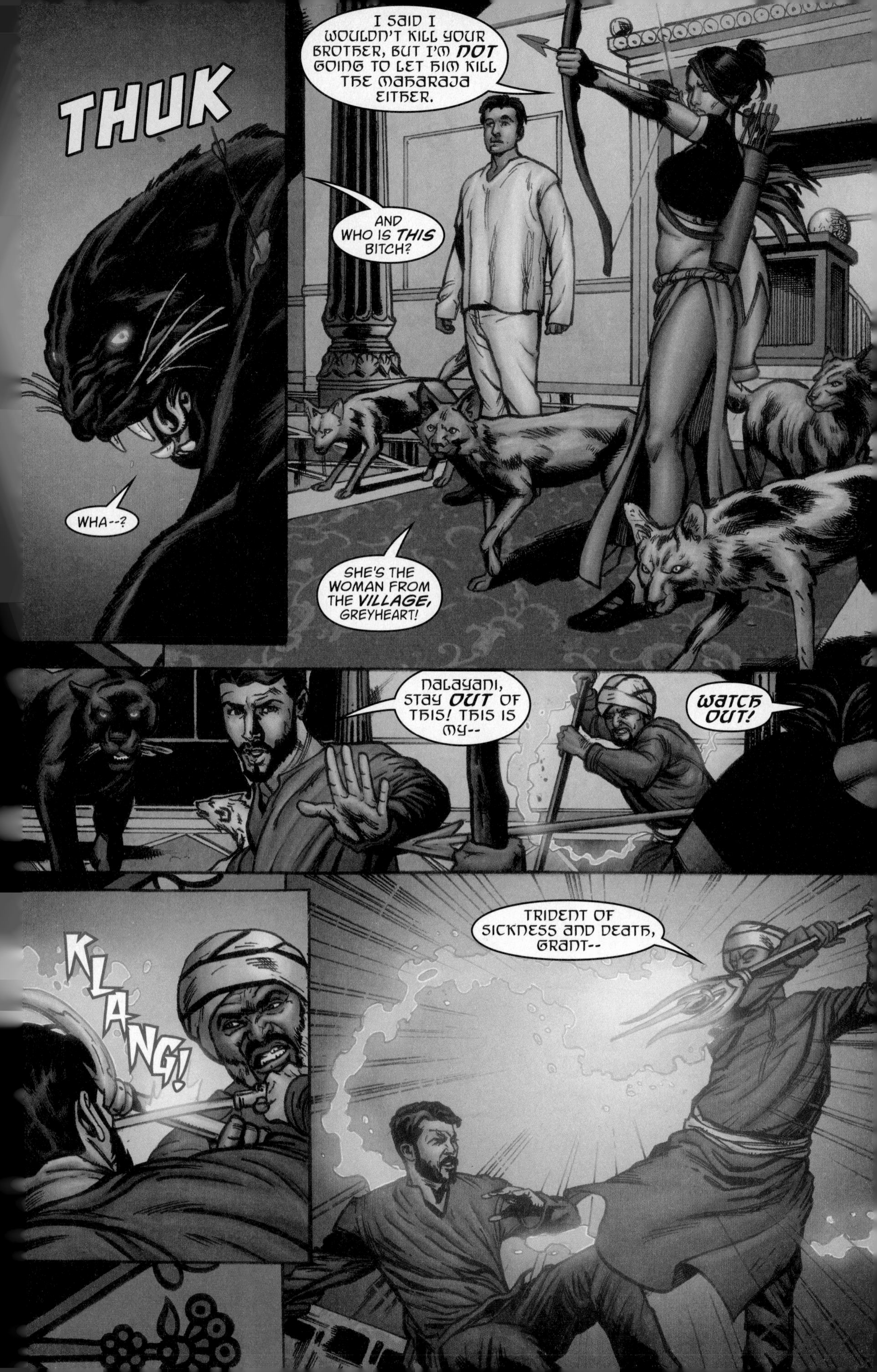
THUK
I SAID I WOULDN'T KILL YOUR BROTHER, BUT I'M NOT GOING TO LET HIM KILL THE MAHARAJA EITHER.
AND WHO IS THIS BITCH?
WHA--?
SHE'S THE WOMAN FROM THE VILLAGE, GREYHEART!
NALAYANI, STAY OUT OF THIS! THIS IS MY--
WATCH OUT!
KLANG!
TRIDENT OF SICKNESS AND DEATH, GRANT--

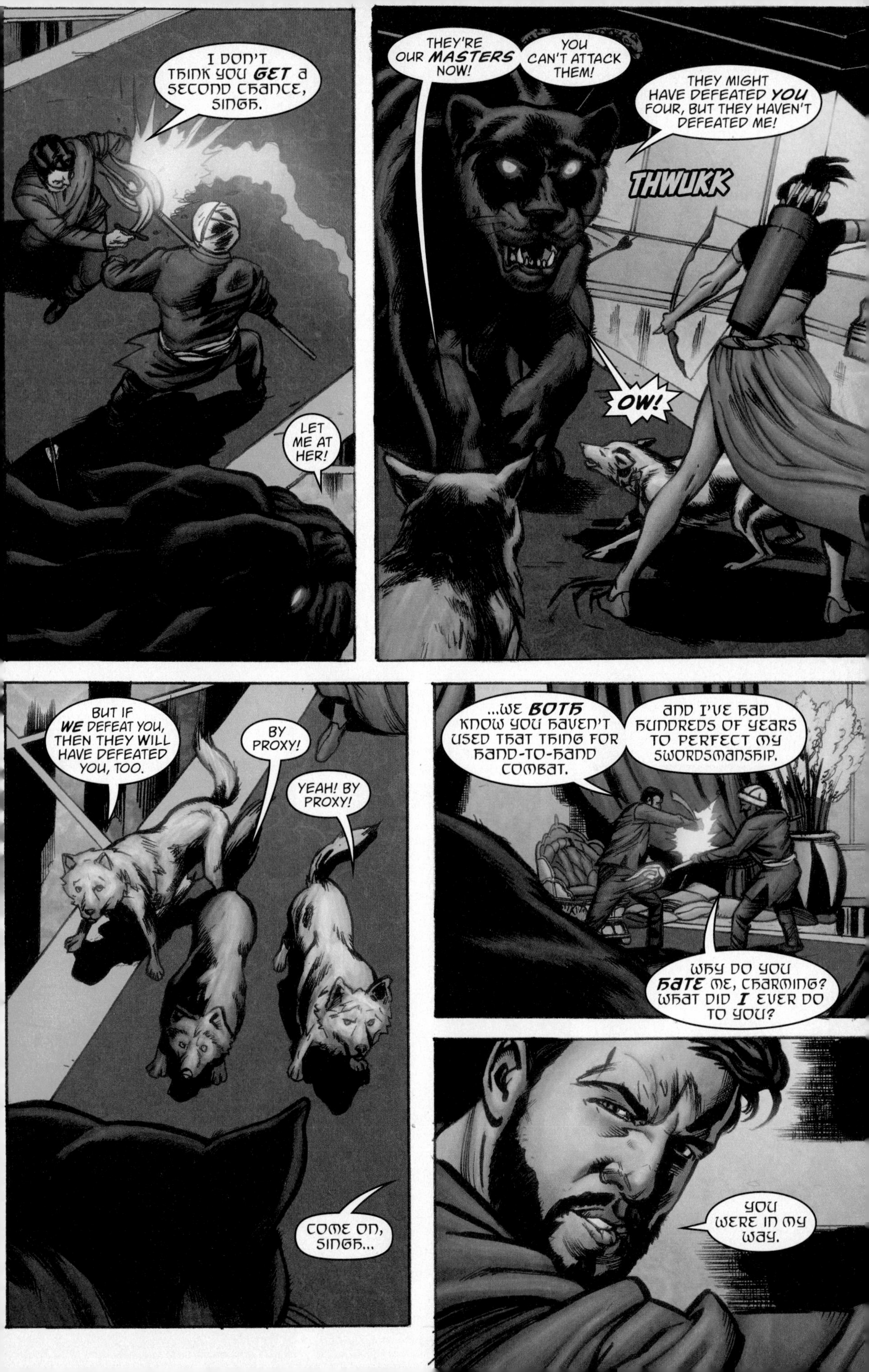

I DON'T THINK YOU GET A SECOND CHANCE, SINGH.
LET ME AT HER!
THEY'RE OUR MASTERS NOW!
YOU CAN'T ATTACK THEM!
THEY MIGHT HAVE DEFEATED YOU FOUR, BUT THEY HAVEN'T DEFEATED ME!
THWUKK
OW!
BUT IF WE DEFEAT YOU, THEN THEY WILL HAVE DEFEATED YOU, TOO.
BY PROXY!
YEAH! BY PROXY!
COME ON, SINGH...
...WE BOTH KNOW YOU HAVEN'T USED THAT THING FOR HAND-TO-HAND COMBAT.
AND I'VE HAD HUNDREDS OF YEARS TO PERFECT MY SWORDSMANSHIP.
WHY DO YOU HATE ME, CHARMING? WHAT DID I EVER DO TO YOU?
YOU WERE IN MY WAY.

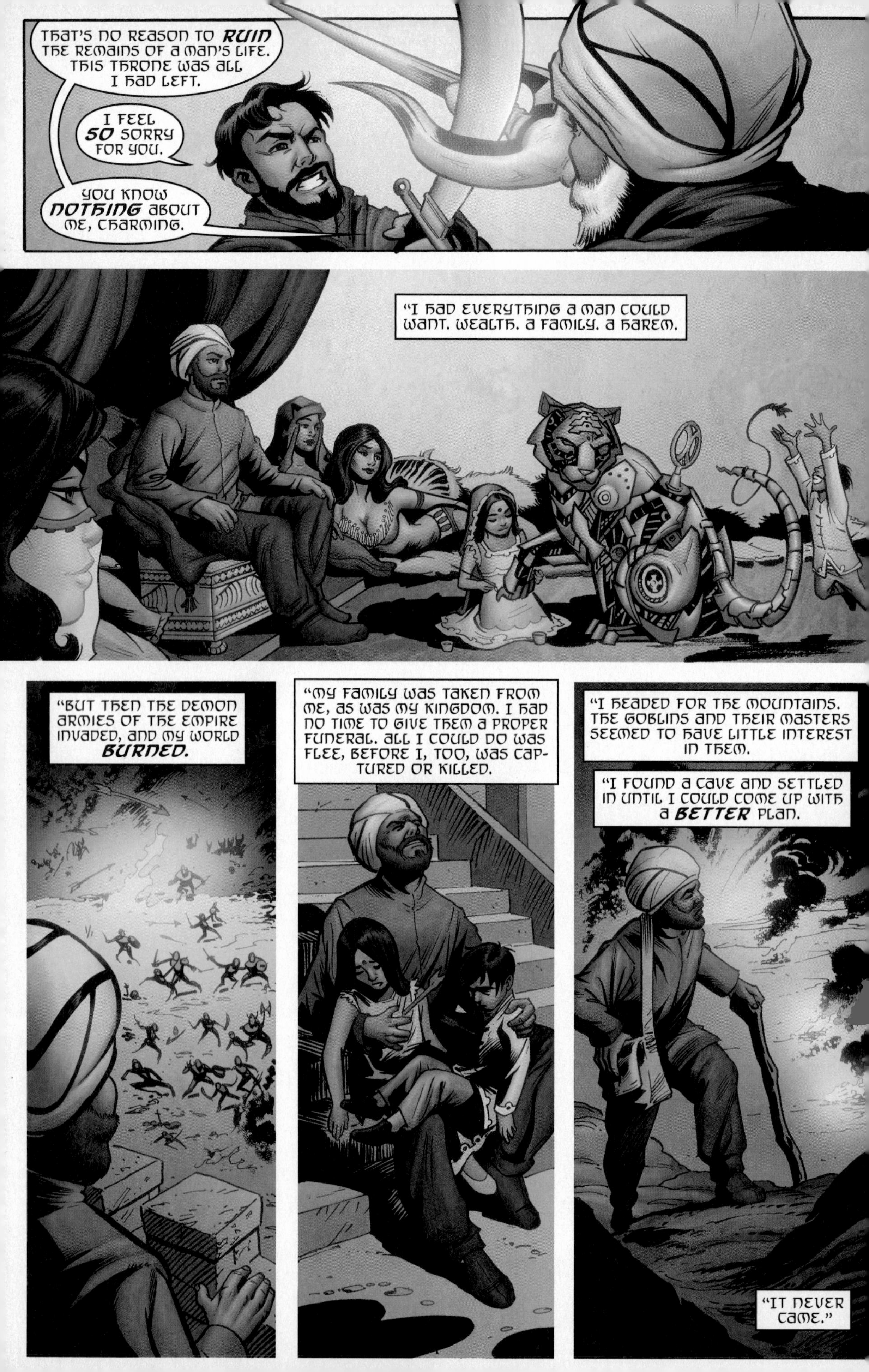
THAT'S NO REASON TO RUIN THE REMAINS OF A MAN'S LIFE. THIS THRONE WAS ALL I HAD LEFT.
I FEEL SO SORRY FOR YOU.
YOU KNOW NOTHING ABOUT ME, CHARMING.
"I HAD EVERYTHING A MAN COULD WANT. WEALTH. A FAMILY. A HAREM.
"BUT THEN THE DEMON ARMIES OF THE EMPIRE INVADED, AND MY WORLD BURNED.
"MY FAMILY WAS TAKEN FROM ME, AS WAS MY KINGDOM. I HAD NO TIME TO GIVE THEM A PROPER FUNERAL. ALL I COULD DO WAS FLEE, BEFORE I, TOO, WAS CAPTURED OR KILLED.
"I HEADED FOR THE MOUNTAINS. THE GOBLINS AND THEIR MASTERS SEEMED TO HAVE LITTLE INTEREST IN THEM.
"I FOUND A CAVE AND SETTLED IN UNTIL I COULD COME UP WITH A BETTER PLAN.
"IT NEVER CAME."

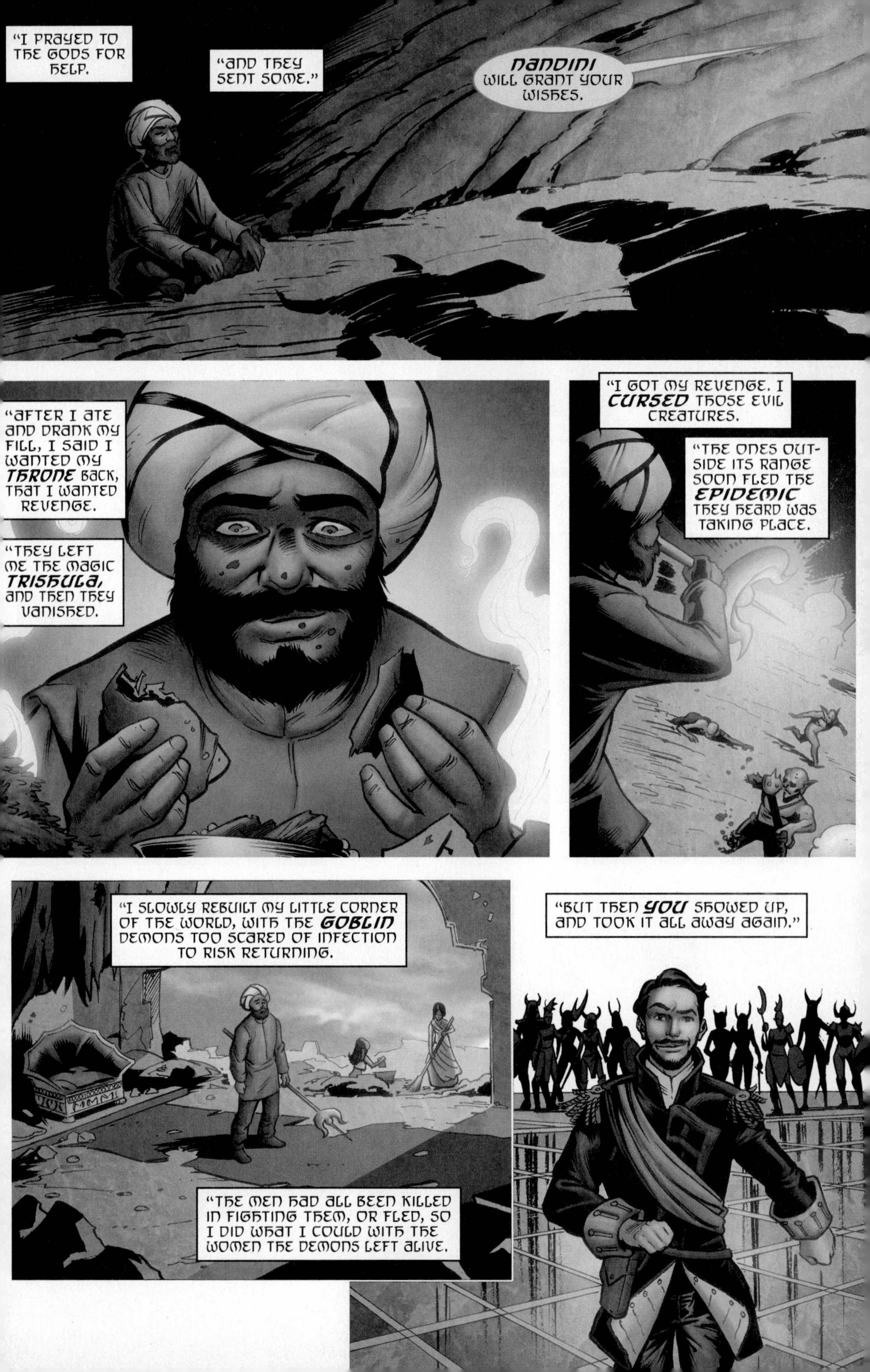
"I PRAYED TO THE GODS FOR HELP.
"AND THEY SENT SOME."
NANDINI WILL GRANT YOUR WISHES.
"AFTER I ATE AND DRANK MY FILL, I SAID I WANTED MY THRONE BACK, THAT I WANTED REVENGE.
"THEY LEFT ME THE MAGIC TRISHULA, AND THEN THEY VANISHED.
"I GOT MY REVENGE. I CURSED THOSE EVIL CREATURES.
"THE ONES OUT-SIDE ITS RANGE SOON FLED THE EPIDEMIC THEY HEARD WAS TAKING PLACE.
"I SLOWLY REBUILT MY LITTLE CORNER OF THE WORLD, WITH THE GOBLIN DEMONS TOO SCARED OF INFECTION TO RISK RETURNING.
"THE MEN HAD ALL BEEN KILLED IN FIGHTING THEM, OR FLED, SO I DID WHAT I COULD WITH THE WOMEN THE DEMONS LEFT ALIVE.
"BUT THEN YOU SHOWED UP, AND TOOK IT ALL AWAY AGAIN."

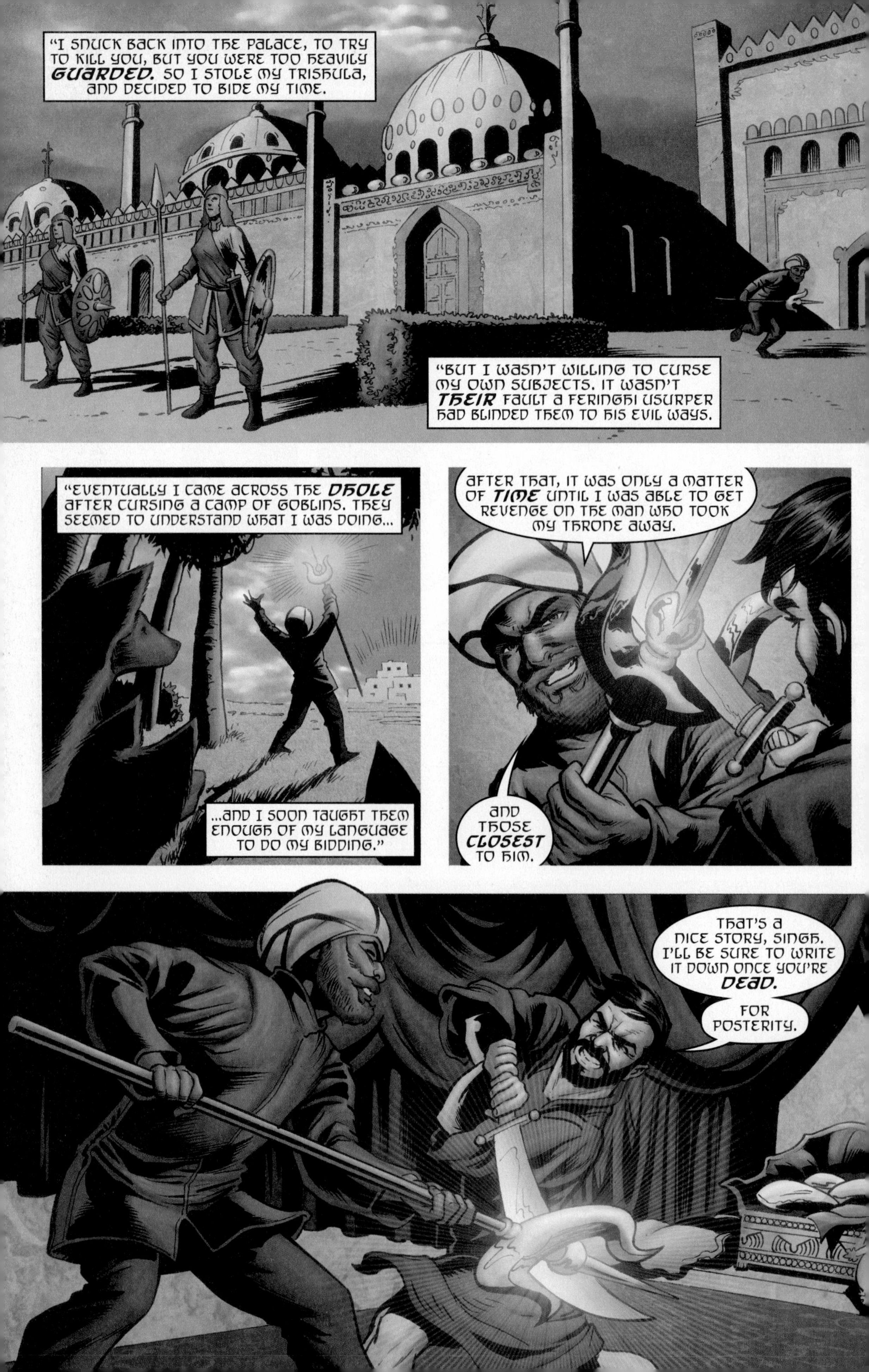
"I SNUCK BACK INTO THE PALACE, TO TRY TO KILL YOU, BUT YOU WERE TOO HEAVILY GUARDED. SO I STOLE MY TRISHULA, AND DECIDED TO BIDE MY TIME.
"BUT I WASN'T WILLING TO CURSE MY OWN SUBJECTS. IT WASN'T THEIR FAULT A FERINGHI USURPER HAD BLINDED THEM TO HIS EVIL WAYS.
"EVENTUALLY I CAME ACROSS THE DHOLE AFTER CURSING A CAMP OF GOBLINS. THEY SEEMED TO UNDERSTAND WHAT I WAS DOING...
...AND I SOON TAUGHT THEM ENOUGH OF MY LANGUAGE TO DO MY BIDDING."
AFTER THAT, IT WAS ONLY A MATTER OF TIME UNTIL I WAS ABLE TO GET REVENGE ON THE MAN WHO TOOK MY THRONE AWAY.
AND THOSE CLOSEST TO HIM.
THAT'S A NICE STORY, SINGH. I'LL BE SURE TO WRITE IT DOWN ONCE YOU'RE DEAD.
FOR POSTERITY.

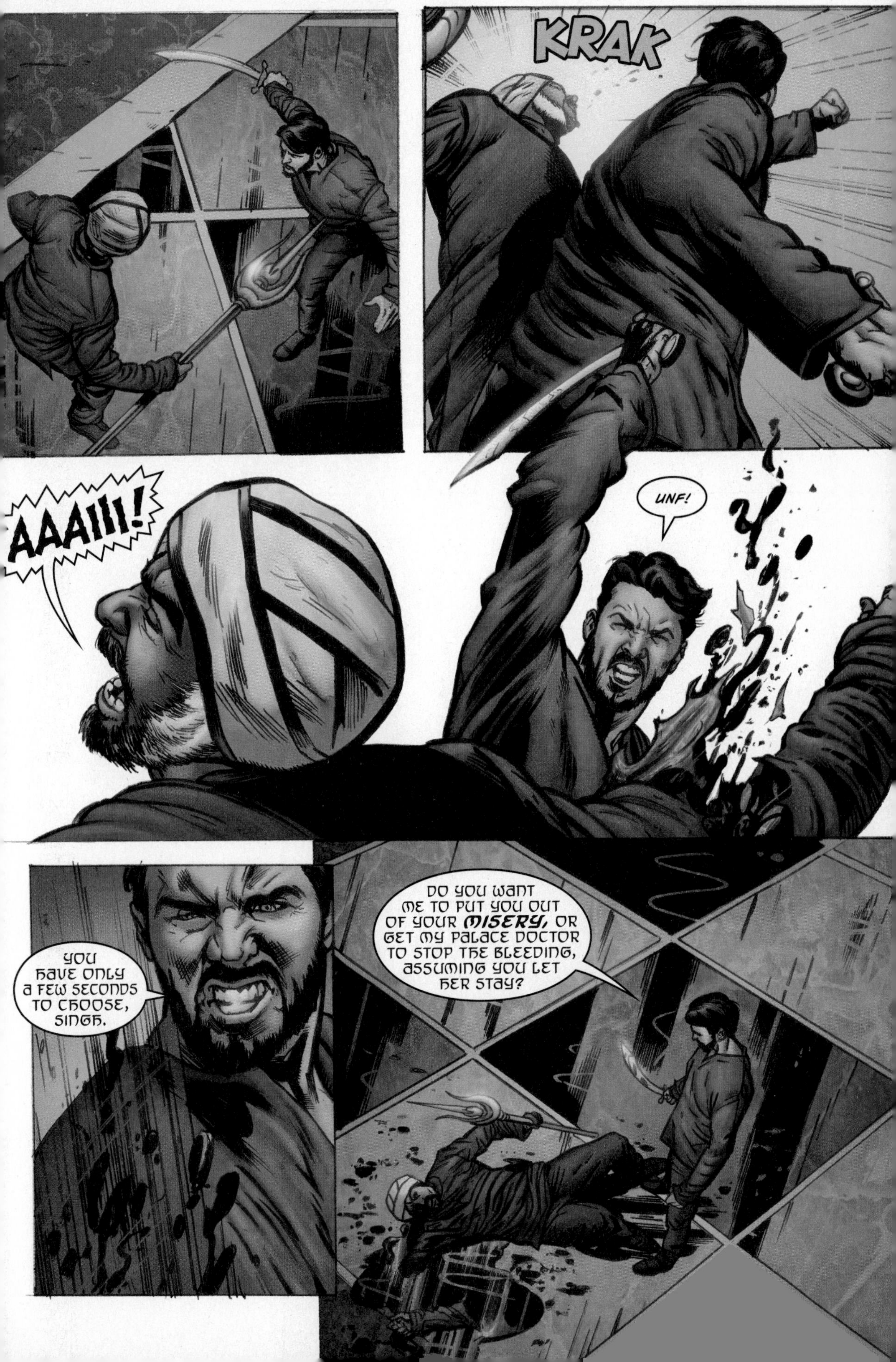
KRAK
AAAIII!
UNF!
YOU HAVE ONLY A FEW SECONDS TO CHOOSE, SINGH.
DO YOU WANT ME TO PUT YOU OUT OF YOUR MISERY, OR GET MY PALACE DOCTOR TO STOP THE BLEEDING, ASSUMING YOU LET HER STAY?

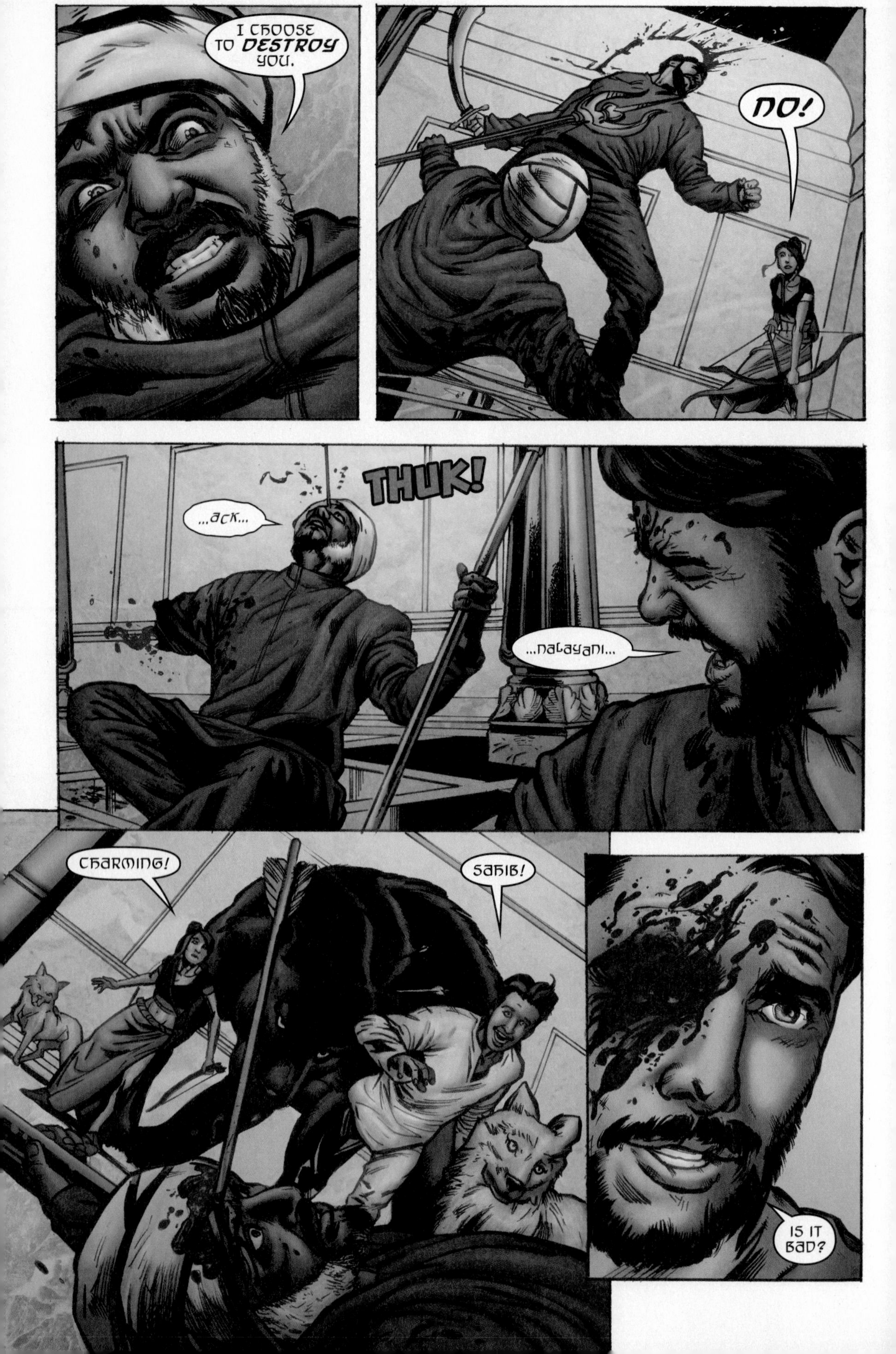

I CHOOSE TO DESTROY YOU.
NO!
THUK!
...ACK...
...NALAYANI...
CHARMING!
SAHIB!
IS IT BAD?

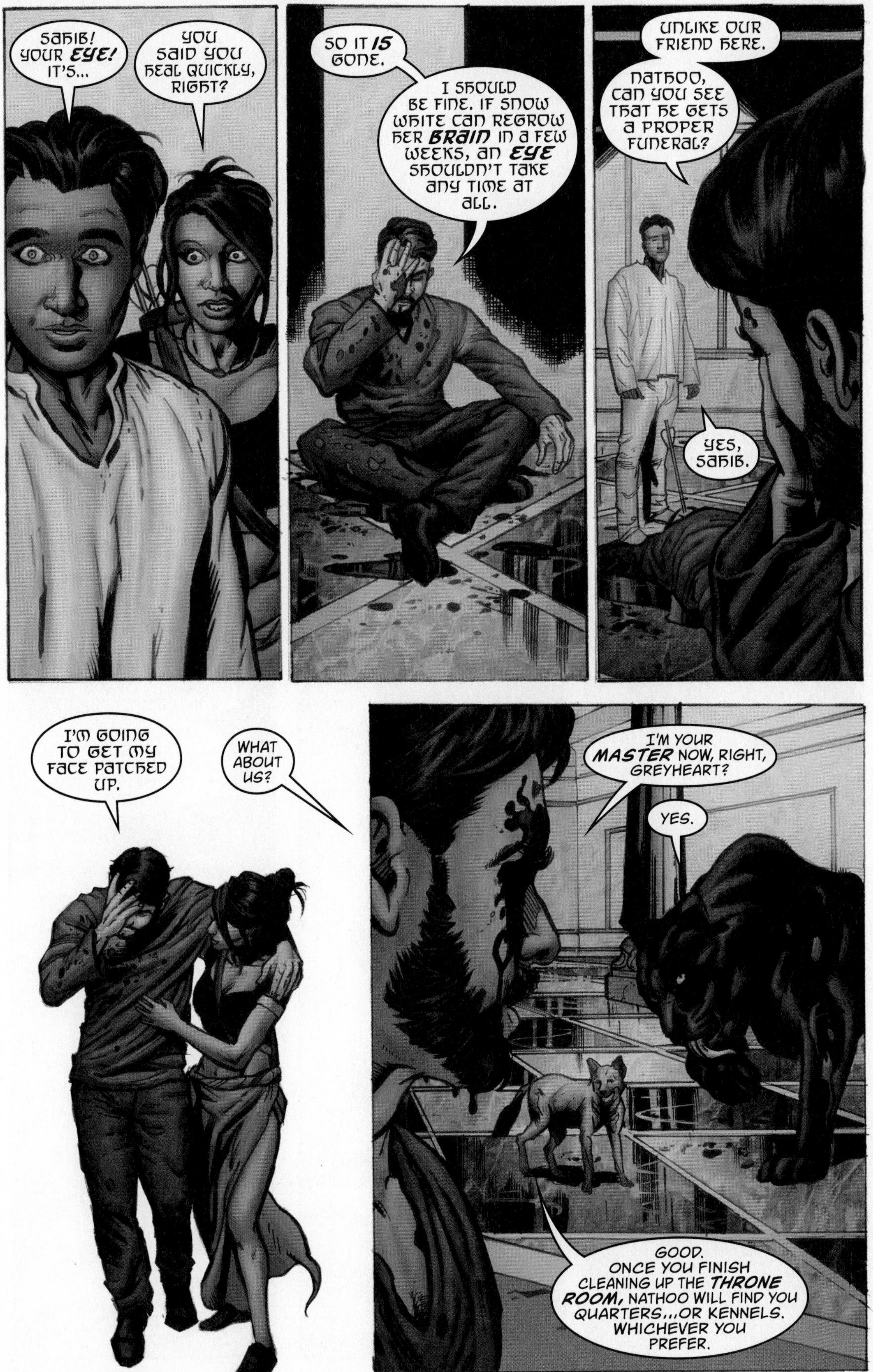
SAHIB! YOUR EYE! IT'S...
YOU SAID YOU HEAL QUICKLY, RIGHT?
SO IT IS GONE.
I SHOULD BE FINE. IF SNOW WHITE CAN REGROW HER BRAIN IN A FEW WEEKS, AN EYE SHOULDN'T TAKE ANY TIME AT ALL.
UNLIKE OUR FRIEND HERE.
NATHOO, CAN YOU SEE THAT HE GETS A PROPER FUNERAL?
YES, SAHIB.
I'M GOING TO GET MY FACE PATCHED UP.
WHAT ABOUT US?
I'M YOUR MASTER NOW, RIGHT, GREYHEART?
YES.
GOOD. ONCE YOU FINISH CLEANING UP THE THRONE ROOM, NATHOO WILL FIND YOU QUARTERS...OR KENNELS. WHICHEVER YOU PREFER.

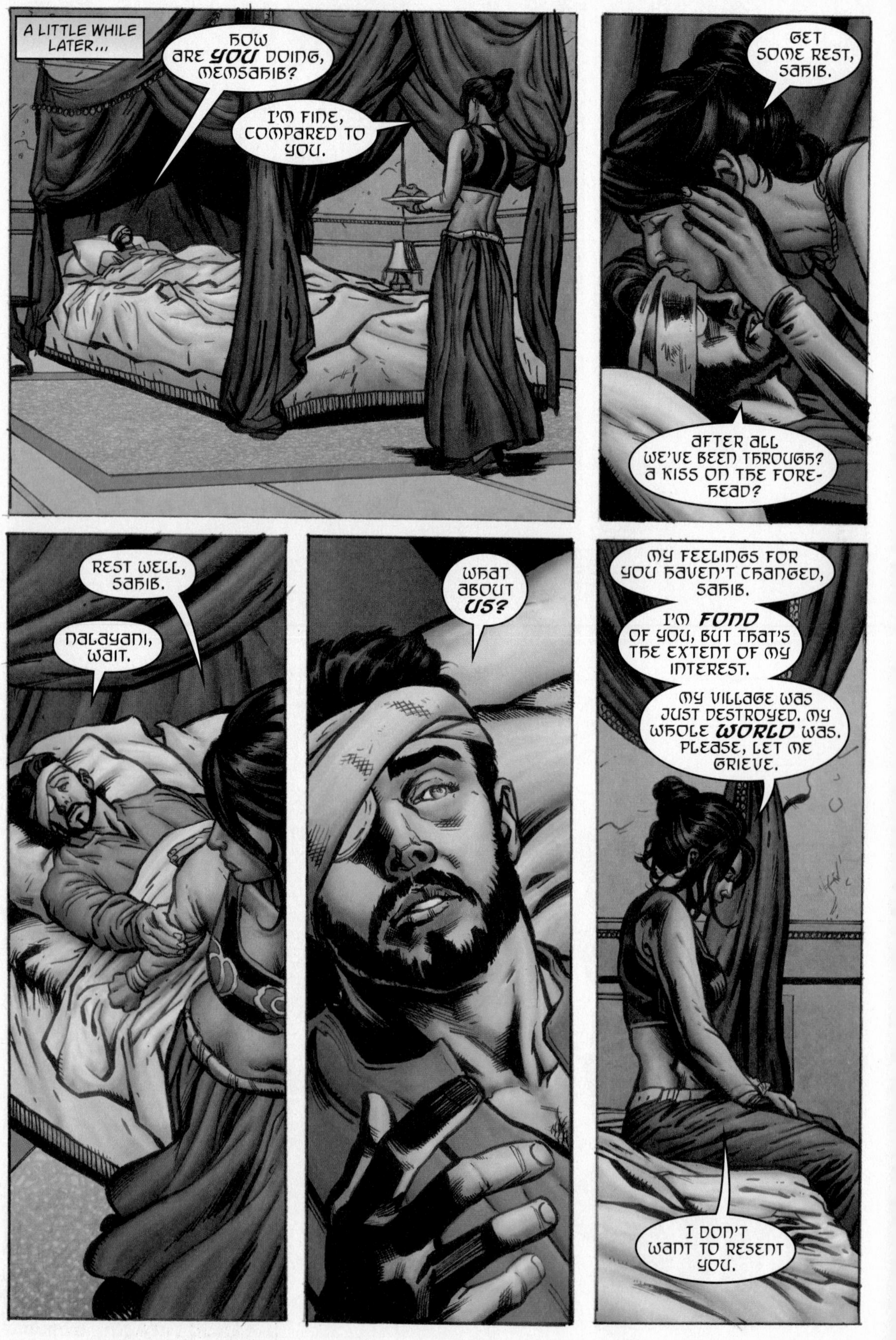
A LITTLE WHILE LATER...
HOW ARE YOU DOING, MEMSAHIB?
I'M FINE, COMPARED TO YOU.
GET SOME REST, SAHIB.
AFTER ALL WE'VE BEEN THROUGH? A KISS ON THE FORE-HEAD?
REST WELL, SAHIB.
NALAYANI, WAIT.
WHAT ABOUT US?
MY FEELINGS FOR YOU HAVEN'T CHANGED, SAHIB.
I'M FOND OF YOU, BUT THAT'S THE EXTENT OF MY INTEREST.
MY VILLAGE WAS JUST DESTROYED. MY WHOLE WORLD WAS. PLEASE, LET ME GRIEVE.
I DON'T WANT TO RESENT YOU.

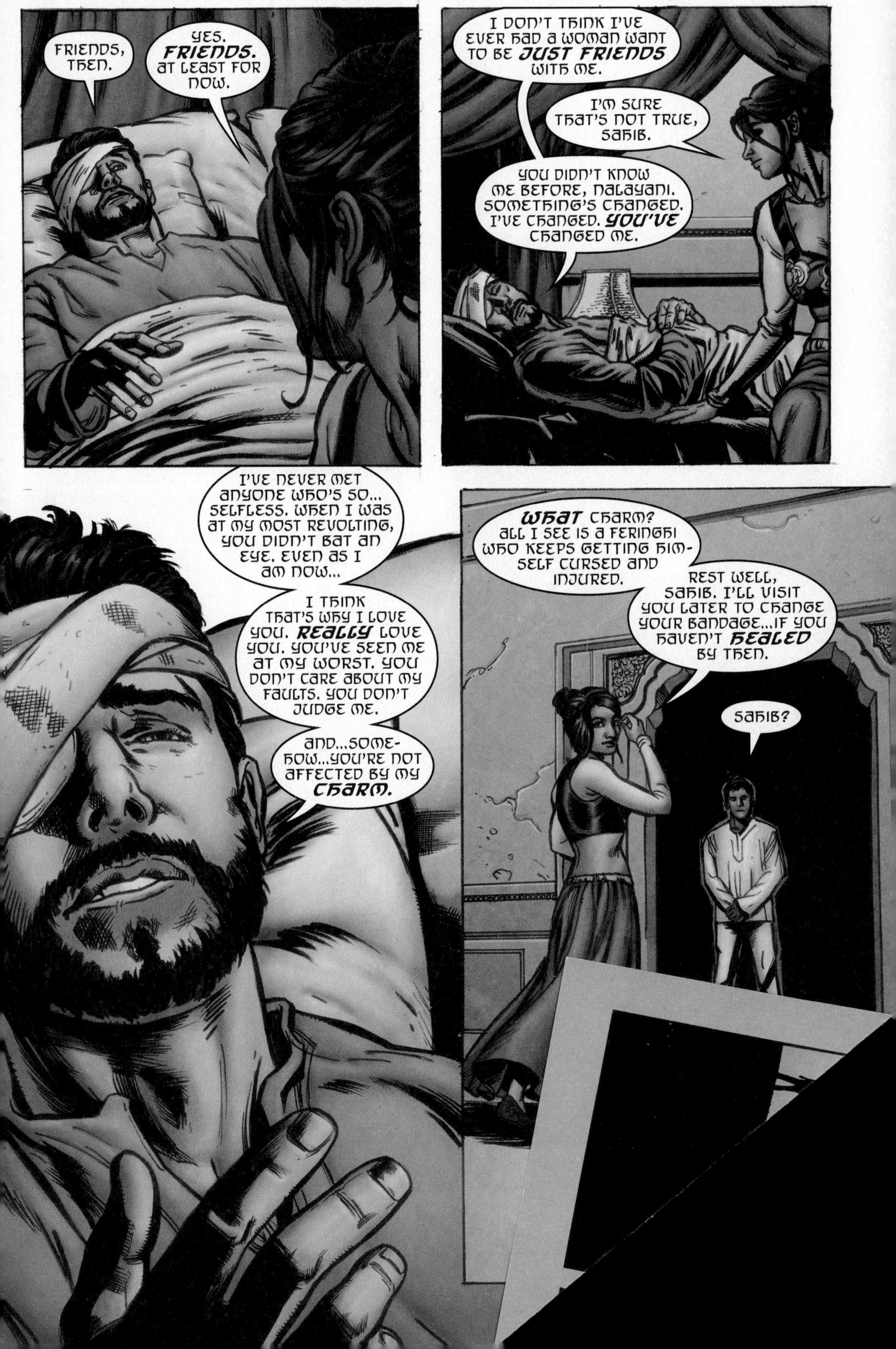
FRIENDS, THEN.
YES. FRIENDS. AT LEAST FOR NOW.
I DON'T THINK I'VE EVER HAD A WOMAN WANT TO BE JUST FRIENDS WITH ME.
I'M SURE THAT'S NOT TRUE, SAHIB.
YOU DIDN'T KNOW ME BEFORE, NALAYANI. SOMETHING'S CHANGED. I'VE CHANGED. YOU'VE CHANGED ME.
I'VE NEVER MET ANYONE WHO'S SO... SELFLESS. WHEN I WAS AT MY MOST REVOLTING, YOU DIDN'T BAT AN EYE. EVEN AS I AM NOW...
I THINK THAT'S WHY I LOVE YOU. REALLY LOVE YOU. YOU'VE SEEN ME AT MY WORST. YOU DON'T CARE ABOUT MY FAULTS. YOU DON'T JUDGE ME.
AND...SOME-HOW...YOU'RE NOT AFFECTED BY MY CHARM.
WHAT CHARM? ALL I SEE IS A FERINGHI WHO KEEPS GETTING HIM-SELF CURSED AND INJURED.
REST WELL, SAHIB. I'LL VISIT YOU LATER TO CHANGE YOUR BANDAGE...IF YOU HAVEN'T HEALED BY THEN.
SAHIB?

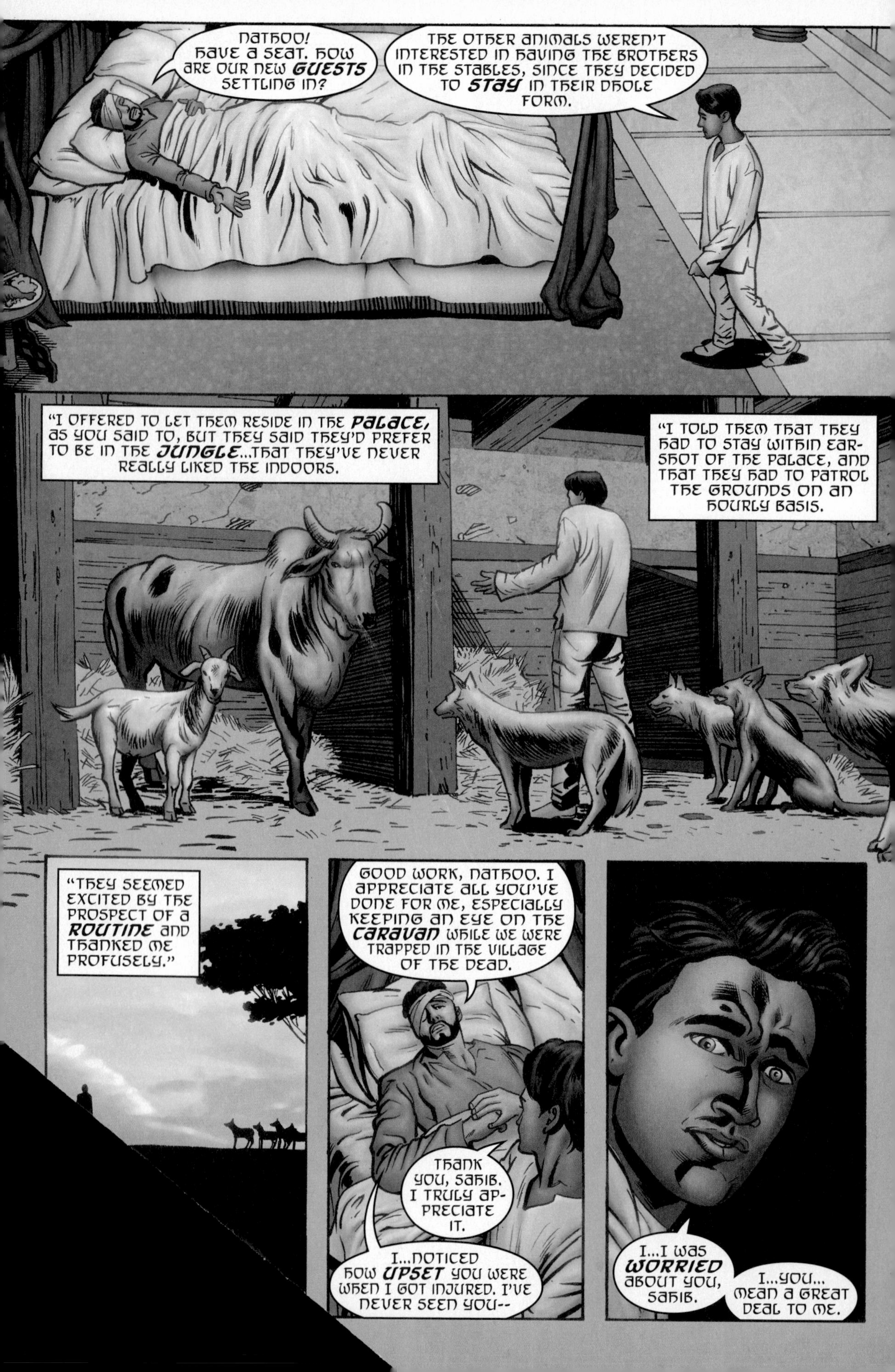
NATHOO! HAVE A SEAT. HOW ARE OUR NEW GUESTS SETTLING IN?
THE OTHER ANIMALS WEREN'T INTERESTED IN HAVING THE BROTHERS IN THE STABLES, SINCE THEY DECIDED TO STAY IN THEIR DHOLE FORM.
"I OFFERED TO LET THEM RESIDE IN THE PALACE, AS YOU SAID TO, BUT THEY SAID THEY'D PREFER TO BE IN THE JUNGLE...THAT THEY'VE NEVER REALLY LIKED THE INDOORS.
"I TOLD THEM THAT THEY HAD TO STAY WITHIN EAR-SHOT OF THE PALACE, AND THAT THEY HAD TO PATROL THE GROUNDS ON AN HOURLY BASIS.
"THEY SEEMED EXCITED BY THE PROSPECT OF A ROUTINE AND THANKED ME PROFUSELY."
GOOD WORK, NATHOO. I APPRECIATE ALL YOU'VE DONE FOR ME, ESPECIALLY KEEPING AN EYE ON THE CARAVAN WHILE WE WERE TRAPPED IN THE VILLAGE OF THE DEAD.
THANK YOU, SAHIB. I TRULY AP-PRECIATE IT.
I...NOTICED HOW UPSET YOU WERE WHEN I GOT INJURED. I'VE NEVER SEEN YOU--
I...I WAS WORRIED ABOUT YOU, SAHIB.
I...YOU... MEAN A GREAT DEAL TO ME.

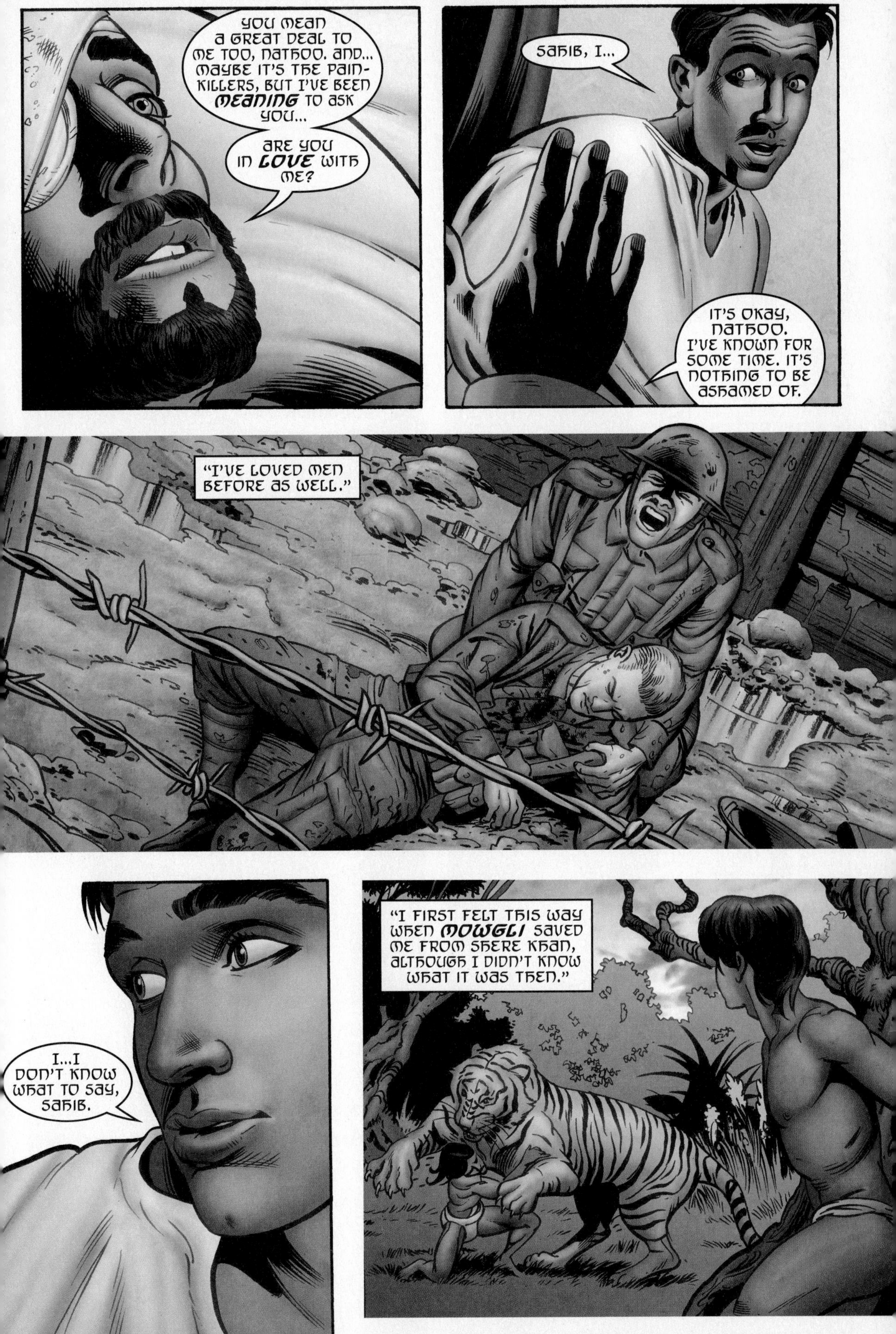
YOU MEAN A GREAT DEAL TO ME TOO, NATHOO. AND... MAYBE IT'S THE PAIN-KILLERS, BUT I'VE BEEN MEANING TO ASK YOU...
ARE YOU IN LOVE WITH ME?
SAHIB, I...
IT'S OKAY, NATHOO. I'VE KNOWN FOR SOME TIME. IT'S NOTHING TO BE ASHAMED OF.
"I'VE LOVED MEN BEFORE AS WELL."
I...I DON'T KNOW WHAT TO SAY, SAHIB.
"I FIRST FELT THIS WAY WHEN MOWGLI SAVED ME FROM SHERE KHAN, ALTHOUGH I DIDN'T KNOW WHAT IT WAS THEN."

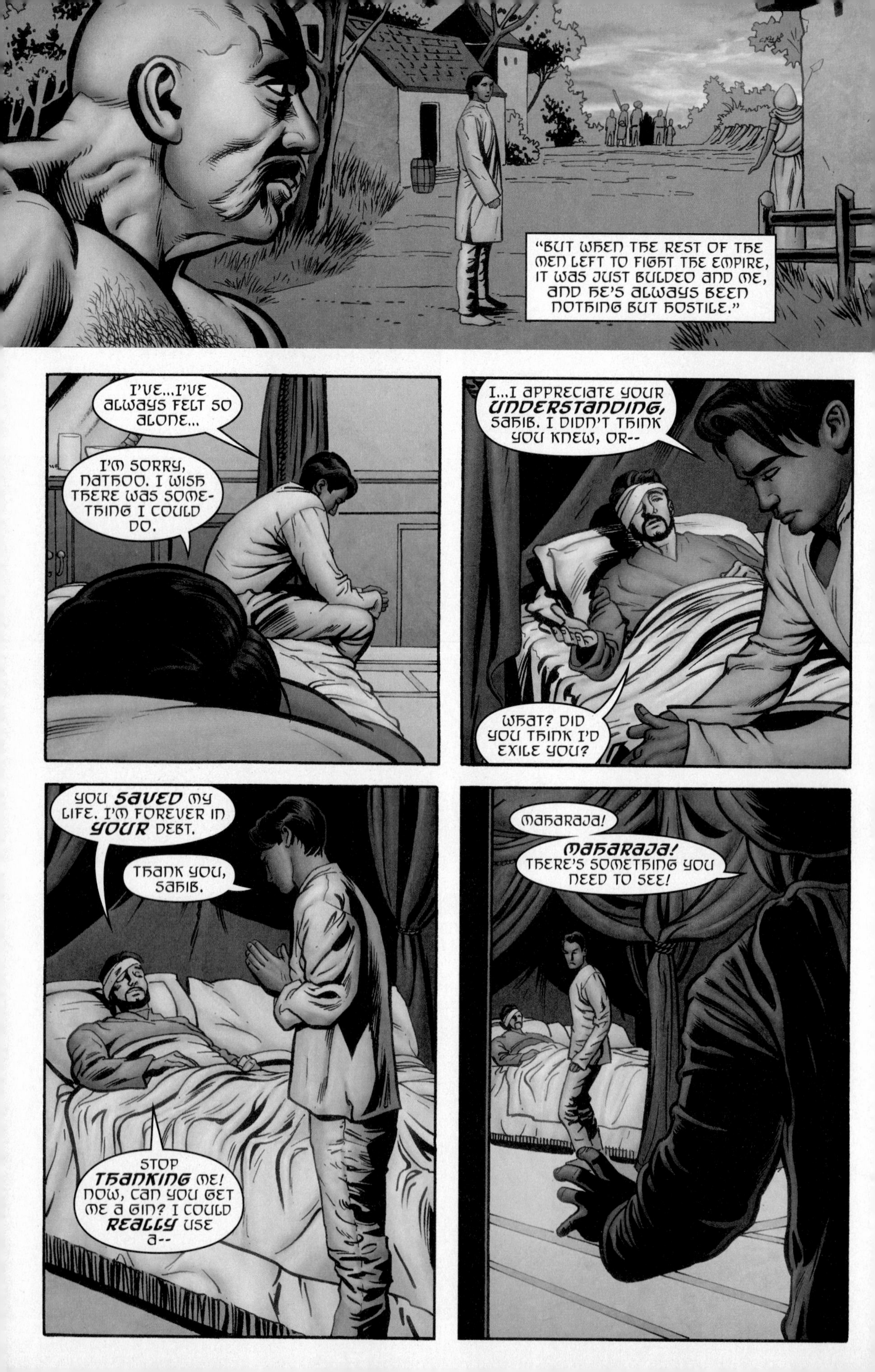
"BUT WHEN THE REST OF THE MEN LEFT TO FIGHT THE EMPIRE, IT WAS JUST BULDEO AND ME, AND HE'S ALWAYS BEEN NOTHING BUT HOSTILE."
I'VE...I'VE ALWAYS FELT SO ALONE...
I'M SORRY, NATHOO. I WISH THERE WAS SOME-THING I COULD DO.
I...I APPRECIATE YOUR UNDERSTANDING, SAHIB. I DIDN'T THINK YOU KNEW, OR--
WHAT? DID YOU THINK I'D EXILE YOU?
YOU SAVED MY LIFE. I'M FOREVER IN YOUR DEBT.
THANK YOU, SAHIB.
STOP THANKING ME! NOW, CAN YOU GET ME A GIN? I COULD REALLY USE A--
MAHARAJA!
MAHARAJA! THERE'S SOMETHING YOU NEED TO SEE!

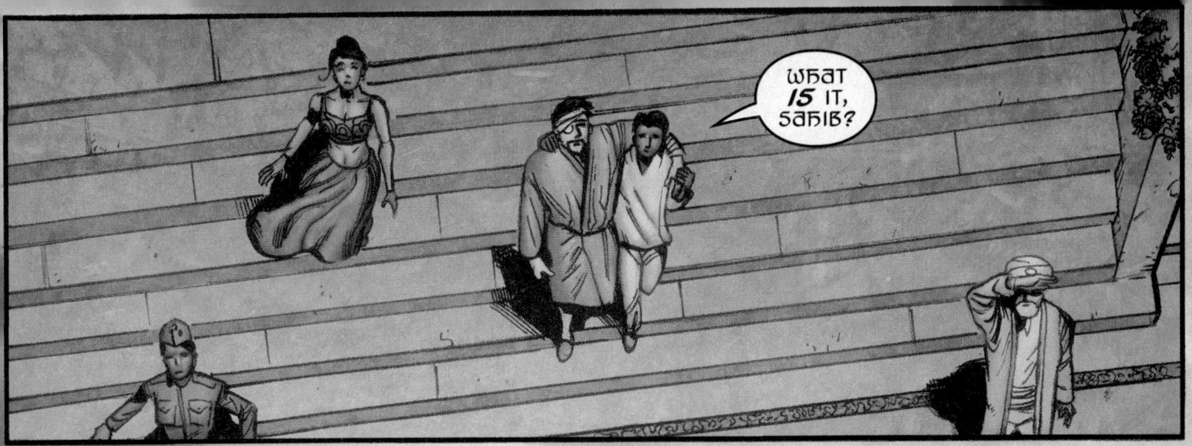
WHAT IS IT, SAHIB?

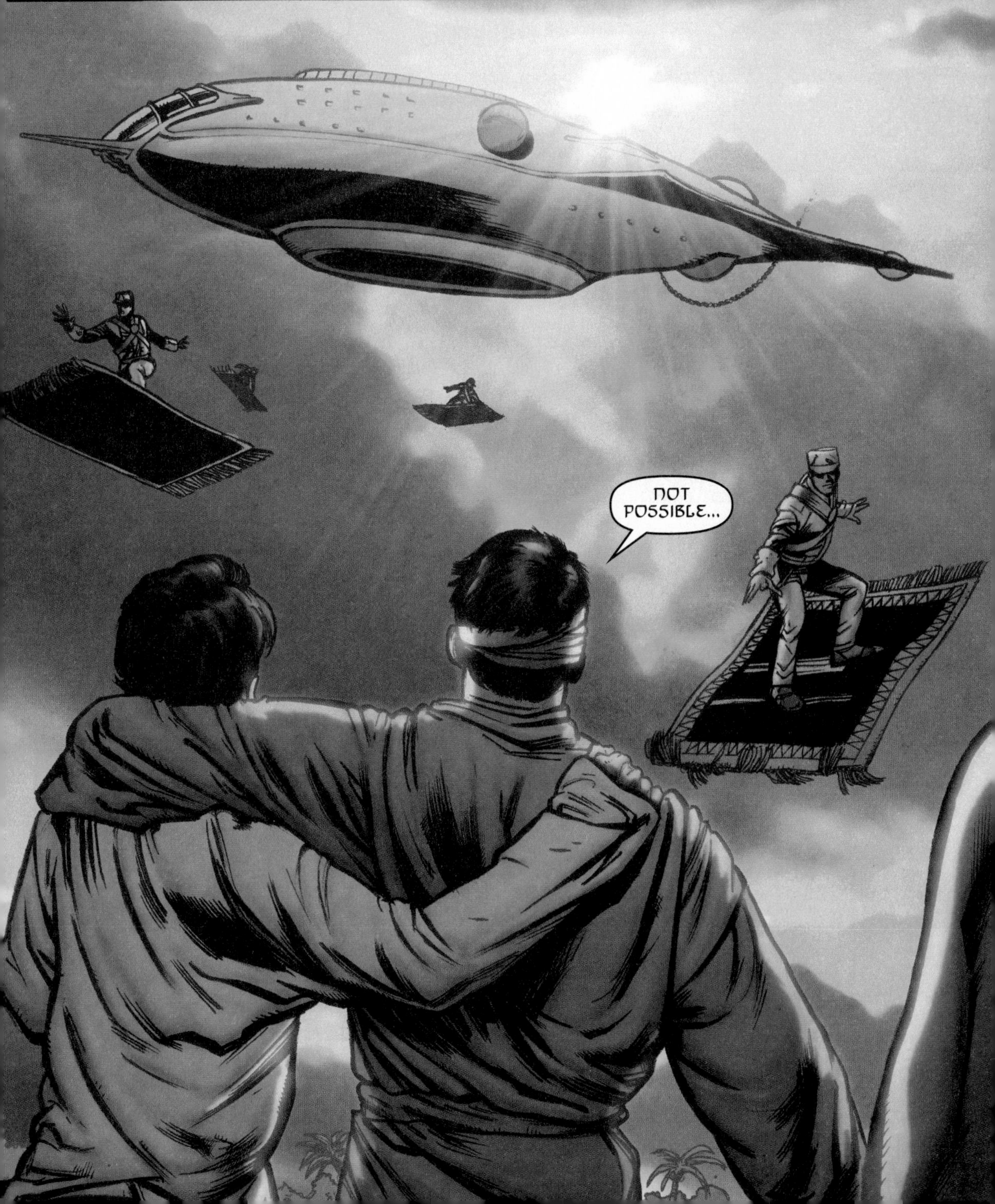
NOT POSSIBLE...

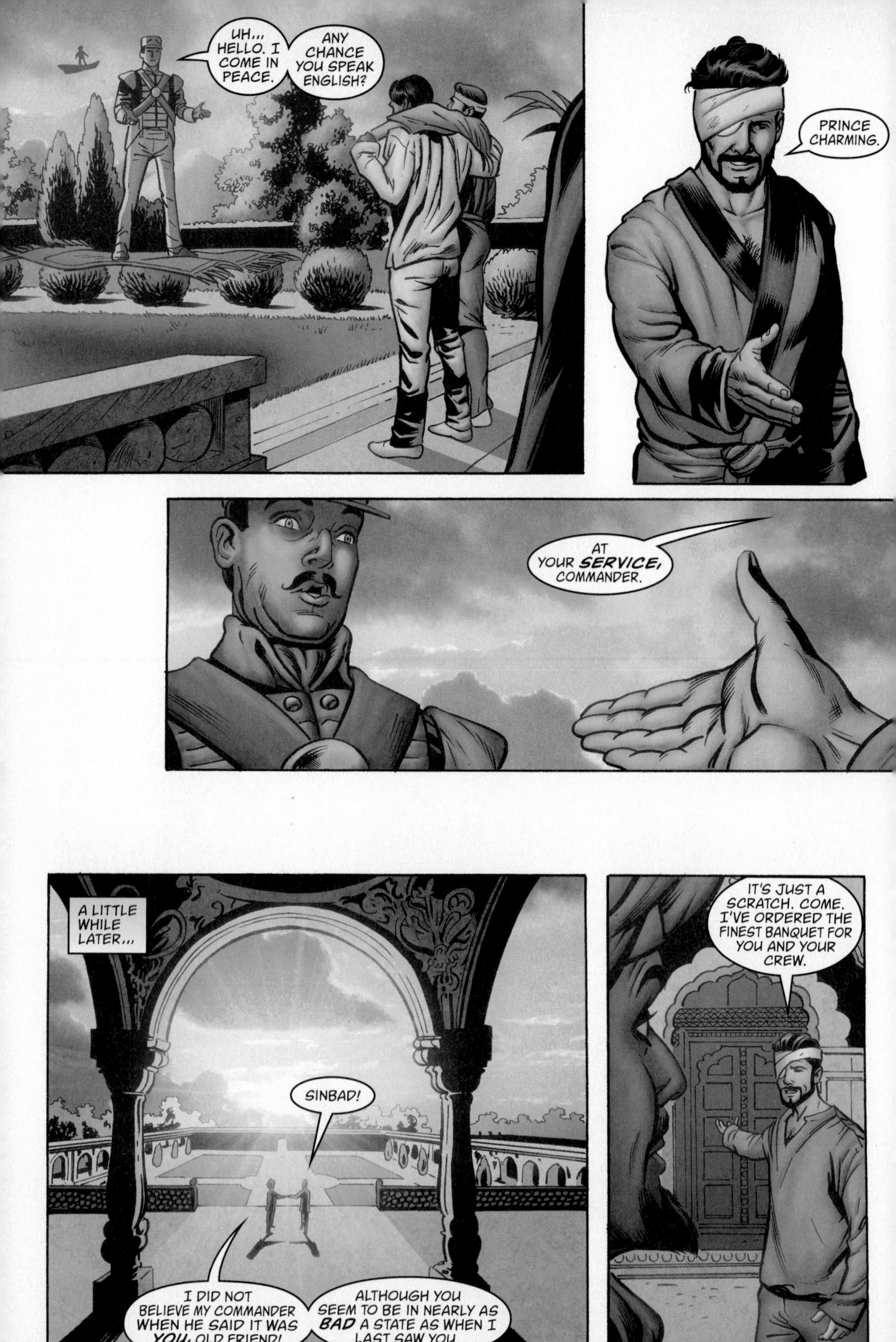

UH... HELLO. I COME IN PEACE.
ANY CHANCE YOU SPEAK ENGLISH?
PRINCE CHARMING.
AT YOUR SERVICE, COMMANDER.
A LITTLE WHILE LATER...
SINBAD!
I DID NOT BELIEVE MY COMMANDER WHEN HE SAID IT WAS YOU, OLD FRIEND!
ALTHOUGH YOU SEEM TO BE IN NEARLY AS BAD A STATE AS WHEN I LAST SAW YOU.
IT'S JUST A SCRATCH. COME. I'VE ORDERED THE FINEST BANQUET FOR YOU AND YOUR CREW.

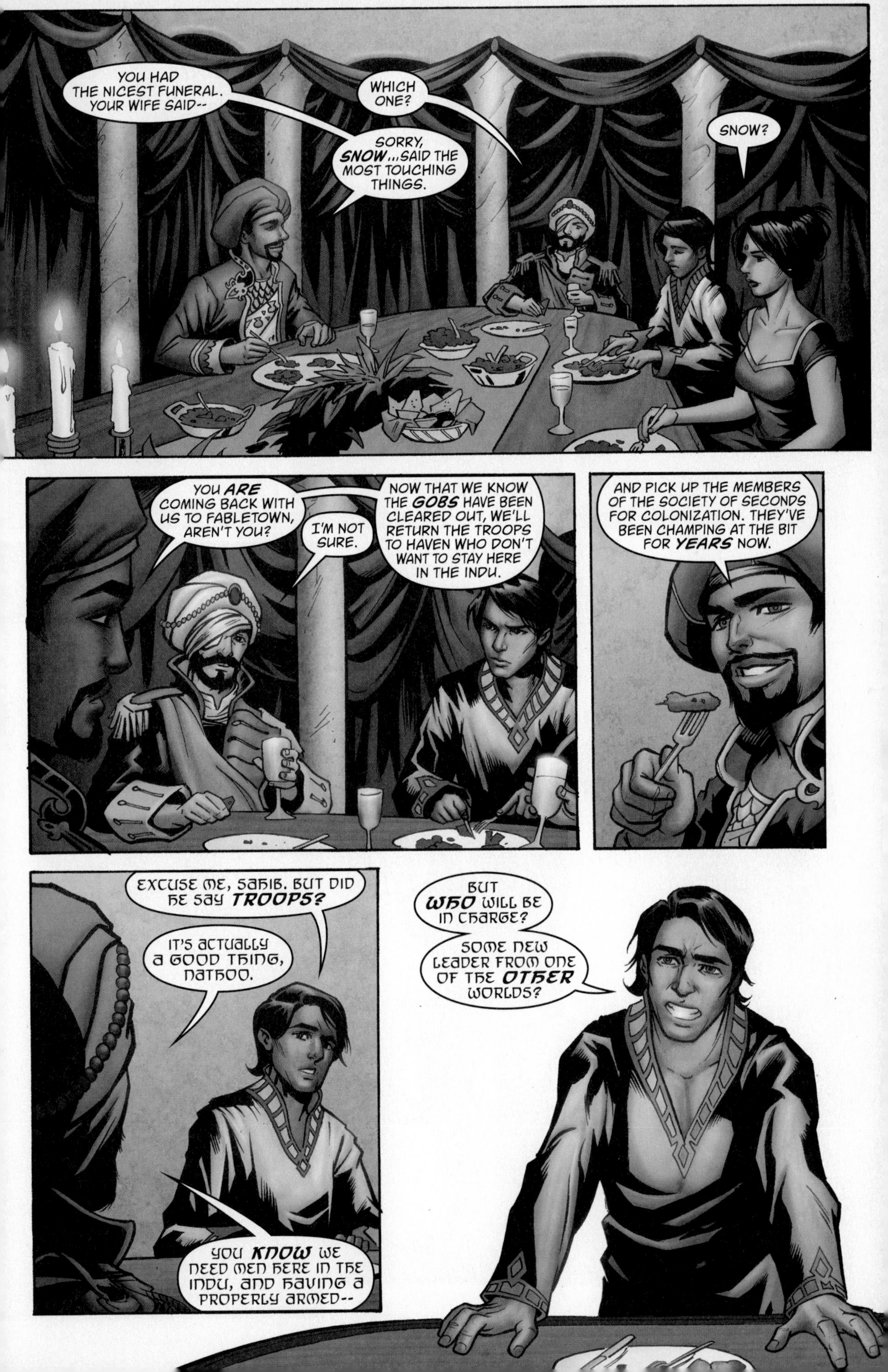
YOU HAD THE NICEST FUNERAL. YOUR WIFE SAID--
WHICH ONE?
SORRY, SNOW...SAID THE MOST TOUCHING THINGS.
SNOW?
YOU ARE COMING BACK WITH US TO FABLETOWN, AREN'T YOU?
I'M NOT SURE.
NOW THAT WE KNOW THE GOBS HAVE BEEN CLEARED OUT, WE'LL RETURN THE TROOPS TO HAVEN WHO DON'T WANT TO STAY HERE IN THE INDU.
AND PICK UP THE MEMBERS OF THE SOCIETY OF SECONDS FOR COLONIZATION. THEY'VE BEEN CHAMPING AT THE BIT FOR YEARS NOW.
EXCUSE ME, SAHIB. BUT DID HE SAY TROOPS?
IT'S ACTUALLY A GOOD THING, NATHOO.
YOU KNOW WE NEED MEN HERE IN THE INDU, AND HAVING A PROPERLY ARMED--
BUT WHO WILL BE IN CHARGE?
SOME NEW LEADER FROM ONE OF THE OTHER WORLDS?

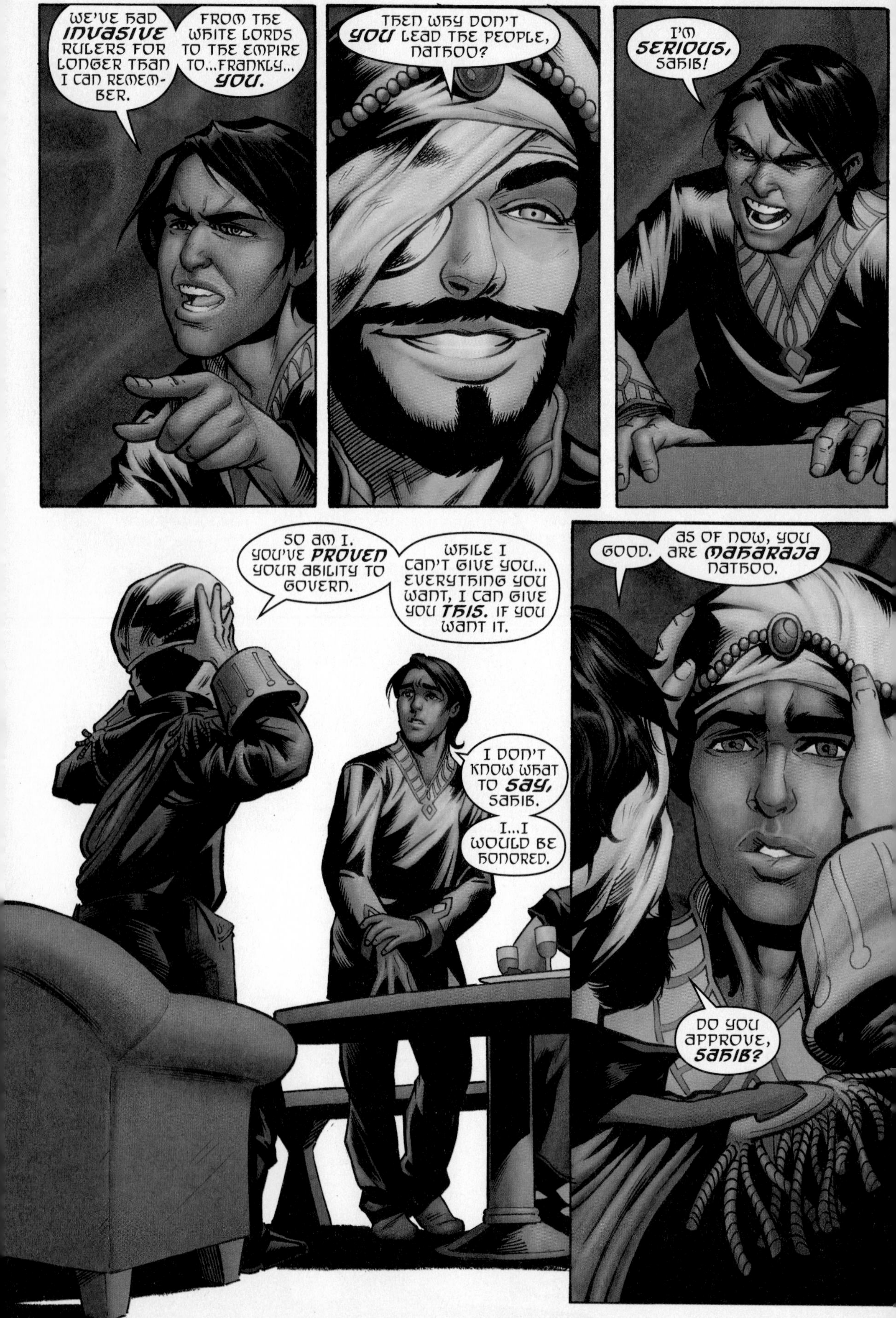
WE'VE HAD INVASIVE RULERS FOR LONGER THAN I CAN REMEMBER.
FROM THE WHITE LORDS TO THE EMPIRE TO...FRANKLY... YOU.
THEN WHY DON'T YOU LEAD THE PEOPLE, NATHOO?
I'M SERIOUS, SAHIB!
SO AM I. YOU'VE PROVEN YOUR ABILITY TO GOVERN.
WHILE I CAN'T GIVE YOU... EVERYTHING YOU WANT, I CAN GIVE YOU THIS. IF YOU WANT IT.
I DON'T KNOW WHAT TO SAY, SAHIB.
I...I WOULD BE HONORED.
GOOD.
AS OF NOW, YOU ARE MAHARAJA NATHOO.
DO YOU APPROVE, SAHIB?

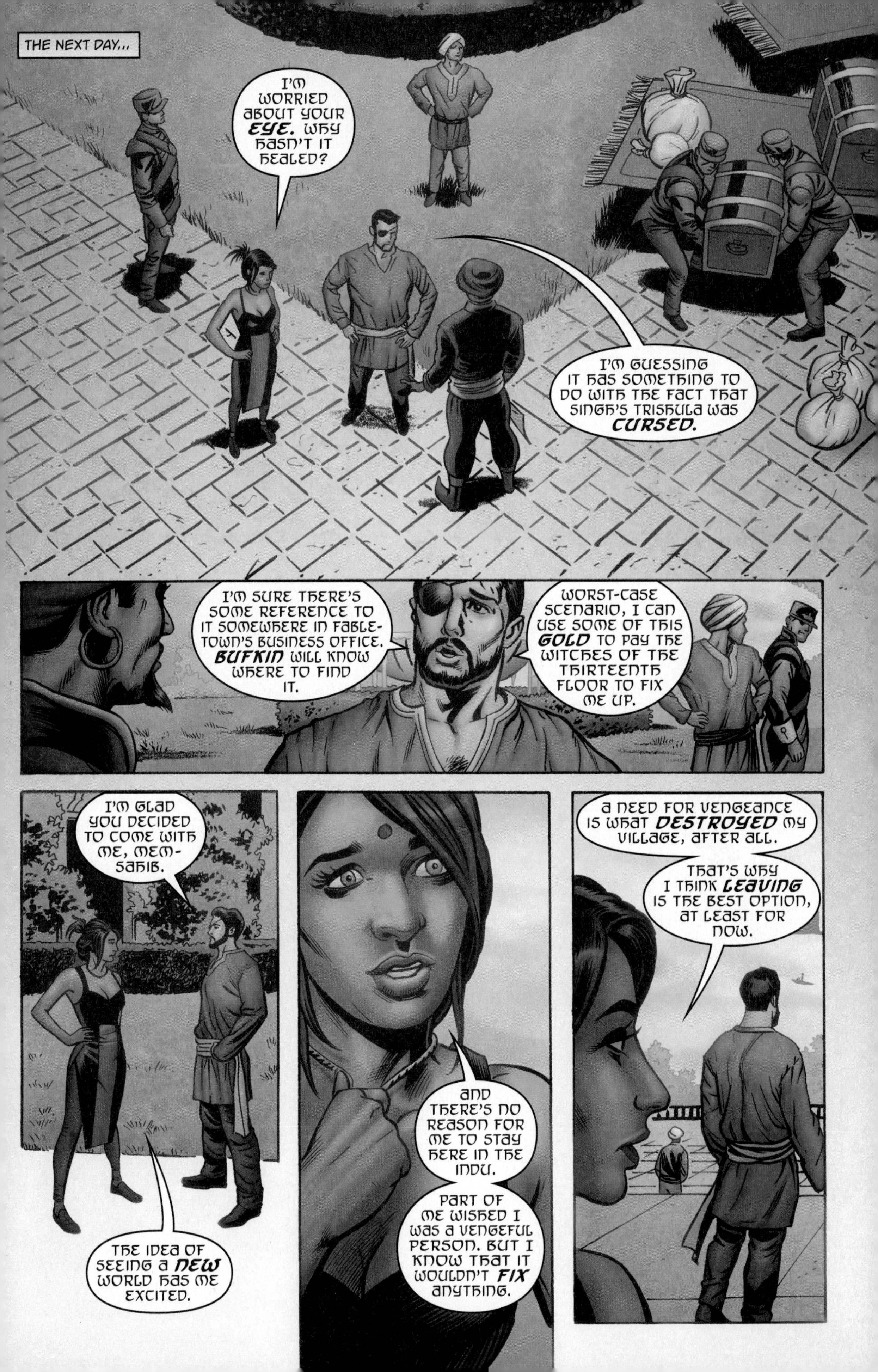
THE NEXT DAY...
I'M WORRIED ABOUT YOUR EYE. WHY HASN'T IT HEALED?
I'M GUESSING IT HAS SOMETHING TO DO WITH THE FACT THAT SINGH'S TRISHULA WAS CURSED.
I'M SURE THERE'S SOME REFERENCE TO IT SOMEWHERE IN FABLE-TOWN'S BUSINESS OFFICE. BUFKIN WILL KNOW WHERE TO FIND IT.
WORST-CASE SCENARIO, I CAN USE SOME OF THIS GOLD TO PAY THE WITCHES OF THE THIRTEENTH FLOOR TO FIX ME UP.
I'M GLAD YOU DECIDED TO COME WITH ME, MEM-SAHIB.
THE IDEA OF SEEING A NEW WORLD HAS ME EXCITED.
AND THERE'S NO REASON FOR ME TO STAY HERE IN THE INDU.
PART OF ME WISHED I WAS A VENGEFUL PERSON. BUT I KNOW THAT IT WOULDN'T FIX ANYTHING.
A NEED FOR VENGEANCE IS WHAT DESTROYED MY VILLAGE, AFTER ALL.
THAT'S WHY I THINK LEAVING IS THE BEST OPTION, AT LEAST FOR NOW.

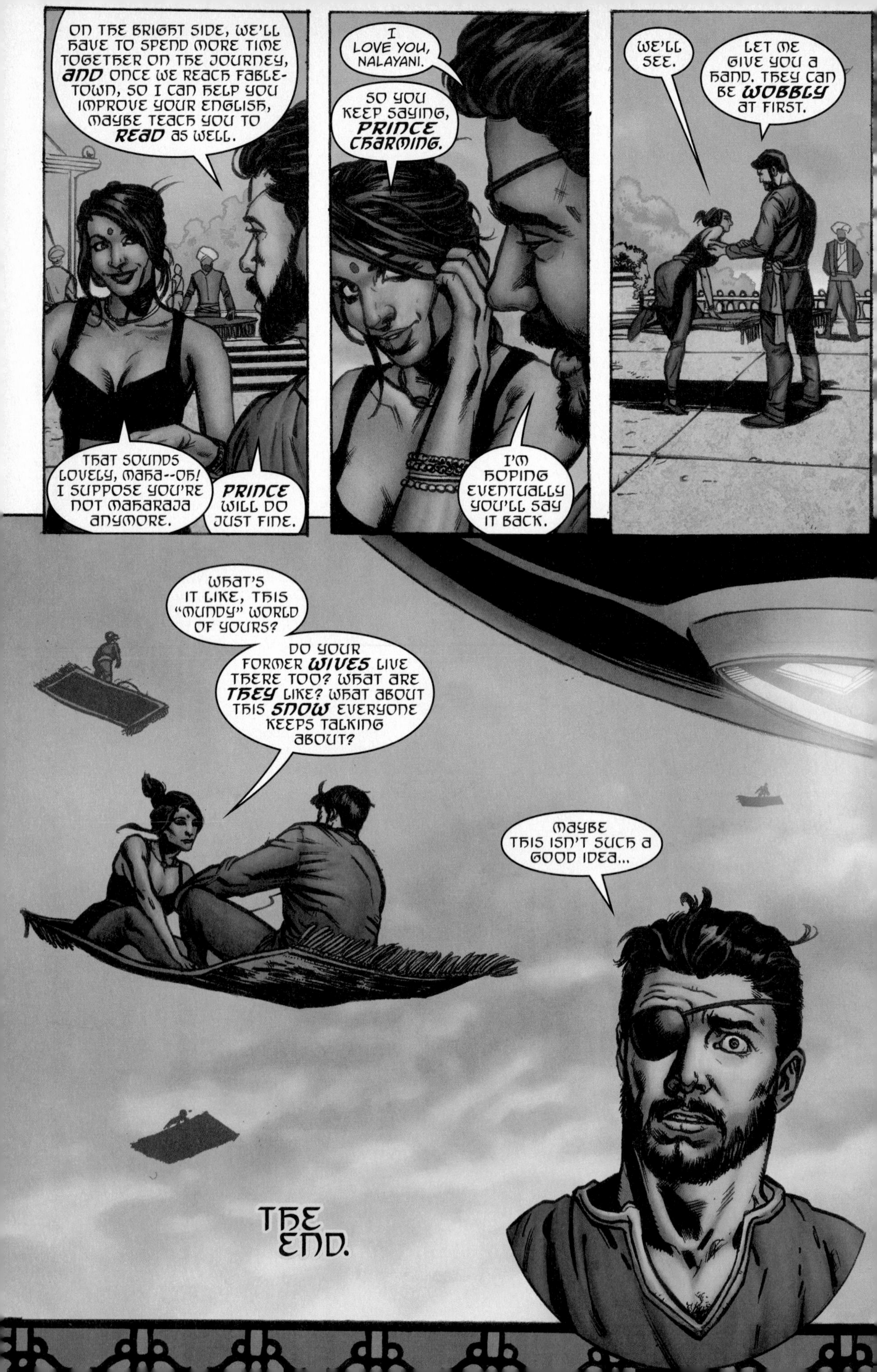
ON THE BRIGHT SIDE, WE'LL HAVE TO SPEND MORE TIME TOGETHER ON THE JOURNEY, AND ONCE WE REACH FABLETOWN, SO I CAN HELP YOU IMPROVE YOUR ENGLISH, MAYBE TEACH YOU TO READ AS WELL.
THAT SOUNDS LOVELY, MAHA--OH! I SUPPOSE YOU'RE NOT MAHARAJA ANYMORE.
PRINCE WILL DO JUST FINE.
I LOVE YOU, NALAYANI.
SO YOU KEEP SAYING, PRINCE CHARMING.
I'M HOPING EVENTUALLY YOU'LL SAY IT BACK.
WE'LL SEE.
LET ME GIVE YOU A HAND. THEY CAN BE WOBBLY AT FIRST.
WHAT'S IT LIKE, THIS "MUNDY" WORLD OF YOURS?
DO YOUR FORMER WIVES LIVE THERE TOO? WHAT ARE THEY LIKE? WHAT ABOUT THIS SNOW EVERYONE KEEPS TALKING ABOUT?
MAYBE THIS ISN'T SUCH A GOOD IDEA...
THE END.

BILL WILLINGHAM

FABLES VOL. 1: LEGENDS IN EXILE